Ad Hoc
Arabism

PETER LANG
New York • Washington, D.C./Baltimore • Bern
Frankfurt am Main • Berlin • Brussels • Vienna • Oxford

Roni Zirinski

Ad Hoc Arabism

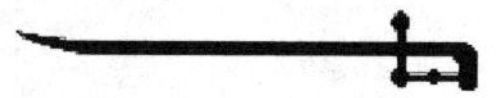

Advertising, Culture, and Technology in Saudi Arabia

PETER LANG
New York • Washington, D.C./Baltimore • Bern
Frankfurt am Main • Berlin • Brussels • Vienna • Oxford

Library of Congress Cataloging-in-Publication Data

Zirinski, Roni.
Ad hoc Arabism: advertising, culture, and technology
in Saudi Arabia / Roni Zirinski.
p. cm.
Includes bibliographical references and index.
1. Advertising—Saudi Arabia. I. Title.
HF5813.S28.Z57   659.1'09538—dc22   2005010088
ISBN 0-8204-7445-2

Bibliographic information published by **Die Deutsche Bibliothek**.
Die Deutsche Bibliothek lists this publication in the "Deutsche
Nationalbibliografie"; detailed bibliographic data is available
on the Internet at http://dnb.ddb.de/.

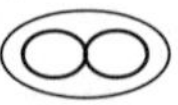

. . . He completely ignored the shirts of Van Heusen, Vestiaco, and Pierre Cardin as well as the one of Sonneti sport. He lingered a moment by the Levi's shirt trying to combine it in his imagination with the Wrangler Jeans. But immediately he moved to the really essential accessories: The Swatch watch with the black background, a bracelet of the same color (although the current dominant fashion is a big watch shaped like a compass), a gold necklace, and another bracelet. However, it seems that this set will not be completed tonight, nor tomorrow, because although they had Sting, Police and RayBan sunglasses, they did not have the ones with the golden frame and the round black lenses, the ones Sylvester Stallone wore in his last movie . . .

Meanwhile the crowd, without women, reached a new peak. The traffic that filled the road moved slowly, and a sort of fever, just like the one usually prior to the last scenes in the movies, took control of everything. A group of teenagers crowded under a large sign with Layla Alawi's image, a sign that disclosed quite a bit of the abundance she was blessed with, thank God. Although the young man showed inexperience at the shoe store, cars were a completely different matter. He started moving his gaze, a look that showed quite some experience, between the lines of cars that swamped the wide road. He ignored the common brands (Fiat) and the classic ones (Mercedes), and knew how to focus immediately on the Honda Civic and the Toyota Corrolla. But then he really got lucky: suddenly a dark-glass Golf emerged, with loud music and a girl, her hair blowing in the wind, her arm, naked up to her shoulder, hanging out of the window, promised much, much more. But then, soon enough, a BMW made her disappear . . ."

Contents

Illustrations

Acknowledgments

Many friends, colleagues, and institutions have helped hone my interest in Middle Eastern communications into the wary enthusiasm I hope to communicate in this book. I owe a special debt of gratitude:

- to Uri M. Kupferschmidt for advising the MA thesis on which this book is based, and for the staunch friendship and lasting encouragement throughout the years;

- to two anonymous readers at Haifa University and two anonymous reviewers at Peter Lang Publishing. All authors should have such perceptive critics;

- to my students at GOV 1968, Harvard University ("International Politics in the Middle East") for their insightful comments;

- to the supportive faculty at the University of Haifa, which will always be my first academic home. Special thanks to Amatzia Baram, Aaron Ben Zeev, Gideon Fishman, Avner Giladi, Gad Gilbar, Tamar Katriel, Amalia Levanoni, Saida Medjidov, and Joseph Nevo;

- to my friends in Saudi Arabia, from whom I learned and with whom I had many fruitful debates. Particular thanks goes to: Hisham & Muhammad Ali Hafez, Abdallah Bajir, Muhammad al-Farisi, Ilyas Harfush, Halah al-Nasser, Fahami Huwaidi, Adel Murad, Nawwal Nur Shasha, Muhammad Mahadi al-Hariri, Abd al-Rahman Zamahshari, Abd al-Razak al-Uthmani, and Faisal Idrisi;

- to members of the Center for Middle Eastern Studies at Harvard University: Steve Caton, Bill Granara, Engseng Ho, Cemal Kafadar, Gulru Necipoglu-Kafadar, Miri Kubovy, Roy Mottahedeh, Roger Owen, Carol Saivetz, and Wheleer Thackston—for the friendship, intellectual guidance, and constant encouragement to publish this and other works;

- to the Department of the History of Science at Harvard, for adopting an academic wanderer and giving him enough ideas for a lifetime of future academic work. Special thanks to Mario Biagioli, Peter Galison, Bruno Latour, Everett Mendelsohn, and Steve Shapin;

- to Ekmeleddin Ihsanoglu and his warm family for the sharp observations and the wonderful days in Yildiz Saray and Buyuk Ada;

- to Itamar Rabinovitch and the many others who aided at Tel Aviv University. Among them: Akiba Cohen, Nili Cohen, Haim Gal, Michael Harsagor, Tamar Hermann, Eitan Hoffman, Gila Holtzman, and Dafna Lemish;

- to the organizers of seminars, conferences, and workshops where I was able to further formulate my thoughts. Among them:

    - the Department of Middle East Studies at Ben Gurion University, Beer Sheva, for inviting me to the engaging Consumption in the Middle East conference (special thanks to Sam Kaplan, Yoram Meital, Haggay Ram, Relli Shechter, Boaz Shoshan, and Dror Zeevi);
    - the Middle East History and Theory Conference, Chicago University, for the invitations in 2001 and 2003 (special thanks to John Wood);
    - the History Department, Concordia University, for the wonderful History and Media conference (special thanks to Matthew Barlow and Anna Ginter);
    - the Graduate Seminar at the Near Eastern Languages Department, Princeton University (special thanks to Michael Cook, Bernard Lewis, and Abraham Udovitch);

- the Middle East Studies Institute, University of Miami (special thanks to Haim Shaked);

- to Damon Zucca—gifted editor—for his enthusiasm, agility, and professionalism; to Bernadette Shade for her technical support; and to Anat Stiendler for the graphics and the laughs;

- to the following institutions and funds that helped finance the project during its various stages: the Gustav Heinemann Institute for Middle Eastern Studies; the Berta von Suttner Fund; The Tami Steinmetz Center for Peace Research; the President & Rector Fellowship—Tel Aviv University; the Rabin-Peres Peace Research Fund; the Fulbright Fellowships Fund; Harvard University: the School of Arts & Sciences, the Center for Middle Eastern Studies, the Department of the History of Science; the Chaim Herzog Center for Middle East Studies & Diplomacy; the Hubert Burda Center for Communications; and the distinguished committee of the Yohanan Hoffman Award;

- to the following cooperations and advertising agencies for the permissions to reprint their ads: Rama Watch SA; Movado Group, Inc. (Movado, Ebel, Concord); Rolex SA; General Motors Corp.; Toyota Motor Corp.; DaimlerChrysler Corp.; Kellogg Comp.; Nestlé S.A; Al-Saudiyya Inc.; Al-Safi Inc.; Mars Inc.; Häagen-Dazs Ltd.; The Coca-Cola Company; Gucci Group N.V.; Unilever N.V.; Reckitt Benckister plc; Van Cleef & Arples Inc.; Royal Philips Electronics N.V.; Telefonaktiebolaget LM Ericson (publ); Simone Pérèle S.A.; Marks and Spencer Group plc; Parker Pen Corporate Gifts & Incentives; Al-Khalejiyah, Inc.

- to my friends and colleagues—Or Alterman, Eyal Ari, Tamar Ashuri, Nimrod Bar-Am, Gabby Berzin, Gabby Blum, Galit Barshadsky-Isler, David Braun, Inbar Cagan, Yoav Di-Capua, Kobi Gal, Yoav Liberman, Galit Goldsobel, Amy Gorelick, Oren (Chumpilino) Harman, Shiri Kalet-Litman, Tami Katzir, Eyal Reinstein, Noa Havilio, Yaron Klein, Leyla Kayhan, Christian Lange, Lihi Lidor, Yoav (Ha-Lipkon) Lipkin, Tal Musseri, Asli Niyazioglu, Shani Orgad, Sharonna Pearl, Amnon Aran, Alma &

Ariel Yanai-Shani, Alberto Ribas-Casasayas, Avi Rubin, Lucila Scimone, Siham Salman, Menachem, Avi & Roi Shmool, Yoav Sroka, Himmet Taskomur, Etty Terem, Rony Tilinger, Ava Vassileva, Dotan Winkler, and Ronen Zeidel–for their continuous assistance and involvement in this project.

And, finally, the warmest hug, to my loving family, my very heart and soul: Imma-Imtse (Miri), Pufah (Yael), Pudah (Tamar), Shoko (Uri), Todo Matoko (Adi), Ziko (Boaz), Nat-Nat (Einati), and Abba (Gadi) who is always present.

Roni Zirinski
Cambridge, Massachusetts, March 2005

Toward a Semiotic Analysis of Advertising in Saudi Arabia

Advertising is the art of our global multicultural world. It takes a product designed for Culture A and puts it through a rigorous process of symbolic manipulation, thus transforming it into a product with a wholly different resonance that is suitable for Culture B. Since suggesting a new way to read and use a product is always much cheaper than manufacturing a new one, this ad hoc manipulation of mental images facilitates the double-headed process of international commerce (export-import) and constitutes the mechanism of global economics in late capitalism. The paradox of this process is that while different people around the world become accustomed to the same products, the ways in which they interpret and use them grow increasingly different. Thus, this process deepens the borders between cultures and becomes a major factor in global culture wars—both virtual and real. This book analyzes one example of this process.

Advertising, like art, is an interpretive visualization of the world, a metonym of a certain lifestyle, a declarative political statement about how things should be. Like art, advertising changes reality continuously through the manipulation of symbols and the propagation of cultural agendas. Indeed, the invitation in all advertisements, no matter the culture, is to stop for a moment the humdrum of daily life and be drawn into a world of fantasy. After all, advertising is an illusion of escape from the present—whether to the past or to the future—offering a vision of a sweeter life.

Let us therefore imagine ourselves for a moment as an advertiser who receives a particularly lucrative contract to publicize a new and promising product—a car, a watch, a perfume—that must be sold to the general public of a certain culture.

It is reasonable to assume that the first thing we will do is gather marketing data by analyzing the specific society, its people, their habits, their dreams and aspirations. Our goal, of course, is to sell as much as possible; our mission, consequently, is to identify the "need" of the consumer—his cultural inclinations and tendencies, which may still be in an embryonic stage, a very narrow fissure, barely perceived—to set a foot in it, and to enlarge it to a huge degree. Thus, a large part of the need of the consumer is actually an *enlarged need* or a *created need*, a new need, better phrased and much more articulated than the initial, primordial need. In order to stretch the consumer's needs further, we the advertisers must combine the product with existing cultural symbols; that is, the historical reservoir or storeroom of the society, a process that will eventually bring about the transformation of the product as well as the widening of the borders of the economic-cultural imagination of a given society.

This process will not bring about the abandonment of the old and the familiar cultural heritage.[1] However, over time, it will expand the ancient cultural dictionary. This process of cultural expansion will occur regardless of how well the product connects to those preexisting cultural symbols, and without regard for whether the product became a hit or completely failed to sell. One way or another, culture gets its way: its symbolic reservoir is being advertised.[2]

Between Advertising and Arabism

During the advertising process, culture plays the role of a centripetal force, bringing objects into the imagined center. In that sense, culture is an essentialistic force: at any given moment it produces a snapshot of itself, using, time and again, the same structural essentials. As we shall see throughout this book, in Saudi Arabia, culture is revealed in the community stories told by Saudi Arabian advertising, in the way the advertiser envisions the readership and uses the symbolic universe, and in the assemblage of characterizations and the store of knowledge by which advertisers put new products through a process of habitualization. "Determinism of the situation" and the advertiser's "position in life," as these terms are explained subsequently, drive the advertiser to use "Arabism"—the culture that is embedded within the Arabic language—as a metalanguage of advertising. In the process this reduced Arab culture copies itself, albeit with changes, by attaching cultural symbols to imported or newly created products.

Daniel Lerner, in his well-known work on modernization in the Middle East, *The Passing of Traditional Society*, claimed that modernization originating in the West, along with the modern media, would bring about the development of "modern," Western societies in the Middle East.[3] In fact, his views were close in spirit to process approaches in communications studies, the view that "the medium is the message."[4] Later views, influenced by dependency theories, regarded the development of modernization and media in the Middle East as a new sort of Western colonialism and imperialism.[5] But, in the context of multicultural approaches, although the media are doubtless pulling Saudi Arabia into the "global village," this is a village in which many rival clans continue to exist, and they wrap their consumer products in different cultural packages.[6] The most prominent cultural package in Saudi Arabia is "Arabism," which participates in a dialogue with "Saudism," "Wahhabism" (the religious-political movement based on the ideas of Muhammad b. Abd al-Wahhab [1703/4–1792], and the dominant state ideology in Saudi Arabia), "Islam," "Westernism," and other cultural influences.

All these terms are in quotation marks, and perhaps it is time to remove them. They are in quotation marks because they are generalizing, essentialistic concepts that do not adequately preserve historical precision in societies and cultures that existed and still exist in different geographic regions and in various historical eras. This, of course, was the scathing criticism of Edward Said, which brought about a revolution in Middle Eastern studies.[7]

In this study, I will demonstrate that in Saudi advertising, and probably in the study of other cultures of advertising as well, taking an "essentialistic" approach is inevitable, since it derives from the material itself and is even explicitly stressed in it. The advertiser, as a seller of cultural knowledge, requires this essentialism, this abstract Arabism. The advertiser needs Arabism in the essential sense of the word, Arabism without quotation marks, glamorous and trivial. The advertisements attempt to reflect, in Habermas's words, the illusion of an "ideal speech situation," a situation of communication without barriers, in which any sentence is potentially acceptable to all participants.[8] Advertisers attempt to "found a truth" in the Foucaultian sense,[9] by a manipulation of knowledge.

The model of Arabism presented in the advertisements is optimal. It is necessarily ethereal, a sort of Platonic idea that makes reality seem pale. It is a celestial Mecca, a mirage that promises a new sort of desert oasis. It is an imagined Arabism that exists only in the "isolated state," as in the title of a work by the well-known nineteenth-century German economist Heinrich von Thünen, an imaginary state sealed off from the rest of the world, located in an infinite, uniform plane. This Arabism is a hymn to the dominant fantasies, an urge to idealize the current social order. Therefore, a study of Saudi advertising is largely a study of Saudi fantasies.

This is an "invented tradition" of Arabism, a symbolic, functionalistic, privatized Arabism.[10] To paraphrase Starrett, it is "putting Arabism to work."[11] Culture—in this case, Arabism—becomes a peddler in a bazaar, a mercenary in a "symbolic economy,"[12] an important, essential element in "public relations identity."[13] This is Arabism in the spirit of Lyotard: "Knowledge is and will be produced in order to be sold, it is and will be consumed in order to be valorized in a new production: in both cases, the goal is exchange."[14]

It is an Arabism of duplication and symbol attachment, a recycled Arabism at the "Xerox level of culture"[15]; an Arabism of images and metaphors, to the point of what Habermas calls "cultural impoverishment"[16]; a trans-Arabism, a hyper-Arabism, an Arabism of "total metonymy."[17] It is a playful Arabism,[18] a visual-virtual journey, a nostalgic, romantic Arabism, a simulation of eclectic, esthetic, synthetic, communicational, performative, theatrical, hedonistic, imaginary Arabism. It is a transparent Arabism that becomes a collection of quotations, passages, and symbols,[19] a teleological Arabism that attempts to construct a tautological relationship between itself and any given product, an Arabism that aims to make the connection between itself and the product appear to be obvious and trivial. In Jean Baudrillard's words:

> When things, signs, or actions are freed from their respective ideas, concepts, essences, values, points of reference, origins, and aims, they embark upon an endless process of self-reproduction, yet they continue to function long after their ideas have disappeared and do so in total indifference to their own content. The paradoxical fact is that they function even better under these circumstances.[20]

At the bottom line, there is only one goal: to use the advertisement to promote sales. This is, therefore, Arabism for a purpose: *ad hoc Arabism.*

So what sort of historiography does this book offer, if at all? In this work, I present advertising texts from late-1990's Saudi Arabia and describe how "history" is reconceived at the present. This research does not set itself the goal of describing, after Leopold von Ranke, "the way it really was" (*wie es eigentlich gewesen*), but rather how the past invades the present in order to serve the purposes of the future, thus creating a complex time that Lyotard dubbed *futur antérieur* and Foucault described as "multi-layered (archaeological) time consciousness."[21] This form of present resembles what Van Velsen called the "ethnographic present."[22] Thus, this is not a study of the history of Saudi advertising but rather a study of how history is reflected in Saudi advertising. For, in the spirit of Walter Benjamin, the function of history is not to preserve the past, but to reconstruct its lost hopes.[23] This is an attempt to locate the submerged traces of history in the life of the present, to sense the warm vapor of its breath in everyday reality.[24] It is an historical description of the mask rather than of the real face that may once have existed. It deals with the history of historical rumors, *ut dicitur* ("as it is said"), to use the coinage of the twelfth-century historian William of Tyre, who lived and wrote in Crusader Jerusalem.[25] It is a sort of description of "optative history": "History as it might have, must have, should have been."[26]

This historiographic approach stands on the shoulders of giants such as Marc Bloch. In his book *The Historian's Craft*, Bloch attacks the view of history as the "science of the past." He claims that not only can we better understand the present by means of the past, but that the contrary is just as true—it is impossible to understand the past if one is ignorant about the present. History, he goes on, should start at the present and move backward—from what is more comprehensible to what is less so. The "science of man in time" requires us to combine the study of the dead with the study of the living.[27]

This is relevant historiography, which chooses its fields of interest according to issues germane to the present. Modern historians are under various conflicting pressures, including the need to be relevant, writes François Bédarida; he proposes, therefore, that they carry on a constant dialogue between past and present.[28]

But this is not an attempt to provide only my own interpretation of contemporary advertising texts. I will try to achieve more than that: to describe how a contemporary Saudi reader, whether consciously or unconsciously, might interpret these texts; that is, I will attempt to attain what Clifford Geertz (following Gilbert Wright) called "thick description." According to Geertz, "Cultural analysis is not an exact science which strives for regularity, but an interpretative science which searches for significance." The "overt presentation" or "thick description" attempts to locate the subtle semiotic interpretations of an event.[29] I will therefore try to attain what Appleby, Hunt, and Jacob call "qualified objectivity" or "practical realism."[30]

The field that combines everyday life, including communications and advertising, with cultural studies and with history is, certainly, "cultural history." Marc Poster shows (following Roger Chartier) that cultural history scrutinizes and blurs three traditional distinctions of intellectual and social history: high versus popular culture, production versus consumption, and reality versus fiction.[31] These three distinctions, writes Poster, can aid in understanding the change in historiographic discourse. They propose new directions for discussion and research. As one of the subjects to be examined, Poster names advertising.

Advertising as a Social Text

Advertising is over 3,000 years old. A placard dating from circa 1000 B.C. promises the reward of one gold coin for the capture of a runaway slave.[33] Similar advertisements have been found all over the ancient world. A notice found in Rome offered property for rent; another, painted on a wall in Pompeii, referred the attention of passersby to an inn in another city. In the Middle Ages, the practice of "oral advertisement" existed in Europe: heralds employed by merchants called out their advertisements. Danesi remarks that this form of advertisement was especially common in marketplaces and prayer houses.[34]

But the birth of modern advertising, or "print advertising," can be dated to the fifteenth century, with the invention of modern printing by Johann Gutenberg (1400?–1468?).[35] Toward the end of the seventeenth century, when newspapers began to be published on a significant scale, the scope and importance of advertising rose as well. The *London Gazette* was the first newspaper to allocate a separate section to advertisement. It was at this time that the first advertisers appeared. The advertisements of this period resembled classified ads—lacking visual material or graphics—but they exhibited many of the characteristics of our own era's full-color ads.[36]

In the eighteenth century, advertisers began to attend to the design of their texts. Words were arranged in blocks, with shorter sentences and contrastive fonts. Coining new slogans and expressions became an everyday activity for the advertiser. The first advertising agencies, an important junction of institutionalization, were founded in the early nineteenth century.[37]

The ideas of advertising and marketing were not foreign to Arab culture, nor were they unfamiliar to the Muslim culture that came into being in the Arabian peninsula in the seventh century. The functions of the well-known *Jahili* poetry and of the bard (*sha'ir*) included propaganda, marketing, and advertisement. The Koran sets itself the task, among others, of propagating the Islamic faith. Likewise, the announcements of the muezzin, cried five times a day from the minaret, are meant to inform Muslim people of prayer times and urge them to perform their religious duty punctually. The sermons of Muslim preachers from the *minbar* platforms in the mosques during Friday prayer also hold great propaganda and advertising importance. Further examples are the seventy evangelistic letters sent by Imad al-Din al-Isfahani, the personal author and aide of Saladin, to the Muslim world after the conquest of Jerusalem (1187). Drori points out that these stylistically polished letters were written for propaganda purposes.[38] The dictionary of professions compiled by Jammal al-Din al-Qasami in nineteenth-century Damascus contains the term *munadi*, defined as the profession of "the man who lifts his voice to make announcements in the markets, according to the wishes of his employer," in the pay of the government or of a merchant (much like the aforementioned European oral advertising).[39]

These, of course, are only a few examples of advertising, marketing, propaganda, and public relations in the Middle East. As remarked above, however, modern advertising is tightly bound with the emergence of print and newspapers. As such, modern advertising in the Middle East is an import from the West.[40] The spread of printing to the Middle East was delayed, for various reasons, until the nineteenth century.[41] It is interesting to note that when the use of print finally did begin to accelerate, it was due to the authorities' desire to publish and advertise laws, rules, and ordinances.[42] Soon after the first Middle Eastern newspapers began to appear (in Lebanon), they came to contain commercial advertisements as well.[43]

In the twentieth century, and primarily in the West, advertising began to focus on promoting consumption and making it into a way of life. "Shopping" came to signify something much wider than a functionalistic activity meant to obtain products necessary for existence and daily life. Purchase became an end in itself.[44] The role of the commercial advertisement was no longer limited to announcing the existence of a given product. In order to affect the purchasing decisions of a wider public, advertisers began to use their advertisements to redesign lifestyles and behaviors, creating a demand for their products. As early as the 1930s, Western advertising came to focus not on the product but on the consumer. Its emphasis was no longer on the description of the product being sold but on issues such as the family, status, and authority. In the 1950s, advertising strove to create a product image with which the consumer could identify.[45] This product-consumer connection involved a return to the product as, in a sense, a mirror of the consumer. Starting in the 1960s and continuing in various ways until the present, the emphasis has been neither on the product nor on the consumer. It is, rather, on the advantage of purchasing the product; the product is only a means, the consumer merely a participant. In the wake of these changes in advertising focus, advertising now attempts to penetrate and manipulate unconscious desires, urges, and passions largely beyond the individual's control. In the early 1960s, James Web Young wrote:

> Advertising, rightly seen, is all about people. And about how to use words and pictures to persuade people to do things, feel things, and believe things. . . . Wonderful, mad, rational and irrational people . . . About their wants, their hopes, their tastes, their fancies, their secret yearnings, their customs and taboos. Or in academic language, about such things as Philosophy, Anthropology, Sociology, Psychology and Economics.[46]

And, one might add, History.

The constant message of the advertising world is an offer of hope on the brink of illusion. It offers higher social status, popularity and personal prestige, health, happiness, and security against aging. To an ever greater extent, the technique of advertising addresses the subconscious, the Freudian id, the sensory stimulations. Danesi phrases it thus: "We are living in a very unstable world which puts much of a premium on satisfying consumerist urges than it does on the attainment of spirituality and wisdom. . . . [The advertiser's] general implicit message is that solution to human problems can be found in buying and consuming."[47]

Or, in the scathing words of author Amos Oz, it is

> a vast industry which manufactures a sort of pornography of consumption: a fetishism of luxury items glowing with colors from the dawn of time, socks crowned with a transcendental halo, digestive pills presented as heralds of apocalyptic salvation, detergents gleaming with celestial light, futuristic toilet bowls whose depths hold a prophecy of the Hereinafter.[48]

Moreover, from a Marxist point of view, the entire media system may be considered a by-product or supplementary industry of advertising. It can be argued that the informative parts of a newspaper are published merely as a pretext for the appearance of advertisements. Why are stories split over different pages ("Continued on page . . .") if not as a way of making the reader leaf through more advertisements? Why are advertisements usually placed on the side of the paper that the eye first encounters in turning the page? I raise these questions without entering into a discussion of the question of public relations and the "purchase" of informative stories, and without considering the fact that both the newspaper and the news it contains are commercial products. The sections explicitly allocated to advertisements are ostensibly less important and less influential, and in this very fact lies their power. Ultimately, the purpose of journalism, which is sliding ever deeper into "mass media," is that the reader should not read, but skim.

The goal of the advertiser, as a sort of modern Mephistopheles, is to lure the reader into performing the desired action. It is to create an appetite in the reader and immediately offer a means of sating it. For this purpose, the advertiser must identify the reader's desires, hopes, tastes, and yearnings and then produce a message that will limit the reader's freedom of interpretation. The advertiser must restrict the possibilities of understanding the message. In the terminology of communications theory, the reader must be guided toward "normal decoding," while the possibility of "aberrant decoding" is minimized.[49] The advertiser increases the "redundancy" of the text and reduces its "entropy."[50] This is aided by the maximal use of conventional symbols, signs, and associations, with an emphasis on the "distinctive features" of the advertising text.[51] If the product is an unfamiliar one, the advertiser's task is to "conventionalize" it. In Islamic terms, advertisers must turn *bid`a* (a forbidden or undesired innovation) into *halal* (a religiously legitimate act). For this purpose, they must address the lowest common denominator of the society in which they operate.

How do advertisers find this lowest common denominator? Most importantly, they are aided by public opinion polls and market surveys. Modern advertising agencies, especially international ones representing mammoth corporations, are in fact research institutes. Behind every advertisement are consumption studies, market analyses, and acquaintance with the target audience; the advertiser uses all these to design a product's "personality." To a large extent, advertising agencies enjoy an advantage over academic and governmental research institutes because of the vast amounts of money in the field. Every study is spurred by a financial incentive. Such studies, of course, are confidential, closely guarded trade secrets. To carry out similar studies for academic research purposes would cost many millions of dollars. Nonetheless, semiotic analysis of advertisements can reveal the study questions used and the answers received. Such analysis can turn advertising agencies and their associated research institutes into assistants in one's own research. This study, then, is a reverse one: it begins with the conclusions and attempts to expose questionnaires, to list the questions and the answers.

But beyond market analysis, the advertiser ("the individual author"), who also fills a social role as an advertiser ("the social author"), operates in the framework of an advertising agency in which many staff members influence the design of the advertisement ("the large author"), and all these staff members are individuals in the specific culture ("the level of culture," "the cultural author").[52] That is, advertisers cannot be detached from the society in which they operate. In this way, culture becomes the author of advertisements. On the other hand, the product itself is metamorphosed into a part of the social order. Product and culture merge so that it is no longer possible to separate message from code, content from form, the vessel from what it holds.[53]

In this approach, the image of the advertising consumer is formed beforehand by the advertisers. In the initial stages of composing an advertisement, they "project" the potential reader for themselves[54]; they derive this image from their social *al-lawh al-mahfuz* (literally: the hidden board), from the ideal master plan of their culture. Since the advertising product is created in a certain society, by individuals within that society, the reader becomes not only the recipient of the message but its author as well.[55] Culture, that abstract, protean, illusive entity, becomes a copywriter, thus propagating and reproducing itself (albeit with changes) with every product. By propagating the dominant ideology,[56] every advertising text is also a political text.[57] Advertising becomes the continuation of policy by other means; consumption becomes the opium of the masses.

Advertising, as Henri Lefebvre pointed out, is becoming the poetry of the modern era,[58] perhaps even its bard, as the term "bardic television," coined by Fiske and Hartley, may also be applied to the study of advertising.[59] Fiske and Hartley claim that television today performs the functions formerly filled by bards: emphasizing the chief features of the social consensus about the nature of reality; guiding individuals in society toward the dominant value system, by supporting that system and demonstrating its behavior; explaining and interpreting the representatives of the culture; guaranteeing that the culture remains relevant and well prepared by confronting its ideologies and myths with the practical world; revealing inconsistencies due to changing external factors or to pressures deriving from the culture itself; convincing viewers that their status and identity as individuals are safeguarded by the culture; and conveying emotions that link individuals to the culture (security and involvement).

These insights apply equally well to the understanding of advertisements as a social integral, as a feuilleton revealing the nature and myths of a society. Therefore, of all the media channels available to the researcher, it seems that advertising is especially fitted for the study of society and culture "from below."

Arabism as a Metalanguage of Advertising

Fiske and Hartley's description of bardic television is useful in understanding the role of advertising in Arab society, as the tremendous influence of poetry and poets as an integrating factor through the course of Arab history is undeniable. The importance of poets was recognized as early as the *Jahiliyyah* period, Arab times before the emergence of Islam, and persists in the Arab intellectual world of the twenty-first century. Chejne remarks, perhaps with some exaggeration, that there is no Arab scholar who has not tried his hand at poetry.[60] Advertisers today praise their products in the same fashion that the poets of the *Jahiliyyah* used to write *mada'ih*, poems celebrating illustrious rulers and noblemen, *amajid al-arab*, "the most glorious among the Arabs."

"New" or "free" Arab poetry is sometimes called "poetry in prose."[61] Le'a Glazman points out that this designation is a conscious dissociation from the writing traditions of classical (and neoclassical) Arabic and their poetic and thematic conventions: rhyme, meter, content patterns, and so on.[62] Reuven Snir notes the extent to which such poetry makes use of the multiple denotations of words both poetically and in the context of everyday life, its fusion of different linguistic registers.[63] Advertising grounds this new Arab poetry into concrete daily reality, exploiting the "tribal" character of the Arabic language, in which every word is linked by kinship to many other words and meanings. Just as in the work of the twentieth-century poet Nizar Qabani, the poems of advertising are "rife with an overflowing abundance of metaphor, symbolism and poetic imagery, with a clear tendency toward overt self-recycling."[64] But in advertising, at least, the goal is not to liberate readers but to enslave them as loyal consumers. The contemporary Arab advertising poetry, then, is a siren song that seeks to entice the seafarer navigating the straits, the nomad roaming the boundless desert of consumerism.

I have referred to reproduction of the dominant ideology, but we must keep in mind that advertising, like poetry, Arabism, history, or any other social product, is not immutable, for "popular culture is always a culture of conflict."[65] Advertisers must account for social tensions, groups, identities, and social relationships. They must take into account the old and the new, consensus and dissent; and even if they do not wish to do so, they are forced to by inherent, subconscious currents. The choice confronting the advertiser is twofold: either to address different groups in different languages or to combine such groups by using a single metalanguage. In order to avoid various sensitivities and tensions, Saudi advertisers employ the metalanguage of "Arabism." This Arabism is not free of other ideologies, even, sometimes, conflicting ones. Saudi culture also contains Saudism, Wahhabism, Islam, Westernism, and Far Eastism. But it is the advertiser's task to fuse all these elements; to propose new cultural alternatives, fitted to a changing reality. This is accomplished by the use of Arabism and with the aid of Arabic narratives. Thus, the constant new arrangement of the dominoes of Arab discourse becomes the cultural glue.[66]

Semiotics, Sociology of Knowledge, and Cultural Studies

There are two main currents in the study of communications. In the first, communications are a process of transmission of messages. The various stages of the production and transmission of a message are examined, usually in a linear fashion.[67] The approach is exemplified in the first model of this school, that of Shannon and Weaver, developed in the 1940s and known as the mathematical theory of communications.[68] The idea of combining mathematics and communications indicates the pattern of thought characteristic to this current: the process of communication is linear and logical, almost logarithmic. Another well-known model of this school is that of Lasswell, which poses the following questions: who says what, by what channel, to whom, and with what effect.[69] That is, it assumes a process with a beginning and an end, in which a message is transmitted from a source S to a receiver R.

The second school of communications theory focuses on the message itself, on its meaning, on examining it as a social text whose interpretation is dependent on time and place. The text is an autonomous entity, the interpretation of which is much more significant than the intentions of its author. The central method of this school is semiotics. A semiotic analysis is particularly appropriate when studying advertising as a social text.

"Semiotics," suggests poet Rachel Halfi, "is the study of signs / The study of signs is the study of scars / The study of scars is a system of ill-healed wounds."[70] Indeed, semiotics attempts to decode the signs hidden in the text, the scars branded in it. Whereas in linear models the text is one of many elements in a process, in the semiotic approach it is everything. In the words of Jacques Derrida, "There is nothing outside the text" (*il n'y a pas de hors-texte*).

A further difference derived from the centrality of the text is the status of the receiver. In the semiotic approach, the receiver plays a much more active role; therefore, the term "reader" is preferred. Reading is an acquired, learned activity, and as such it is defined by the cultural experience of the reader. A reader is always a participant, not a mere spectator, and possesses previously accumulated cargo without which reading would be impossible.[71] Texts, by their very nature, demand understanding and invite interpretation, imagination, and association. The reader is always a *mujtahid*, an extractor of meaning, an interpreter, of the text, and the gates of interpretation (*ijtihad*) are always open. The reader not only decodes the text but also negotiates with it. This creative activity prompted Umberto Eco to suggest, with his poignant humor, that "[s]emiotics is in principle the discipline studying everything which can be used in order to lie."[72]

Semiotics consists of three main fields of study: (1) the study of signs, that is, the examination of different kinds of signs and the ways in which they convey messages[73]; (2) the study of codes and systems, that is, an examination of the ways in which signs are organized and combined[74]; and (3) the study of culture, that is, an examination of the specific culture in which the signs, codes, and systems operate.

In my analysis, I focus on the third level, the study of culture. Here it is crucial to keep in mind that our very understanding of reality is cultural. According to Schapera, "Culture is not merely a system of formal practices and beliefs. It is made up essentially of individual reaction to and variation from a traditionally standardized pattern."[75]

In this sense, all of reality is a social construction, according to the title of the now famous book by Peter Berger and Thomas Luckmann.[76] In this work, the authors take as their starting point the sociology of knowledge (*Wissenssoziologie*), a term coined by Max Scheler. This field deals with the relationship between human thought and the social context in which it develops, with the "existential determinism" (*Seinsgebundenheit*) of thought. In other words, values and opinions are founded on a social basis. This basis leads to a "determinism of the situation" (*Standortsgebundenheit*) and a "position in life" (*Sitz im Leben*); that is, to seeing the world from a specific standpoint within it.[77] This is why the social order, despite being relative, seems to the individual to be the natural way of looking at the world. Scheler called this a "relative-natural worldview" (*Relativnatürliche Weltanschauung*). Karl Manheim, whose views were more extreme than Scheler's, saw society and culture as determining not only the ways in which human ideas are expressed but also their entire contents.[78]

According to Berger and Luckmann, society conveys much more than ideas, opinions, and theoretical concepts. Society and culture convey "common sense"; they convey subjective meanings presented as a complete, coherent world. They convey all of the everyday life that individuals in the society take for granted. Among the "plurality of realities" is one reality that presents itself as *the* reality par excellence.

Language defines the coordinates of life in society.[79] I use the term "language" in its widest sense, to include its images, metaphors, humor, proverbs, and so forth. Language guarantees that reality is preserved, even when it develops and changes. Here lies the connection between language (the carrier of culture), semiotics (which exposes its meanings), and history. One's relationship with other individuals in one's culture is not limited to contemporaries; one is related both to distant forefathers and to one's descendants. This relationship is affected by semiotic-linguistic means, which enable the expression of meanings beyond the here and now. Language, in its widest sense, including all semiotic means, becomes a repository that stores all the previous experiences and significations of the society. As the poet Aaron Shabtai writes, "A dictionary is never a thing-in-itself, it is never neutral."[80]

Therefore, the ways of being "human," "cultural," or "social" are as numerous as the number of existing cultures, maybe even as numerous as the cultures that could possibly exist, or that could be imagined or initiated—perhaps an infinite number. "Humanity" is a sociocultural variable. Human beings create themselves as individuals in a society; *Homo sapiens* is always *Homo socius*. The social order is a human product, or more precisely, a continuous process of human production. Social knowledge undergoes a process of habitualization, which averts the need to define each situation anew, stage by stage.

The knowledge of a given social group becomes public by the means of common history, by an assemblage of attributes. Thus, legitimacy in a culture is based on signs, imagery, and linguistic constructions. "Logic" becomes bound up with the social order, the store of knowledge, and is taken for granted. Any essential deviation from the social order strikes members of the culture as an escape from reality. The social world becomes a sort of all-embracing court in which all events take place.[81]

The idea of reproduction, that a society reproduces itself endlessly, appears as early as Friedrich Engels' work *The Origin of Family, Private Property, and the State*.[82] This is the social phenotype, to borrow the terminology of evolutionary biology: the sum of all attributes of the individual formed by a combination of genetic heredity and contact with the environment.

Language is also the means of creating a "symbolic universe," of bringing into being an entire, full-fledged world. The symbolic universe defines the course of all history taking place within it; it unites all events into a single whole comprising past, present, and future. With regard to the past, it creates a "collective memory."[83] With regard to the future, it produces a common reference point that will direct individual actions.

This is, to a large extent, the "imagined communities" described by Benedict Anderson. Early in his book of that title, he proposes "in an anthropological spirit" a definition of the term "nation": "an imagined political community, imagined as inherently limited and as sovereign." This community is imagined because a member of even the smallest nation can never know the majority of the other members, meet them, or even hear of them. Yet the mind of every member contains an image of the entire community.[84] Anderson's ideas were, of course, intended to describe the phenomenon of nationalism; nonetheless, they are equally applicable to the "virtual nationalism" of advertising.

From another viewpoint, Gary Hoppenstand writes:

> The ability of the individual to effectively describe those things of his social being which are meaningful is useful as a mechanism of survival. The individual is a consummate social storyteller, and the stories of his community, his past and future assist him with his day to day struggle with life.[85]

Saudi Arabia: An Exporter of Media and Arabism

To discuss advertising is, above all, to discuss purchasing power and consumption ability. Such ability may be real (by economic parameters), or it may exist only in the conception of the manufacturer and the advertiser. The two may be interrelated, but mental conceptions can change long after (and, possibly, also before) economic reality. Since the end of the 1970s, Saudi Arabia (with a population of more than 24 million in 2003, more than 40 percent of it under the age of 14, and with an annual population growth rate of more than 3.2 percent) is perceived as possessing tremendous purchasing power, mainly due to the oil boom—which has returned once again recently—and the almost inexhaustible accompanying reserve of petrodollars (Saudi Arabia has the largest reserves of petroleum in the world, 26 percent of the proved reserves, and ranks as the largest exporter of petroleum),[86] but also because of industrialization and various development programs (still, the petroleum sector accounts for roughly 75 percent of budget revenues, 45 percent of GDP, and 90 percent of export earnings).[87]

In the 1990s, despite the drop in oil prices, consumption was not reduced. On the contrary, one of Saudi Arabia's constantly worsening problems is the rising trade deficit.[88] This deficit indicates a meteoric rise in imports: in 1994–95 the total cargo passing through Saudi ports amounted to 79.4 million tons (compared with 68.2 million tons in 1990–91).[89] According to World Bank data, per capita income in that period reached $7,500 ($11,400 in 2002); inflation in 1996 was only 1.9 percent (1 percent in 2002)[90]; and the unemployment rate remained around 25 percent (which was financed with oil revenues). All these factors turned Saudi Arabia into a leading consumer state, or at least earned it the image of one, increasing its importance to foreign and domestic advertisers.[91]

One must keep in mind that data on per capita income are largely misleading because of the considerable gaps between different sectors of the population,[92] despite Saudi efforts to develop few features of a welfare state.[93] Of course, the gaps are even greater between Saudi citizens and foreign workers, Arab and non-Arab.[94] In addition to social tensions and those between citizens and foreigners, religious tensions also exist in Saudi Arabia. There is a large Shi'i minority, mostly living in the al-Hasa district, where almost all of Saudi Arabia's oil reserves are located. There is also a Zaidi minority—a branch of Shi'i Islam—in the Asir region, in the southwest of the kingdom, on the border with Yemen.[95] Furthermore, there exist radical Sunni groups, which aim to recover power for pure Salafi Wahhabism (Islamic Salafi movements hold fundamentalist ideologies, calling for the return of the pure, untainted religion that characterized the beliefs and actions of the prophet Muhammad and his immediate successors).[96]

Saudi Arabia's socioeconomic situation, then, confronts the advertiser with both challenges and opportunities. As previously described, the advertiser's (as well as "society's" and "hegemony's") way of overcoming tensions and conflicts in Saudi society is by an appeal to Arabism. After all, the deserts of the Arabian Peninsula are the cradle of Arabism. Saudi Arabia, of course, is also the cradle of Islam, its king the "guardian of the holy places" (Mecca and Medina), and its official ideology is Wahhabism. No doubt, there is also a process of "regional diffusion" by which Western ideas infiltrate Saudi Arabia.[97] Cultural change and social variation are not to be considered "stratigraphic change," however, but rather "divergence change," even tending toward "hermeneutic change."[98] The interpretation of culture typically chosen in Saudi advertising is the "Arab interpretation." It is exactly because "Arabism" is perhaps the least relevant ideology for everyday life that it serves advertising so well. This is why it is "ad-hoc Arabism": an Arabism used only when needed. It usually is needed; it is the ideology that addresses the broadest, most distant, and least charged common denominator, and, ultimately, elicits the highest profits.

The Saudi advertiser also wraps products in Arabism because Saudi Arabia is a major exporter of Arab media.[99] Geographically, it is located in the center of the Arab world and is visited yearly by many foreign Arabs and Muslims during the *hajj* (pilgrimage). Therefore, Arabism enables the advertiser to reach an audience located in Arab countries and communities all over the world. A study of advertising in a Saudi weekly is for this reason not just a case study of a single Arab country; it makes possible cautious inductive conclusions regarding other Arab countries and communities, or rather regarding the ideas exported to them from Saudi Arabia.[100] It reveals a worldwide imagined Arabian community created through advertising—an advertised Pan-Arabism.

A further reason why advertisers turn to Arabism is Saudi censorship. The 1998 *Europa World Yearbook* states that Saudi media "is subject to no legal restriction affecting freedom of expression or the coverage of news."[101] However, Saudi Arabia's Basic Law of Government (the Saudi constitution) states, in Article 39:

> Information, publications, and all other media shall employ courteous language and the state's regulations, and they shall contribute to the education of the nation and the bolstering of its unity. All acts that foster sedition or division or harm the state's security and its public relations or detract from man's dignity and rights shall be prohibited. The statutes shall define [the implementation of this Article].[102]

The brunt of Saudi censorship is directed against opposition Islamic elements, both Shi'i and Sunni. The journal *Al-Jazirah al-Arabiyyah*, an Islamic political monthly published in London with the reputation of being a pro-Iranian publication opposed to regimes in Saudi Arabia and the other Gulf states, occasionally runs stories on Saudi religious censorship, free speech restrictions, confiscations, and so forth.[103] Censorship can also be indirect, for example, by regulation of paper prices, importation, and distribution.[104] The appeal to Arabism enables advertisers to bypass socioeconomic gaps, Islamic ideologies, and other burning political issues, preventing them from straying into social minefields. Arabism becomes a neutral, distant ideology, somewhere between Western liberalism and radical Islam.

Research into Saudi Arabian media and advertising is still lacking. The few studies of Saudi advertising, conducted by graduate students, have not been comprehensive and have never been published. Al-Fardi has written about the historical development of commercial advertising on Saudi television.[105] Al-Yusuf has carried out a content analysis of Saudi television commercials,[106] finding that most commercials are thirty seconds long, are broadcast on evening prime time, employ Arabic of a non-Saudi dialect, and feature non-Saudi actors. Al-Kheraiji too has performed a content analysis of commercials on Saudi television, from their first appearance in 1986 until 1989. He found no Western influences but identified Arab influences (mostly Egyptian and Syrian).[107] Other scholars have chosen to examine television advertising by collecting field data on the attitudes of Saudi Arabian men toward commercials.[108] I have therefore elected to focus on a *semiotic* analysis of the advertisements in a Saudi weekly family magazine, *Sayyidati*.

Why Sayyidati?

The ads in this work were taken primarily from one Saudi journal. This strategic decision might raise questions on whether this study reflects the entire Saudi advertising industry. Obviously, it does not. But, as discussed below, choosing *Sayyidati*, a major publication of the most important company publishing magazines in Saudi Arabia, a company that reproduces the same ads in many of its publications, creates a very solid base for a thorough case study. Any criticism of the inductive technique used in this book—that is, its way of reaching general conclusions on the basis of a case study—will have to argue that a study of CNN can tell us nothing about American culture, that ads in *Le Monde* do not accurately reflect French advertising, and that an in-depth analysis of hidden messages in the newspaper *Akşam* (one of many dozens of papers printed daily in Turkey) reveals nothing about Turkish society in general.

The weekly journal *Sayyidati*, founded in 1980, is published by a company called Saudi Research and Marketing, whose main offices are in Riyadh, Jiddah, and London. Other company offices are located in Cairo, Kuwait, the United Arab Emirates, Jordan, Morocco, and Washington. This company, the leading and most prominent such company in

Saudi Arabia (and one of the most prominent in the Middle East), publishes myriad newspapers, weeklies, and journals, including an English-language daily (*Arab News*), an Arabic daily (*Al-Sharq al-Awsat*), a weekly titled *Al-Muslimun* (The Muslims), a children's weekly, a sports weekly, a horse-riding weekly, and a few others.[109] The broad range of publications indicates the nature of the target audience. The presence of the word "research" in the name of the company hints at market studies and information gathered for purposes of distribution and advertising. Indeed, the company occasionally places in the journal various prize-bearing questionnaires asking how the journal was purchased, to what extent the reader is satisfied with it, what subjects the reader would like to find in the journal in the future, and so on. These questionnaires are placed at the beginning of the journal and are obviously considered highly important.[110]

The weekly is printed in a luxury format, on high-quality chromo (glossy) paper, and in full color. Its departments include stories about men and women from the Arab world, cosmetics and care, recipes and cooking, quizzes and crosswords, and so forth. A special department intended to consolidate ties with the journal's readership is *Asafir* (Birds): every issue of the weekly devotes several pages to pictures of babies and young children sent in by readers in Arab nations and communities all over the world, and one such child is awarded the title "Bird of the Week." The cover of the journal displays Arab women in modest, though usually "modern," dress.

It should be kept in mind that the purpose of the public opinion polls, the various departments, and in fact the entire journal, is one: to sell products. Each issue is 150–200 pages long, with every page of articles facing a page of advertisements; there are also double pages of advertising. Many issues contain over 100 pages of advertising; that is, more advertising than articles. When single pages of advertising appear, they are mostly printed on the left-hand page; that is, the first page the eye encounters when reading Arabic from right to left. The chief advertisers are both large international corporations and local Saudi companies. The products advertised are mostly consumption products: cars, perfumes, cosmetics, watches, foods, and the like. The journal's main English-language advertising agency is Al-Khaleejiah International.[111] The advertisements themselves are usually produced at local advertising agencies, or in the graphics studio of *Sayyidati* (usually in the cases of

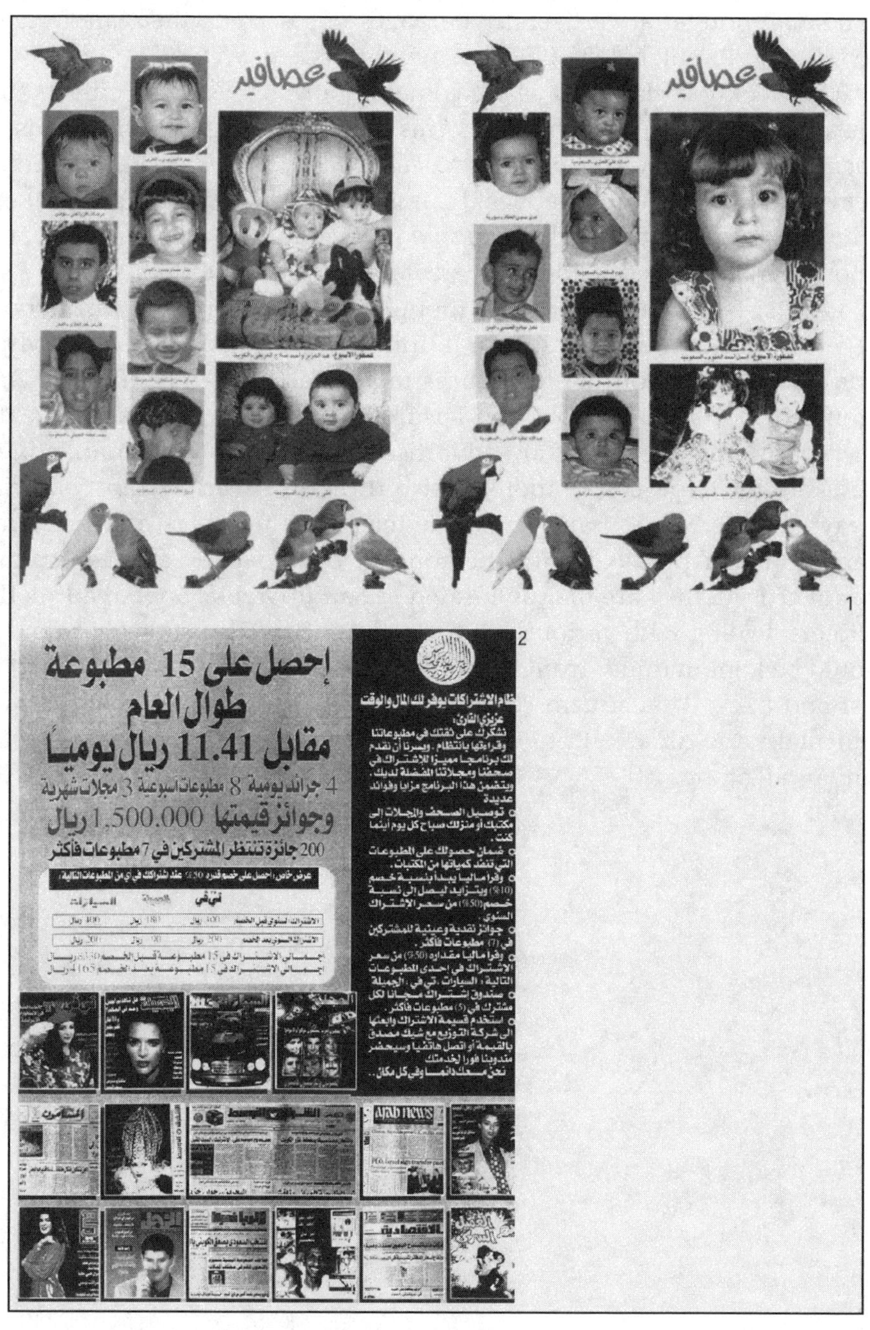

Fig.1 (1) the Asafir department of *Sayyidati;*
(2) ad for various publications by Saudi Research and Marketing.

local small-budget advertisers). The pages of *Sayyidati*, then, are a modern *'ukaz*: a vibrant, colorful bazaar, a vigorous *qaysariyyah*.

The weekly is classified as a "women's journal,"[112] but its editors (the chief editor at the end of the 1990s was Matar al-Ahmadi) define it as "a magazine for the Arab family" (*majalat al-usra al-arabiyyah*). Indeed, it seems that as a high-quality weekly, issues of *Sayyidati* are typically kept for a long period and read by people other than the buyer (that is, the exposure it enjoys is considerably greater than its distribution).

It must be remembered that, though the weekly is sold throughout the Arab world and in Arab communities worldwide, it is primarily a Saudi journal. The journal has offices in several cities in Saudi Arabia; a significant portion of culture and leisure articles deal with Saudi events; when perishable foodstuffs are advertised, they are always Saudi; advertisements by large corporations with offices in several Arab countries always list the Saudi branch first, the telephone numbers of other Arab branches being prefixed with the country code; when sales campaigns are advertised, they are mainly located in Saudi Arabia. So in reading the chapters dealing with various products, the cyclical directions of research should be kept in mind: from Saudi Arabia outward, and from present to past and back. This stream of advertising consciousness, which is fundamentally the direction of every cultural-building process, will accompany us all along.

Ilm al-Miqat, The Science of Times: Timepieces and History

Henry Kissinger, returning from one of his shuttle trips to the Middle East, said he had learned a new word: *bukrah* (spoken Arabic for "tomorrow"). Asked its meaning, he replied with a smile that it was much like the Spanish *mañana*, but "without the sense of urgency."[1]

My analysis of Arabism in advertising begins with a study of the advertising of timepieces. Time—as a clock or a watch, in its most physical manifestation—becomes Saudi time, a sociocultural variable. I begin with timepieces because they represent a subject that appears throughout this study: the constant connections between past, present, and future that are involved in the creation of new products; the indissoluble tie between future generations and social legacies.

"Time" has fascinated humankind throughout history, not only in the twentieth century, which turned time on its head, but starting with very early periods. References to time are found in the ancient cultures of the Middle East, in ancient Egypt and in the Fertile Crescent.[2] The *perception* of time is a sociocultural variable. The differences between cyclical, linear, relative, and other models of time are well known. These currents appear throughout the history of philosophy, Western and Eastern, up until the development of such theories as relativity and quantum mechanics. The Koran, the Sunna, and the works of almost every Muslim philosopher reflect an attitude toward the concept of time.[3] Likewise, advertisements for timepieces in *Sayyidati* also reflect attitudes toward time, perceptions of history, and the relationship between Saudi time and other kinds of time.[4]

The concept of time conveyed by Saudi advertising, as well as by contemporary Western advertising, is a fractal image, a patchwork: it is time in its disjoined state, drops of time dripping onto the pages. When a certain company takes over one time period, "finders keepers," its competitors grab another. In this way, every company defines its timepiece, the period-identity of its product, by means of a different piece of history; and collective, cultural consciousness creates a mosaic of times and eras. The advertiser becomes a "time person," to use al-Sakhawi's term slightly differently.[5] Advertisers take their readers on a voyage through time or through a time tunnel, each "chapter" dealing with some historical event. And so, when the advertiser employs a pseudohistorical commercial language to talk about time, the reader is forced to give up the belief that time passes.[6] Time, in Saudi advertisements, does not grow or develop due to causality; it consists of a collection of events from different periods that appear in the same journal. Naturally, like any researcher constructing a subject, I have tried to rearrange the advertisements in an historical, comprehensible order, in their "correct" historical sequence. But this, of course, is an academic fiction whose purpose is really the opposite: to explain the lack of change, the chill of commercial death, the advertising-time dish made up of a potpourri of different eras. I will show how advertisers choose, in the words of Ibrahim al-Ati, "a new way of regarding the past of our ever-renewing heritage, bringing us . . . to encounter the real life of that heritage."[7] In other words, how advertisers continue to "produce" history in time.[8]

Selling Products via Ancient Egypt

In Saudi advertising, the earliest historical period that sells products is ancient Egypt. The use of the Sphinx, the Pyramids, the Nile, or the desert and its Bedouins (which we will encounter later on) are all recurring themes in other cultures of advertising (European and American advertising included). In Saudi Arabian advertising, though, these motifs are not part of an Orientalist exoticism and perception of otherness, but part and parcel of the representation, and thus formation, of a "genuine" historical self-identity. Ancient Egypt (and ancient Arabia) is being brought closer: not only as part of human civilization, but as part of "our own" genealogical roots.

In an advertisement not translated into Arabic, the EBEL Corporation, the "Architects of Time," invited readers to "explore new dimensions in time."[9] The advertisement shows a long boat propelled by six oarsmen, on a wide river or sea. On the boat is a strange vehicle, shaped something like a sphinx, inside of which is a human figure. In the background can be seen another rowboat, a sailboat, desert dunes, a full moon, and the tops of three pyramids. The "architecture" of time, at night and on the water (miracles always work best on water, a fluid surface that allows manipulation of time and space), makes it possible to move *Abu al-Hawl*, the Sphinx, out of its place and time—to float it on the water and turn it into a vehicle. This "architecture" can connect the modern world of automobiles with the ancient one of the Pyramids, and modern clocks with the moon, probably one of the first two timepieces. It can change the location of the Pyramids and place them near a body of water; in reality, the Pyramids are not visible from the Nile, the Mediterranean, or the Red Sea. The geography of time creates an air of mystery produced by the combination of night and water (which together indicate high tide, with all its cultural significance). The manipulation of time produces the fear of a higher power. Over the entire picture hovers the question "Why?" Why are these people rowing in the dead of night with a sphinx-automobile in their boat? What sort of occult ritual is being enacted? The advertisement exploits the reader's inability to fully understand history: something always remains beyond comprehension. The reader can approach the past only in its deconstructed state, as a rhapsody of signs, or in this case a raft of symbols. The lack of answers to existential questions exalts time, and consequently timepieces, to the rank of a deity: a deity for whom a ritual, perhaps one of sacrifice, is being held. Although Umar Ibn al-As and Umar Ibn al-Khattab ended the practice of sacrificing virgins to the Nile,[10] it is as if pagan rites live on in this imagination.

Pictorially, the advertisement consists of two thirds water and one-third sky, separated by a narrow strip of land. Land, the place where real human beings live their earthly lives, is of negligible importance here. Human events in this advertisement take place on the water; the Nile is no longer a giver of gifts, but the gift itself. It is the fantasy of desert dwellers.

The Pyramids, monuments that challenge time and were intended to do so (as eternal tombs for divine rulers), occur often in advertisements in *Sayyidati*. The Swiss clockmaker Rama advertises two of its clocks as the "Pyramid Collection." The picture shows the two clocks on a background of two shaded pyramids, all lighted by a rising or setting sun (a time of transition, in either case) that paints the sky orange. The slogan reads, "The Passion Has a Name." The reader is left to decide: is the name "Pyramid"? Or possibly "Rama"? The latter name bears some resemblance to "Ramses," a name from a famous Egyptian royal dynasty, and is also the name of the temple containing the earliest known Arabic-language inscription.[11] Another advertisement by the same company declares that "skilled hands have created wonderful, elegant forms, with an extremely flat mechanical movement. . . . An experience in the world of Rama clocks." The skilled hands recall the ancient Egyptians, with their sundials and clepsydrae.

The first moon the reader encounters in this historical-commercial journey, in the first advertisement described above, is a full moon: a perfect, round shape, which, according to Aristotelian science, contained no motion.[12] The company, as mentioned above, calls itself the "Architects of Time"; Avraham Vachman, in a fascinating thesis presented to the Faculty of Architecture at the Technion in Haifa, showed how architecture developed from round building shapes, which still dominate religious construction.[13] The appearance of angular shapes was a later development. The well-known semioticist and philosopher of culture, Roland Barthes, spoke of roundness as a perfect shape in his mythologies of everyday life.[14] The circle and the sphere are perfect symmetrical objects. All the shapes in the advertisement tend toward roundness: time acts on them like water on pebbles. The sand dunes are domed, as though imprinted with the moon. All the shapes are rounded by time except the pyramids, the glory of ancient Egyptian architecture, a construction that withstands nature and challenges time—and, not surprisingly, with the further exception of the square black EBEL logo in the lower left-hand corner of the advertisement. The EBEL clock is a late formal development of the spherical moon and the angular pyramids; it is more sophisticated than either. The "history" in this advertisement, then, is also a journey through the history of shapes. But here, all these geometric forms appear together, in temporal coexistence.[15]

The moon and the sun, which appear implicitly in the advertisement, were of course the first timepieces; they symbolized the separation of day and night. Solar and lunar eclipses were mystical events, as was the possibility that the sun and moon might stop. It seems the moon, with its changing shape, made a better clock. Despite being only a mirror of the sun, it came to define the day, the month, and later the year (the solar year is a subsequent development). Even today, this ad suggests, the sun and moon still signify time: the light we now perceive as sun and moon, the light reflected by this advertisement, began its journey through space thousands of years ago, perhaps indeed in Pharaonic times.

Bedouin Arab History: The Stuff of Legends

A second historical period expressed in watch advertisements is that of Bedouin Arab history. The Concord Corporation chose to sell its time-pieces with the aid of magical Arab legends. Each advertisement is designed as a story, and all of them taken together, appearing in different issues of the weekly, form an enchanted collection of fairy tales. Of course, each advertisement was repeated several times in different issues, sometimes in two-page versions, thus leaving its imprint on the reader's mind. The advertising legends were "Concord: The Beauty," "Concord: The Desire," "Concord: The Romance," and "Concord: The Imagination."

The advertisement titled "Concord: The Beauty"[16] shows a woman wearing a black *abayyah* dress, gazing into a mirror designed to resemble the face of the watch being advertised. The mirror is held by celestial, feminine hands emerging from the clouds; they are covered with clouds exactly up to the wrist. The woman stands with her back and profile to the reader, and eye contact with her is possible only through the heavenly mirror, which shows a narrow strip of human skin not covered by the black dress: a pair of dark eyes and shapely black eyebrows. This advertisement reveals the motif that returns throughout the "Concord legends," and in many other Saudi ads: the eyes, *al-Karimatani*, "the two dear ones." The eyes are the windows of the soul, in this case the female soul; they are the only place where male penetration can begin. The only parts exposed by the Islamic-Saudi dress covering the woman from head to toe are the eyes and the hands. The eyes represent a possibility of expressing emotion, desires, and wishes. In this ad, the eyes of the Saudi woman are her only imagined means of communication with the outside world. "Imagined" because this is really an earthly manifestation of the male paradise: the *huriyat* with the perfect pupils, legendary women in the Islamic paradise, become reality. The fingernails of the delicate, feminine hands holding the magic mirror are unpainted. For a woman to paint her fingernails is forbidden by the Saudi ideal of purity; foreign women entering the kingdom at the airport are handed cloths dipped in solvent to remove their nail polish.[17] The dream is always fitted to social reality.

The text of the advertisement reads as follows: "Concord: The Beauty, Wonderful harmony and "delicate" and "refined" motion, in a frame of precious diamonds and pure gold. Babiun [the name of the model]: Concord's gift to magical eyes." The ideal of feminine beauty is connected with wonderful harmony between the eyes and their reflection, and with "delicate and refined" motion accompanied by diamonds and pure gold. It undergoes a reduction from "woman" to "gaze." Moreover, the figure of the real, covered woman, looking into the mirror, resembles a cartoon character or a computer design. Only the parts in the celestial reflection look like real flesh and blood. In other words, the ad suggests that the only way for a woman to reveal herself and become flesh and blood, her only way of being alive, is by an infinitesimal analytic deconstruction, by mediation and filtering, by turning her back on the beholder, by games of covering and revealing. And also by deception and reversal, for the mirror does not convey what is really happening: it inverts things and events. The young woman's left eye becomes her reflection's right eye, and vice versa. So, of the three basic feminine characters in the scene, who is the real woman here: the covered woman, her reflection, or the female reader of the weekly?

On the actual watch in the ad, the surface in which the woman is reflected contains a diamond-studded image of a butterfly. The band of the watch is also "decorated with 18-carat gold butterflies." In the celestial, eternal watch, the woman, a chrysalis in its cocoon, replaces the butterfly. Only by accepting the feminine dress code and avoiding direct eye contact is she able to fly, to be a butterfly (and see the Sadefco advertisement in the chapter on foodstuffs: *khali al-ta'am yufarfash*—"the sweetness of the taste makes you feel you are flying like a butterfly"). Only in the imaginary advertisement can a black dress turn into a white cloud (though it still covers the body to the wrists, in exact accordance with the desired dress code). Roland Barthes, in his book *Camera Lucida*, expressed the hope that a "history of looks" might someday be written[18]; here, a Saudi advertisement fulfills his wish. The entire Concord series is a paean to the Saudi code of looking, and to the code of behavior related to looking (which is rooted in and bound in with history). According to the historical interpretation suggested here, this is a history of miserliness in looking, of preventing and supervising it; a history of lowered eyes, of what may and may not be looked at; and of the difference between male and female looking, between the direct gaze and the indirect, embarrassed glance. These advertised women are always spectators, rather than active lookers. They must mind where they glance. Such looks are in no way a means of real communication; they are far too brief.[19] The covering, the lack of communication, turns the woman into a secret. This secret, these looks, are an immanent part of the mechanisms of the Saudi advertised culture.

It is the woman's looking away from the man, her remaining in a state of desire (*al-raghba*), that ultimately brings about the arrival of Concord, the Arab knight, as the story of another advertisement in the series suggests.[20] This time the covered woman may turn her direct gaze on the reader, for the object of desire, an Arab knight in a headdress riding a white Arab horse, is behind her. She may not look at him; he may see her and keep his eye on her. She can only desire. Here once again is the "presenceless presence" of the man: his look, like that of a miniature god, also contains the woman. Even in the free expanse of the desert, the woman is always in a harem, under the man's watchful eye. He measures her with his gaze, and it is this measurement that makes her real. The separation of looks between men and women also appears in the traditional Bedouin tent, where the men sit with their backs to the women. If he does not see her, she does not exist. She is "his-story," as the fantasy of romantic love is always founded on dependency.[21]

The plot of this advertisement takes place at sunset, when the desert hills turn orange, or, as the text puts it, "Glittering diamond pieces swimming in eternal harmony in a sea of gold . . . A watch [also: a time of day] to charm hearts . . . It is the passionate desire to accept beauty." The enchanted, eternal hour when the Arab knight rides past the yearning woman in the desert-turned-sea is incarnated in the Swiss watch. The elegant SL model, one of those advertised in this story-ad, features a mosaic surface: an ancient art form of the Middle East. The man is linked to motion, while the woman is immobile. "Time cannot be described [or 'drawn'; *yatasawwar*] except by motion, and what lacks the quality of motion lacks the quality of time" (Avicenna).[22] The woman, it appears, does not have a time of her own.

Desire, the burning, primitive passion, is likened to a swift, wild horse galloping in the desert. But the process of courtship is a slow and lengthy one. Mutual courtship goes on "no longer riding a steed of blind passion, but the mule of patience, stubborn and reluctant."[23] Desire continues in the oasis, among the palm trees, where one goes to draw water (another mirror, like the celestial one) for one's herds. Of course, the oasis needs a watch fitted for its purposes, and this advertisement, unlike most others in the series, stresses that the watch is water resistant up to a depth of thirty meters, apparently referring to the gushing oasis waters. Again, the man stands on a high cliff, looking at the woman, who is not looking at him. This time the watch is made of "glittering pieces of diamond" on a surface made of *"al-yakut al-ahmar." Yakut* is a collective noun meaning variously colored precious stones occurring naturally as minerals, just like the ones sometimes found in an oasis. The watch, the advertisement continues, is characterized by "flowing wave motions carved in gold and glittering light amber . . . The Verona watch by Concord . . . The devotion of this creation signals the birth of a new watch [or hour], the diamond that keeps time." By preserving the oasis, the palm tree, the dress, the correct look, one can also preserve (keep) time and history; that is, the desired hierarchical social order.

In the oasis advertisement, the man is clearly older than the young woman. Even if in this case he represents the father, guarding her from any unwanted suitors who may stare at her through the pages of the journal, the remaining two advertisements in the series make it clear that the male lover is indeed older than the girl. The age difference is a time gap that no watch can bridge, except, of course, a Concord. The man's age and experience represent power and strength, in contrast to the girl's tender innocence; they signify control and status. Ultimately, who really desires whom, who defines whose tastes, whose preferences are being molded? Women are supposed to learn what they are to love, what they are to fantasize about.

The next advertisement, "Concord: The Romance," brings the reader closer to the man. He wears a white *jalabiyyah* (a long, loose, hooded garment with full sleeves) and a white *kaffiyah* (cloth headdress), which is held by a black *aqal* (a thin cord fastened around the crown). His black moustache, the symbol of manliness, is clearly visible. He is out in the scorching sun, playing an *ʿud* for his beloved, who is in the shade of a massive wall (again, not looking in his direction). The man is in the hot sun, fighting against the world; the woman is shielded by shade. The building beside them is decorated with geometric forms, ornaments, and latticed windows. The lattices too are part of the game of covering and revealing, of light and shadow: one can look through them without being seen, one can fantasize and yearn for what they hide. The size of the

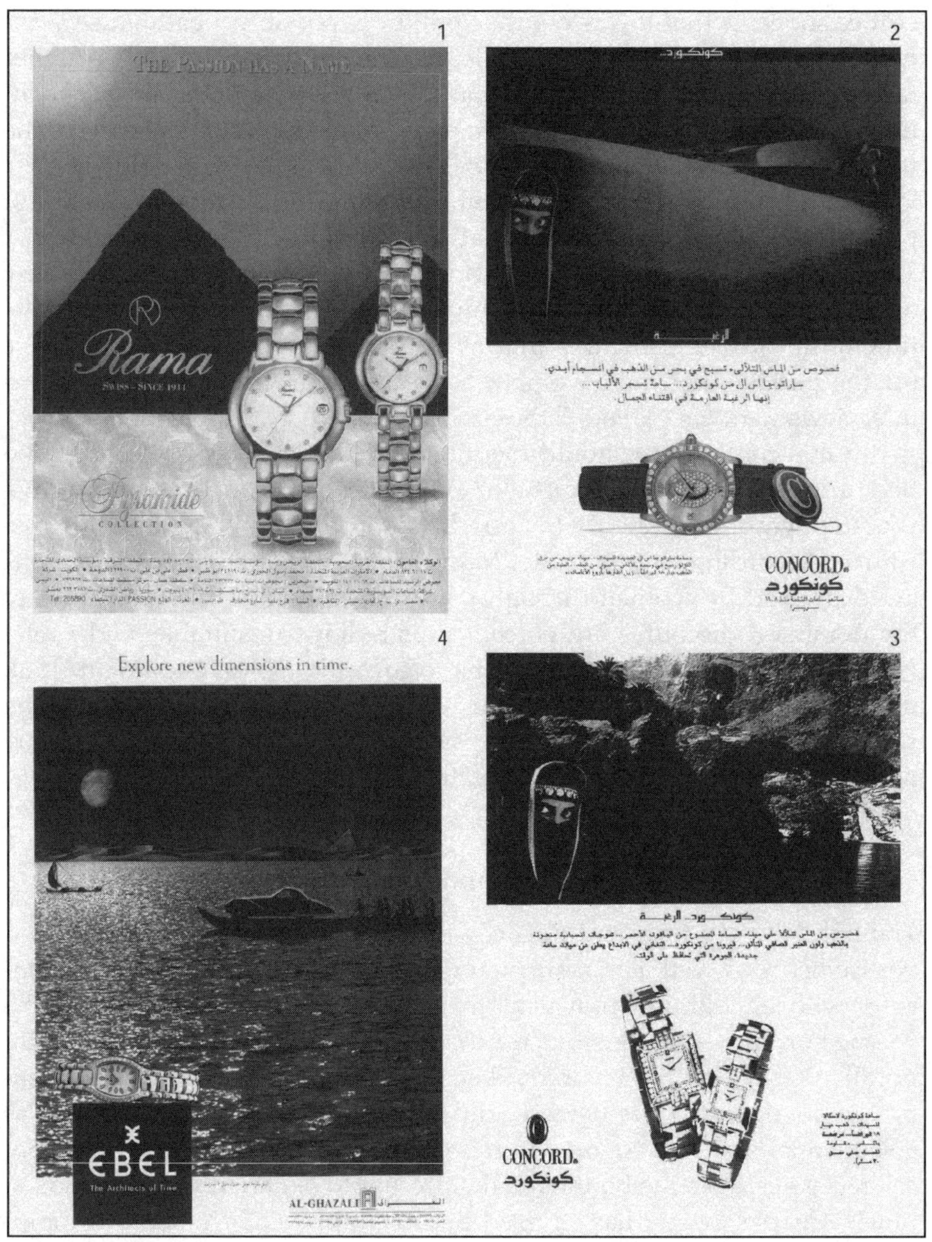

Fig.2 (1) Pyramid Collection by Rama; (2) Concord: The Passion (desert); (3) Concord: The Passion (oasis); (4) Ebel–nile and pyramids.

edifice suggests that this is a public building, possibly a bathhouse, *hammam*, outside of which the lover lies in wait for his beloved.[24] Another factor suggesting a bathhouse is that this is the only other ad that mentions the watch's resistance, and it too describes the watch in terms of the flow of water: "A unique experience with time . . . A gift of flowing . . . Wonderful moments with the sheen of a glittering diamond on a sea of pure gold . . . Enchanted times that pass by quickly, without delay . . . The Swiss Concord watch . . . does not know the limits of time." The flow of Arab music, like that of water, mixes with the flow of Arab time. The time of this advertisement is that of the active Arab man making music for the passive, listening woman. *Sayyidati* often prints articles on and interviews with `ud players[25]; these musicians are invariably men.

In this context, we should mention Lila Abu-Lughod's research into Bedouin poetics among the *Awlad Ali*.[26] Her study focuses on the discourse of emotions, one that contradicts and distorts the masculine discourse. According to this study, in everyday social situations, emotions are expressed by women through the use of music, while the values of the dominant discourse are perceived as hollow, unsuitable, and irrelevant.[27] The advertising dream seems to turn the tables: one might think that emotional discourse is invading masculine discourse, that the *grand récit* (to use Lyotard's term) is collapsing. But again, this can happen only in dreams, only in moments of time that can never be reached.

Time and Music

The link between time and music, which we will encounter in other advertisements as well, is not surprising. The famous physicist Roger Penrose, with an opinion prevalent in modern physics, believes that the passage of time is an illusion and that past, present, and future are temporally coexistent. He has remarked that the musical experience is supratemporal; that is, we perceive music as a single whole, rather than as a sequential series of sounds. In moments of inspiration, he writes, consciousness escapes the bounds of the present to experience other kinds of time.[28] Charles Seeger has stressed the role of music in "speech communication."[29] Theodor Adorno has revealed the politics of music and its symbolic uses.[30] In the case of advertising, it is the metaphor of music, the sounds heard in the reader's brain, that are socially and politically exploited.

Fares al-Shidyaq, a Lebanese Maronite who converted to Presbyterianism, lived in Europe between the years 1830 and 1850. He worked in Malta and studied the differences between Arabic and "Frankish" music. He appreciated the polyphony of Western music and the variety of instruments it employs, but was bored by its "dissonance" and the "lack of emotion in singing." Al-Shidyaq remarked that the "Franks" he met in Egypt found Egyptian music saddening; his explanation for this was the difference in the Arabic way of expressing tenderness and love, which, he said, was more flexible than in the West.[31] (Zeldin states that "Arabic love reached the French troubadours not through philosophers, but by music."[32]) According to al-Shidyaq, the main characteristic of Arabic music was *tarab*, a feeling of lightness that may be caused by joy or by grief.[33] Likewise in advertising, the function of the frozen music is to affect readers and magnify their emotions. In Peirce's terminology the sign and the interpretant of music are both culturally dependent.

Past and Present, Man and Woman

The connection between past and present, and between man and woman, is stressed in another advertisement in the series, "Concord: The Imagination." This time, the woman is passing by in a car with a half-open window; the horizontal slit of the window reveals the horizontal slit of her facial covering, which in turn reveals her eyes. Again, it is a picture inside a picture, a slit inside a slit, a fantasy inside a fantasy, a covering beneath a covering. The woman is not driving the car,[34] only looking out the passenger-side window; she is being driven, not holding the wheel herself. The glass of the window reflects the man; he is standing on a raised mound releasing a falcon that carries something shiny in its talons (a watch?) toward the woman. Falconry is a traditional male pastime among Saudi Bedouins. Once again, the woman is not looking at the man. He is standing at the right of the picture, while she is looking left, possibly at the mediating falcon. This time, the picture looks more like a parting, the end of a relationship. The lovers exchange one last look, and the shiny object is the souvenir of an enchanted time, conveyed by a flying go-between. Here the mediation is still necessary, unavoidable; there is no direct, simple contact. "Dream pictures offer us delicacy and beauty, when the imagination hovers in the world of the noble design and taste of a special hour . . . The Swiss Concord watch . . . Its beauty surpasses dreams."

The parting implicit in every meeting, the yearning for the beloved, are imprinted deeply in Arab culture and recur in literary, theatrical, and cinematic narratives. This is the "sweet sorrow that is such a prominent mood in so much of contemporary Egyptian popular culture,"[35] a claim equally true for other Arab states. Theodor Zeldin adds that "more and more people today have Arab or Persian hearts, for romantic love is a Middle Eastern invention."[36] He continues to say that the Bedouin nomads in the Arabian desert, whose lifestyle was extremely simple, had no need for passionate love. But, according to Zeldin, the Bedouins allowed intimate relations between the sexes; mutual jesting was part of the code of conduct, and men and women could say almost anything to each other. It is to this kind of lighthearted playfulness that the extraordinary idea that two people can love each other enough to give up all else owes its development. Sometimes, banter between a young local woman and a foreign guest (to whom the Bedouins' tradition of hospitality allowed freedoms they denied to themselves) could test her loyalty to the tribe. Humor, the security valve of this system, could fly out of control, and the thrill of breaking the rules, taking risks, braving the unknown, thinking oneself right and the whole world wrong, preferring the mysterious to the familiar, bind the two in a conspiracy of passion.[37]

Advertisements exploit these desires, which are stamped into the collective subconscious. Furthermore, it makes them possible, for in reality their realization is severely punished; the most obvious example is the murder of the Saudi princess Mis'al bint-Fahd ibn-Muhammad in a Jeddah parking lot for defiling the honor of the family (following a love affair with Khalil Mahlal, who was also executed).[38] The love that destroys lovers is the strongest kind of love in Arab culture and has formed the plot of stories, poetry, and songs from the very beginnings of Arab literature, at least since the third century after the Hijra (the famous *"hadith al-'ashk,"* the "telling of love" by Ibn Da'ud is a case in point).[39]

All the Concord advertisement texts contain frequent ellipses (. . .), which evoke a childlike, naive, expectant concept of time. The sentences stretch out in time, just like time itself. And complementing this naiveté is a sense of passion, of social transgression, of secrecy. But this is an organized passion, a prefabricated, patterned transgression, which must take place within a social framework that dictates its limits and character. This social framework is the contrast, the careful observation of clearly defined boundaries. And indeed, all the advertisements, as reflections of Saudi life, employ contrast: woman versus man, eternity versus transience, water versus desert, heaven versus earth, light versus shadow, white versus black, event versus reflection, observer versus observed. The only mediator between these social contrasts, the only possibility of flying like a falcon or a soul out of the present and into eternal time, is the Concord watch. Advertising liberates.

Islamic Time: Knowing When to Pray

The next historical period is the Islamic period, whose beginnings overlap with the Arab period. This connection is made by the Corum watchmakers, designers of the "Special Watch," advertising their Shahrazad model.[40] "This is a Shahrazad watch [the noun is feminine], glittering with gold and diamonds, with a movable window, which Corum presents to the woman who wishes to be the Shahrazad of her time." The connection between time and Scheherezade, the legendary storyteller of Arabian Nights, itself produces a "movable window" relating the present, Arabism, and Islam. For *The Arabian Nights* is a collection of stories from Eastern sources (Persian, Arabic, and other) thought to have been gathered into a single corpus during the Abbasid caliphate (750–1258). Just as these stories, with the passage of time, became "Arabic" and "Islamic," Scheherezade can now become a modern-day Saudi woman.

The history of time continues deeper into the Islamic period, reaching "Islamic time." The science of time and timekeeping was of great significance in Islamic civilization, as stated in verse 103 of the Koranic *Surat al-Nisa* (Chapter of Women): *"an al-salah kanat `ala al-mu'minin kitaban mawkutan"* (Prayer for the believer is a timed book). The importance of determining the precise times of prayer and the direction of Mecca (*qiblah*) brought about considerable development in the sciences and gave birth to new scientific disciplines. Timekeeping required substantial knowledge of mechanics, optics, atmospheric physics, mathematics, and other fields[41]; therefore, Islam stressed scientific development almost from its origins.[42] Determining time was closely bound with heavenly bodies and astronomical phenomena. Astronomical tables, *zij*, contained information on dates, prayer times, and direction of prayer. As a result, the study and development of astronomy was considered to be *fard kifayah* (a collective duty); the well-known theologian al-Ghazali (11th–12th cent.) declared that every Muslim community must possess at least one expert on astronomy.[43] The philosophy of Avicenna is also indissolubly bound with the concept of physical time.[44] Almost from its early beginnings, the Muslim world contained a large number of astronomers, and the Abbasid caliph al-Ma'mun (reigned 813–833) founded two observatories, in Shamsiyyah and Qasiyun. In the following seven centuries, twelve more observatories were established by Muslim rulers, and many others by private individuals.

In fact, interest in the stars and in astronomy predated Islam; for the desert nomad, the sun and moon were insufficient guides for navigation and orientation. Just as the Kabah and the worship of the black stone existed before the appearance of Islam, the duty of praying toward Mecca was adapted from the nomad's system of navigating toward Mecca, turning it into a form of virtual navigation fulfilled only once in a lifetime, in the *hajj*. Star calendars also existed in the Arabian peninsula.[45] Ryckmans claimed that such calendars were used for commercial purposes in ancient Arabia, while the lunar calendar served religious and ritual functions.[46] Thus, Islam's debt to Arabism includes use of the moon for ritual purposes and the stars for navigation and trade (two practices that can already be found in the pre-Islamic cultures of the Sassanians, the Hebrews, and other civilizations of the Fertile Crescent and the ancient Middle East).

Saudi advertising alludes frequently to this historical knowledge of astronomy. The Movado Corporation created a series of watch advertisements titled "A Wonderful Work of Art" (*tuhfah faniyyah ra'i'ah*). The first advertisement shows one of the models accompanied by an astrolabe "from seventeenth-century Morocco." Another features a pocket sundial "made in seventeenth-century Iran . . . whose front and lid are engraved with the names of the most famous Islamic countries . . . and which shows the exact time in all these countries simultaneously." The third advertisement shows another astrolabe, whose design suits that of the advertised watch (the Etwal model, whose name suggests the French *étoile*, "star"); the Arabic letters are replaced by diamonds in the new model. The astrolabe is "of yellow copper engraved with celestial symbols." The picture, it is stated, is from the *Islamic Encyclopedia* compiled by Dr. Jasim Abd al-Latif of Bahrein. The Swiss watch, which is displayed in "over 22 museums worldwide," would not have been possible without Islamic knowledge. Swiss time, despite the difference in zones, adapts itself to Saudi time. So, "Why decorate your wrist with an ordinary watch when you can purchase this wonderful work of art?" All the advertisements in this series, which connect hourglasses, astrolabes, and modern Western watches, echo the opinion of Muhammad Ilyas: "What Muslims preserved and developed during the next 500 years became a phenomenal asset for the Western renaissance of later centuries—a debt modern science owes to Islam."[47]

Another company whose watches are adapted to Islamic time is Mido (Swiss, est. 1918).[48] In the center of the advertised watch is a world map; the frame contains the names of important world cities, including Mecca, Cairo, Tehran, and Dubai. "Yesterday I was in Jakarta, today in Mecca al-Mukarrama ['honorable Mecca,' an Islamic designation for the Holy City that appears whenever it is mentioned, advertisement texts included], tomorrow in New York. My companion [feminine] is the Mido World Timer [transcribed in Arabic letters], the only Swiss watch [again feminine] that automatically changes to local time at the press of a button."

The Geneva-based Patek Philippe company also advertises a watch suited for sale in Islamic countries—studded with 114 diamonds, corresponding to the number of *surat*, or chapters, in the Koran ("lay the foundation stone of a noble tradition").[49] But none of these watches, which are marketed for a relatively large audience and address foreign readers as well, reaches the level of Islamization of item 95 in the 1995 Sotheby's watch catalog (the watch itself dates from the 1950s)[50]:

> A pink gold center seconds wristwatch with a map showing Mecca, Lusina, circa 1950: 18k, nickel lever movement with 17 jewels, champagne chapter ring with applied faceted baton numerals, the center with polychrome enamel map of Saudi Arabia showing Mecca, the back of the case engraved with a map of Saudi Arabia and inscribed *Al-Mamlakah Al-Arabiyyah Al-Sa'udiyyah, Al-Ka'bah Al-Sharifah*. Diameter 37 mm . . . £800–1,000.

Such collector's items exist as well, but are not for mass advertisement in *Sayyidati*. For everyday products, it is enough to adapt models designed for marketing in the West.

The Ottoman Era: Time in Wooden Boxes

The Rolex Corporation also makes use of Muslim history. Its advertisement features two timepieces: above, a "Turkish" clock from the mid-eighteenth century; below, a modern Rolex watch.[51] Until the twentieth century, Turkish (Ottoman) time differed from Western time; not only did the Ottomans use the Muslim calendar, but their Western calendar too was not the one utilized in the West. Only on March 1, 1917, did the Ottomans convert from the Julian to the Gregorian reckoning.[52] Western timepieces were exported to the Ottoman Empire and were highly popular as gifts (the clock that Louis Philippe presented to Muhammad Ali in "exchange" for the famous obelisk that stands today at the Place de la Concorde stopped after a few months and was regarded as a symbol of the asymmetry between the "exploitative" colonialist power and "exploited" Egypt[53]). The Turkish clock "is equipped with three boxes, each of which covers the surface of the clock with absolute precision . . . These clocks were fitted with two, three or four boxes, in order to maintain their interior motion." The text continues in a larger font, separating the upper and lower parts of the advertisement: "In the many centuries past, clockmakers have known that the roots of beauty are deep and firm." The advertisement, then, shows the reader an historical watch and provides the historical knowledge needed for understanding its design. It answers an historical question: why were such watches made with so many boxes? All this information is presented in order to promote the "Rolex Lady Dith watch . . . manufactured with absolute precision, kept in a single pearl-like box of strong, expensive metal to preserve the mechanics of its motion, to a depth of 100 meters." The "absolute precision" of the eighteenth-century clockmakers is matched by that of Rolex. Furthermore, the same desire for accuracy that characterized the Ottoman clock with its insulating lids is reflected in the single lid of the Rolex design. Progress finds a concrete expression: the removal of two lids. The insulation of the watch is expressed by the "pearl-like" metal, waterproof to 100 meters. Here the depth is a metaphor for quality: after all, no one would buy such a diamond-studded watch in order to dive 100 meters below sea level with it. This is a conventional sort of abstract and detached advertising boast; it would have sufficed to say that one could take a shower with the watch (and even that would probably have been superfluous). For readers in the Gulf countries, this too is a link with history, since one of the traditional industries of the region is pearl diving.

Another company that uses the sea as a metaphor for time is Consul, also a Swiss firm.[54] The text reads, "The Golden Bay collection, a yacht which 'whispers words of love' to the sea shyly yet proudly . . . The

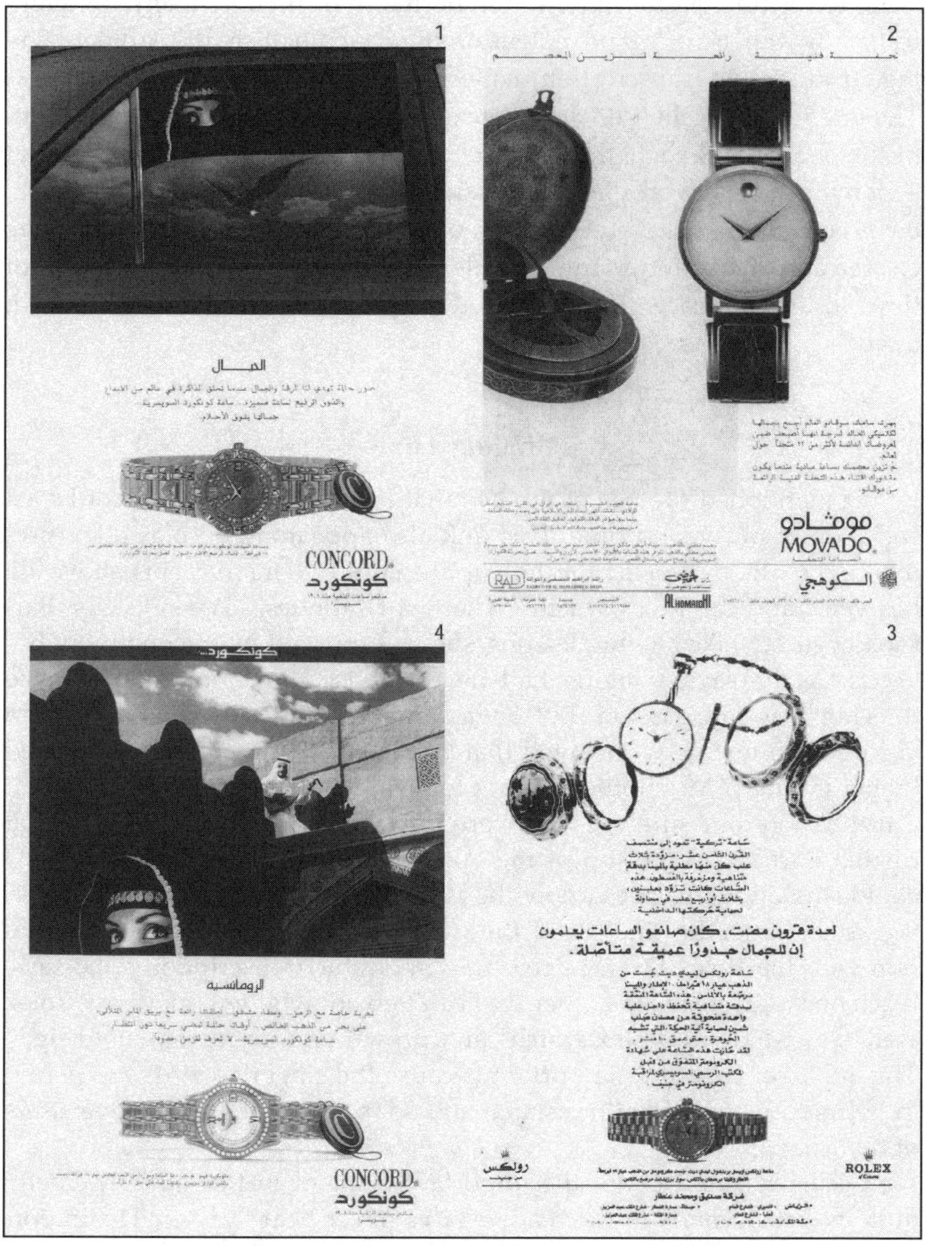

Fig.3 (1) Concord: The Imagination (Falcon); (2) Movado–sundial;
(3) Rolex–"Turkish" watch; (4) Concord: The Romance ('ud).

elegance of time [*al-zaman*] and the harmony of time [*al-waqt*] are manifested by the beauty and splendor which embellish the Golden Bay
[again in Arabic transcription] collection from Consul. Golden Bay . . .
The quality of excellence." In this text, the advertisers exploit the wealth
of the Arabic language, the ultimate cultural tool, with its abundance of
synonyms, puns, wordplay, expressions, and idioms. Repetition in Arabic is considered good style, a form of emphasis that makes the message
clearer and more important. The elegance of time and the harmony of
time: in the first case, the word used for "time" is *zaman*, in the second,
waqt.[55]

Singing Time

I have mentioned the use of the *'ud*, that is, of music, and Concord's association of music and time. This link also appears in a Rolex advertisement. The title is "Cecilia Bartholi appreciates two instruments above all:
her voice and the Rolex watch." The text continues, "When Cecilia Bartholi began to take singing lessons, she was amazed by the quality of her
voice. Cecilia says, 'Singing had never aroused my interest. Flamenco
dancing was my passion. But I was amazed to discover I had such a
voice.'" The text goes on to tell that Cecilia's talent was first recognized
by her mother: "My mother did not force me, but she asked me to give it
a try. Slowly but surely, I discovered my voice." This is the voice that
carried Bartholi to the top of the opera world: "Today I love to sing. I
could sing all night, but I know the audience has to return home." Later,
the article links the singer and the watch: "Cecilia feels the same sensa-
tion with the Rolex Oyster Perpetual [in Arabic transcription]. She says,
'Each one of us needs the other . . . I can't go anywhere without my Rolex
watch, just like my Rolex watch can't do without my companionship.'"
The quote, of course, is important because the singer's words are placed
in her mouth, or at least translated and adapted, by the Arab advertisers
of the watch.

Cecilia Bartholi is not the important element in this advertisement;
quite possibly, many of the readers have never heard of her. The important fact is that she is a singer. Singing and poetry were of great importance in the oral Bedouin Arab culture, and it was Arab poetry that
preserved "history." The Jahili poetry was already closely bound with
the experience of time,[56] but it was in the twentieth century, with the

arrival of mass media, that singers, especially women, were granted royal receptions in the Arab countries. The most prominent Arab women singers were Um Kultum (Kawkab al-Sharq, "the Star of the East") and the Lebanese Fayruz. The importing of advertisements and women singers together is suited to Arab culture.

Mickey Mouse Time

The history of time reaches up to today's Arabian peninsula, which is also used in advertisements. An ad titled "The History of Tremendous Achievements" describes the accomplishments of the Rolex watch since 1914, when it was awarded "a certificate declaring it to be the first wristwatch to perform better than pocket watches."[57] Landmark years are listed, among them "1986: The Royal Geographic Society relies on Rolex watches in its study of the al-Wahibah desert in Oman, due to the watch's resistance to unnatural desert temperatures."

At first glance, one might think that contemporary "Western time" is also invading Saudi time. The al-'Ata watch company marketed, as a "holiday gift" (for the *'Id al-Fitr* festival), four Mickey Mouse watches: "The first and only [such] watch . . . Beware of imitations . . . Look at the back of the watch to find the name of the model beginning with M."[58] But this watch is not sold in a vacuum; the Arab Mickey Mouse is not necessarily the same as his American counterpart, as Allen Douglas and Fedwa Malti-Douglas demonstrated in their book on Arabic comics. They showed how the Mickey Mouse character is used to create Arab narratives: Mickey, portrayed as the hero of Arabism, wears a *jalabiyyah* and wields a *misbahah*.[59] There is also an Arabic-language children's magazine called *Miki*, tracing the adventures of the mouse, who speaks Arabic. The use of an Arab Mickey Mouse recurs in other products as well.[60] The watch itself does not change physically—its inscription still reads "Mickey Mouse"—but the mental concept it evokes is completely different from that of the Western world, Mickey's birthplace.

Back to the Future

The next period of time an advertiser can use is, ultimately, the future. Patek Philippe, with commanding authority, advises its readers to "lay the foundation stone of a deep-rooted tradition that is uniquely yours."

The vowel marks in the Arabic equivalent of "yours" make it clear that the form is masculine; in another version of the advertisement, it is clearly feminine. The first version shows the feet of a "father" in Western dress teaching his pajama-wearing son to play the piano. In the second, a "mother" is seated in the back of a car with her "daughters" (all the women are blonde, with a Western appearance and modern dress).

This is an example of an advertisement imported from the West. The only change is in the text, but it is a considerable one. The suggestion of laying a "foundation stone" (*hajar al-asas*) is a distinctly deep-rooted Arabic one. The association of time and stones is not surprising when one thinks of the black stone (*al-hajar al-aswad*) in the Ka'ba in Mecca, which hundreds of thousands of Muslims every year attempt to squeeze against in order to escape the flames of hell. The same structure houses another, often forgotten, stone, the "happy stone" (*al-hajr al-as'ad*), while Jerusalem possesses the "drinking stone," from which the whole world emerged, also sacred to Islam (according to the interpreters, the Hebrew word *shtiyah* means both "drinking" and "a place of origin"). Stones are also the only objects that survive the all-obliterating desert sun. They are a landmark for wanderers in the journey through time. Raising a family is a milestone in time. This is also an example of the importation of advertisements that are suitable for Saudi-Arabic-Islamic time. Photographs stressing family values, showing modestly dressed women, do not cause a "time gap." Of course, it is impossible to change the watch itself, which in this case shows both the Gregorian calendar and the days of the week, and perhaps a more acute advertiser would have created a new ad with a musical instrument other than the piano, but the connection with "foundation stones" and "deep-rooted tradition" is kept even when new options are presented. In a sense, the appearance of the Western piano and the blonde women actually strengthens Arabism: it is an antigenic vaccine of reduced Westernism, which ultimately preserves hegemonic Saudi values. After all, the text is in Arabic, and the separation of men and women is strictly observed. The invasion of Western time takes place in a quieter fashion: in almost all the advertisements for timepieces, the time is 10:10 (or somewhere between 10:08 and 10:11). This arrangement of the watch hands, creating a V-for-Victory sign, is an advertising technique meant to emphasize the name of the company, which usually appears in the upper part of the watch; it is common practice both in the West and in the Far East.

The digits in the imported watches are Roman or Western (so-called Arabic) numerals; watches featuring actual Arabic numerals are not advertised (though such models have been manufactured in the past). This is no surprise; remaking the models to contain real Arabic numerals would increase manufacturing costs. The function of advertising is to take the same product and turn it into "something else." This role is simplified by the manufacture and importation of watches without digits, watches in which the digits are replaced by diamonds, lines, or dots,[61] or in which only certain digits appear (e.g., IX and VI). The use of Roman numerals helps to dissociate the watch from the modern West and lend it an historical flavor and classical prestige; the Roman Empire also encompassed the Middle East. Indeed, among the watches imported and advertised are many models in which the digits are replaced by other symbols.

Most of the imported watches feature round surfaces. This fact, interesting in itself with regard to the development, representation, and perception of time, may not be surprising since watch surfaces are usually manufactured in circular shapes.[62] But one may say that the direction of the "ticking" of Arab time in these advertisements is, in a sense, reversed: from right to left, through the top of the circle, in a counterclockwise direction. Again, of course, the manufacturers have not changed the model. But when Rolex advertised three of its watches, they were described from right to left. The picture showed the three watches, with the central one raised slightly above the other two. When the text is read or the picture examined in an "Arabic" fashion, the direction of eye movement is reversed. The reading direction conflicts with the "real" motion of the watch hands.

The watches advertised in *Sayyidati* should be seen as jewelry; they are meticulously designed and made of precious metals and stones. The slogan in Rolex advertisements was "Guaranteed Value Watches." In one ad, the watch was pictured on top of a sort of wooden treasure chest or jewel box.[63] That the value of jewels, including watches, should be preserved is of special importance for Saudi women: these are the assets they keep in the event of a divorce.

The Potpourri of Times and Eras

Thus modern Saudi advertisers construct the histories of various periods, or various histories. The timepiece ads juxtapose the Pharaonic period, the nomadic period, the age of Islamic scientific discovery, the Saudi future, and others. The advertisements demonstrate how advertisers control historical information, for information is a form of order: they utilize clothing, eyes, the desert, falcons, music, the ʻud, and other symbols of special significance to Saudi readers.

But above all, the time of Saudi advertising is also timeless or supra-temporal: it contains all times. It is a time whose reality is relative, an invariant time. Ultimately, it is a quiet time. There is no ticking, no history; there are only frozen, imaginary, never attainable events—a pseudotemporal reality. The transient nature of time disappears; the Saudi, Arab, or Islamic symbolic universe becomes a collection of situations of equal reality status. Advertisers distort "space-time," deliberately sacrificing the creative aspect of time, blending different events and places. They provide security and pleasure for a temporary period; if to misuse the words of *Surat al-Baqra*—the second chapter of the Koran—verse 36: "You shall have stability and pleasure on the earth for a time." Advertising denies the existence of social evolution, preserving the hegemonic order. Thus, it functions as a conservative force.

Without changing anything, advertising solves the problem identified by Ibrahim al-Ati: "Time is probably the missing chapter in our contemporary Arab Islamic life. This may be one of the deep-seated, hidden reasons behind our civilizational underdevelopment, a reason which researchers do not sufficiently attend to. Perhaps this study may be a step toward discovering the civilizational time of this nation, a time which links its past to its present and spurs it towards the glowing future, with God's will."[64] In this sense of a magical solution, timepiece advertising in Saudi Arabia is the advertising of salvation. Ibn Hanbal, founder of the Hanbali school (*madhhab*) of Islam that is prevalent in Saudi Arabia, quotes a hadith of the prophet Muhammad: "The hour [also 'the clock'] will not come until time draws near, and the year becomes a month, the month a week, the week a day, and the day an hour."[65] Or, according to al-Maʻari, "The smallest segment of time contains all forms of awareness [*al-mudarakat*]."[66] Reducing history to fit into a single weekly journal allows the advertiser to keep the clock moving, to bridge gaps in space and time, to satisfy the living and the dead.

In other words, these advertisements are timeless, although they are taken from a weekly published in the late 1990s. To interpret them requires a knowledge of other time periods. But history cannot be wholly expressed in this array of timepieces; it is for exactly this reason that advertisers conjure up ancient periods in a sort of shamanic ancestor worship. All the historical possibilities of existence undergo a process of historicization and are resurrected. Amorphous, abstract history becomes accessible. But this is really a form of time without memory: turn the page and you find yourself in another period, the miracle of nostalgia takes place before your eyes, you are in a previous incarnation. This may be seen either as frozen time or as infinitely fast time, as the two are actually the same. It is an ecstasy of times. Into the leisure time of reading a weekly are compressed all other times: the Creation, the end of the world, and everything in between. These watches bring the reader scents and secrets from other ages. "Time talks. It speaks more plainly than words. The message it conveys comes through loud and clear"[67]: God is the machine, the machine is God.

CHAPTER TWO

The Camel and the Wheel: Automobiles in the Desert

This chapter deals with *al-'arabah al-'arabiyyah*, the Arab car (cf. Turkish *'araba* "car"), or, more precisely, with how foreign automobiles become part of the `arab `uraba', "the pure Arabs."[1] The number of cars in Saudi Arabia increased dramatically from the 1970s to the 1990s: in 1970 the total number of cars was 65,000, in 1978 it was 235,000, in 1983–85 it was already 2.85 million, and in 1992 it reached 3.58 million.[2]

An especially fascinating advertisement is for the classic American brand GMC.[3] The model advertised is a large field vehicle, so the ad itself is also an extensive one, spread over two pages. Some two thirds of the ad, including all of the left-hand side, which the eye encounters first, are taken up by the image of a large, ancient-looking papyrus, on which a family tree is drawn in black. The boxes enclosing the names in the genealogy are in the form of Arab ornamental designs—a kind of geometric arabesque. In the lower right-hand corner of the ad is the photograph of the car: black, immobile, and set against a rocky terrain. A bright light emanating from the right of the ad, the source unseen, illuminates the car and the lower-right portion of the papyrus: the enlarged box of the family tree containing the name Suburban ("Subarban"). Only certain parts of the advertisement are illuminated, while the rest is dark. A stylus, apparently the one with which the family tree was drawn, points at the car and at the enlarged box. Most of the text in the advertisement is on the right-hand side, above the picture of the car. It is in white letters against the dark background of the stony desert landscape.

The title of the ad is printed in a font resembling handwriting: "Subarban, the family car that is part of the family." The text reads, "The GMC Subarban . . . The car of perfect calm and wide dimensions, built for nine, presents you with unending luxury and all-encompassing quiet. The GMC Suburban, a car for many tasks, guarantees a strong connection [*tarabutan wathiqan*], whether driving on paved roads or in rocky areas, thanks to its wonderful power and superb performance, and thanks to its long structure and standard double air cushions, [it really] guarantees the safety of the whole family . . . So no wonder the family considers it an integral part of itself." The only text underneath the picture of the car is "GMC Subarban."

The family tree drawn on the papyrus is constructed as follows:

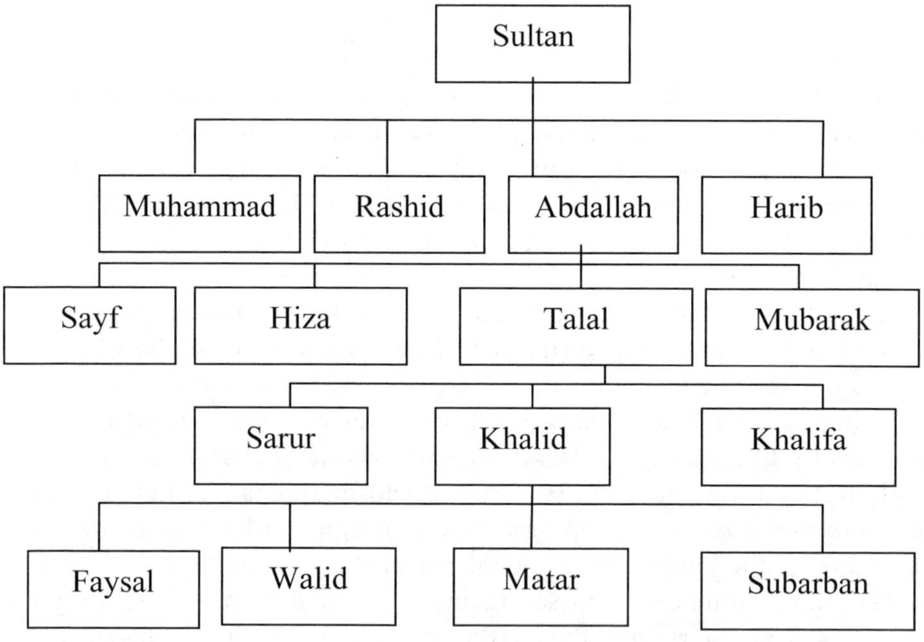

Fig.4 Genealogical tree from a GMC Suburban ad

This advertisement, therefore, has a single purpose: to make an American brand of automobile into a part of the Arab family. The size, strength, and durability of the car, and its capacity for driving through various terrains, are a clear symbol of the cohesion and continuity of the Arab family. The car is associated with a tribal consciousness and all the important qualities of this consciousness: *al-nasab* (lineage), *rabitat al-dam* (blood relation), *silat al-raham* (womb relation), and so on. In Arab culture, that which is rooted, original, aristocratic is superior to that which lacks "pedigree." To give only a few examples: when caliph Umar ibn al-Khattab distributed the *ata*, payments and rewards for Islamic warriors, he did so according to their families' historical service and loyalty to Islam. When the Abbasids decided to wage a war against the Umayyads, they claimed that the son of Muhammad ibn al-Hanafiyyah had transferred the patrimony to them. Ibn-Khaldun stressed that *'asabiyyah*, or tribal solidarity, can be fortified by a family tree of common ancestors, *real or imaginary*.[4] This is also the reason why most royal houses in the Arab world strive to found their legitimacy on descent from an ancient forefather.

The black vehicle planted in the expanse of the desert, with its elongated shape and air cushions, resembles the inside of a traditional Bedouin tent: a "tent" like the huge automobile-shaped houses built by Sheik Hamd ibn Hamdan al-Nahayan from Abu-Dhabi in the middle of the desert.[5] The size of the advertising desert is emphasized by the choice of an expensive two-page format and suggested by the dearth of punctuation marks in the text. GMC, just like the Arabian desert, symbolizes perfect calm and wide dimensions. In the sound of its engine is the all-encompassing quiet of the desert. Just like the camel and its rider (in the watch ads we encountered *Abu al-Hawl*, the sphinx; it is now time for *Abu-Ayub*, the camel), the car and its driver develop a staunch friendship. Just like the camel, this car is built for many tasks; just like the camel, it can penetrate the rocky desert areas; like the best camels, it has two "humps" (in the form of air cushions), grants security to the entire family, and thus becomes an inseparable part of it. It is as if the automobile becomes part of the camel economy described by Bulliet.[6] In fact, the word *sayarah* (car) previously meant "caravan."[7] A *sayyar* is someone who is often traveling or roaming. This vehicle, then, is a tent that can stand up and walk like a camel, or a camel that can plant itself in the ground like a tent; it is anything but a mere car.

The illustrious Arab genealogy, the line of those who trace their lineage back to the sultan himself, is now joined by a glorious new scion: Subarban. The phonetic similarity between the two names, both of which start with *su* and end with *an*, is no accident. The two mythological fathers of the southern and northern Arabs (the *qays* and the *yaman*) were named Andan and Qahtan. The advertisement creates an imaginary forefather whose name ends with the same phonemes, uniting all Arabs. It is even more "ancient" than Andan and Qahtan. Ihsan Muhammad al-Hasan writes that in many Arab tribes "the ancient forefather is imaginary rather than historical,"[8] so the tribe of which Subarban is a member is no oddity. In this case, the forefather is Sultan, and his descendants are members of the royal, almost "sharific," family. The title of sultan goes back to the rulers of the Seljuk dynasty, a Turkish lineage of the Sunni Islamic persuasion (reigned 1038–1194, in today's Iran and Iraq). The meaning of the title is "wielder of power," and it was adopted by later dynasties.[9] The genealogy in the advertisement contains Arab names that may be identified with various Islamic groups and countries. Subarban is a descendant of Abdallah, a name born by the father of the prophet Muhammad, by the founder of modern Jordan, and by the Saudi crown prince. According to Islamic tradition, "Since the creation of the first man, the essence of the divine light was bestowed on the best of Adam's seed, generation by generation, until it reached the loins of the grandfather of Muhammad and Ali."[10] Shi'i tradition states that at this point, the divine light split in two: one part went to 'Abdallah, the Prophet's father, and the other to his brother Abu Talib, father of Ali.[11] The same spark of genetically transmitted divine light, it seems, now falls to Subarban, whose picture is illuminated with a celestial glow. But Abdallah is not the only illustrious name in the dynasty; all the names bear various Arabic connotations. Subarban's brother is one of the prominent figures of modern Arab nationalism, Faysal (rapier), whose importance in the post–World War I history of Syria and Iraq is considerable[12]; his uncle is the present Egyptian president, Mubarak; he is even related to the Prophet of Islam, Muhammad. This glorious family is now joined by Subarban, the "eternal" (*khalid*, the name of his grandfather)—he becomes all the names, he becomes *the* name.

It is interesting that any Arab reader, from any country, can find a figure to identify with. Subarban is beyond family disputes. The use of names that are significant to citizens of different Arab countries exalts Subarban above all conflicts and associates him with the "merciful father" of all Arabs. Thus the advertisement, in a weekly distributed all over the Arab world, manages to break the shackles of narrow parochialism. Subarban is emphasized, enclosed in a larger box than the others, and strongly illuminated. Most of the dynasty that the ancient stylus wrote "along the generations" is now in the darkness of "history." The bright light shines on the present. Subarban is the chosen one of his generation, he is the eldest (first from the right), his hour has come.

The reduction of Arab history to five generations is not arbitrary. The strongest cultural mechanism for preserving family cohesion, that of "blood vengeance" (*al-ahz bil-shi`r*), is founded on a five-generation concept. This is the *khums* structure, which forms part of *asabiyyah*, tribal solidarity. Every individual is obliged to avenge the blood of a family member two generations back (father and grandfather) and two generations forward (son and grandson). Subarban has, in fact, entered an immutable structural system, in which roles never change. Subarban arrives at the bottom, he is the promise of the future, a finger of the *hamsah*, the palm that averts evil. He has entered a motionless present, in Clifford Geertz's sense. Geertz's famous article on the Balinese concept of humanity, "Person, Time, and Conduct in Bali," is illuminating in this context. His main thesis is that Balinese perceive each other as "generalized contemporaries"; that is, as instances of types, as occupiers of roles, titles, positions, and so forth. This is a form of time in which all possible types of people coexist simultaneously; while names (at most) may change, social roles remain. Individuals existing in the present are depersonalized; people are their social functions. In this sense, the time of the Saudi car is also a perpetual present in which all generations coexist, "a motionless present, a vectorless now,"[13] a time that marches in place ad infinitum. The irony, of course, is that the American automobile is introduced with "natural artificiality" into a culture that so stresses the distinction between the "internal" (*batin*) and the "external" (*zahir*).[14]

The dynasty in the advertisement is patriarchal. All the names are masculine; there is not a single woman. Women are erased from history. This fact is a dramatic link between advertising fictions and everyday Saudi reality: women in Saudi Arabia are not allowed to drive.[15] During the Gulf War, when Saudi women demonstrated, demanding the right to drive, the authorities responded by activating the *mutatwwi'un*, or "volunteers," a "modesty brigade" corps. The demonstration was spurred by the sight of American women soldiers driving on the kingdom's roads, as well as Kuwaiti women fleeing the troops of Saddam Hussein. Among the arguments of the Saudi women was the fact that, unlike the Kuwaiti women, they were unable to protect their children, as well as the fact that some 20 percent of an average family's income was spent on keeping a chauffeur; at the outbreak of the war, 300,000 men were employed as full-time chauffeurs in Saudi Arabia.[16] In the context of advertising and consumerism, it is interesting to consider the place where the women chose to dismiss their chauffeurs, and where a quarter of them began to drive by themselves: the parking lot of the *al-Tamimi* supermarket in Riyadh, a famous shopping center. The women who drove were all dressed in accordance with the Islamic code and possessed foreign drivers licenses. All the demonstrators were from "good" families, some of them related to the royal family, most of them with a Western education. In a letter to Prince Salman ibn Abd al-Aziz, the governor of Riyadh, considered a liberal, the demonstrators stressed that in the time of the Prophet, women rode camels, then the chief means of transportation.[17] In Saudi Arabia, even opposition to authority must be expressed in Arab-Islamic terms. The harsh response of the regime, despite a slight disposition to lenience immediately after the demonstration, was encouraged by the conservative chief *alim* (religious authority), Abdallah ibn Abd al-Aziz ibn Baz. According to Doumato, the treatment of women, including the prohibition of driving, is the Saudi regime's way of introducing change while symbolically preserving Islamic values.[18] The ban on women's driving is not the only restriction; despite the rise in the number of female students in the Saudi education system, the decision whether a girl is to receive an education or not is still in the hands of her father.[19] Subarban, then, is part of the patriarchal family, the "gender monarchy." The patriarchal grid of cultural masculinity is being imposed upon this imported Western car, thus becoming an immanent part of its image.

The advertisement also emphasizes the vehicle's carriage capacity: nine people. Another advertisement for the same model stresses that the car is "considered . . . the number one selling car in the Middle East." The slogan selected for this ad was "When you need support."[20] In view of the size of Saudi families, the ability to carry a large number of passengers is emphasized in many automobile ads. So also "Avalon . . . rest and security for six passengers."[21] Avalon enables its owner to explore "new horizons," since it is "designed to carry [*li-tahtadan*] six passengers." The verb translated here as "carry" is one usually employed to describe a mother carrying her children. Once again, the car is a metaphor for a large family.

But this is a Saudi-model family, as a Chrysler ad demonstrates.[22] Chrysler also chooses for its flagship model a large family car, with the slogan "A splendor that increases with time . . . to fit the increased size of your family." The picture tells the story of a family: in the middle, an

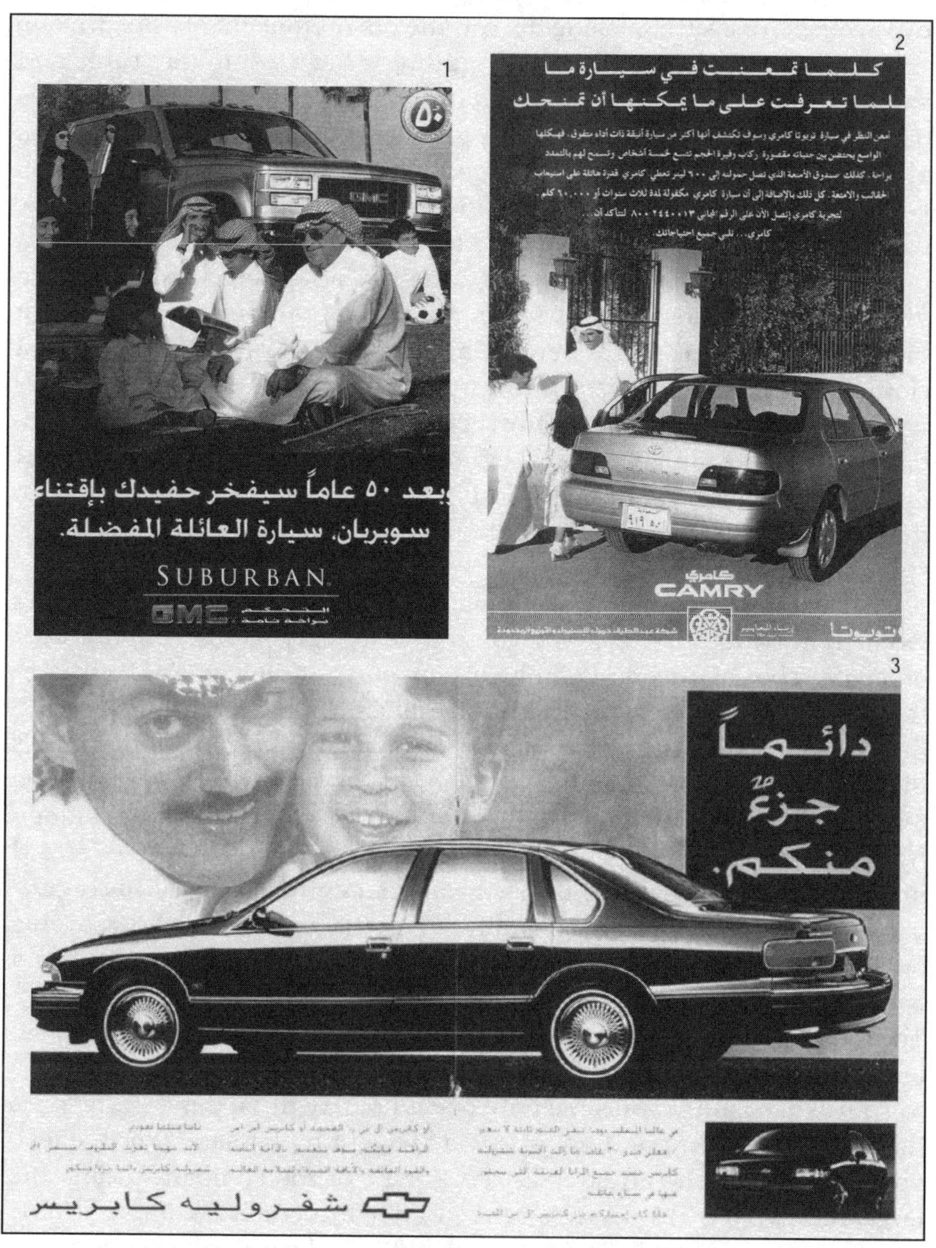

Fig.5 (1) GMC Suburban ad; (2) Toyota Camry ad; (3) Chevrolet ad.

elderly man ("grandfather") is giving his grandson a soccer ball, while two women (one sitting inside the car, the other crouching beside it) look smilingly on. On the right, a boy is putting a bicycle into the trunk, and an elderly woman is conversing with a young man. The impression is that the family has been visiting the grandparents. The elderly mother is giving her son a box of foodstuffs, while the grandfather presents his young grandson with the ball. All the men are dressed in bright white, while the women are in dark black. The black and white ball is a modern representative of the father's and grandfather's checkered headdresses, a dichromatic male continuity. Clothing is of great symbolic significance in the Middle East. Bernard Lewis, in several of his works, notes that clothing in the Middle East is an arena of confrontation and dialogue between East and West.[23] Geoffrey Lewis pointed out that while the prohibition of the caliphate in Turkey excited little interest and provoked little protest, the 1925 "hat law" forbidding the fez, the "traditional" hat that had in fact become fashionable only a century earlier, aroused widespread opposition.[24]

An interesting element of the ad is the presence of the two young women; in Saudi Arabia it is legal and customary to marry more than one wife. The callouts describing various parts of the vehicle emphasize the possibility of "carrying many objects" and "guaranteeing the children's safety." The *"maqsurah"* is not just a cabin; in Islamic tradition it is the special, luxurious chamber in a mosque, reserved for the ruler. The terminology of the ad makes the family in the car a royal family, hidden from the eyes of commoners. The advertisement stresses that "we created it [the car] while envisaging the shape of your entire family." This car can turn *any* family into a royal family. "For the first time: two movable doors on each side of the vehicle double the ease of entry," almost like a Saudi house, which possesses separate entrances for men and women. The house is "drawn" onto the road. This is why this car "is the future . . . in family transport" and is "the luxury car your family prefers."

Since the Saudi man is the only one who may drive this vehicle, he is the one who road tests it, in an advertisement by Nissan ("For the test, only Nissan").[25] The ad stresses the luxury of the company's cars, the large variety, and the services offered after the purchase. Nissan "thus maintains the pioneering spirit to which it has always accustomed you." The escort the driver receives after delivery of the car grants him the "serenity of the fully content soul" (*rahat al-bal al-tammah*), vocabulary typically used to describe the longing of the desert nomad. Since only the man drives, he is the one who does the shopping, suggests a joint ad for Volvo and the IKEA store chain.[26] It shows a Saudi man shopping with his car; literally, the vehicle is transformed into a shopping cart that he pushes along. Likewise, only the man can drive the children to school and elsewhere, as a Toyota Camry ad shows.[27] A Saudi man is opening the door for two small children so they can get into the back seat. As may be seen from this ad, Saudi license plates are black on white, with the word *al-Sa'udiyyah* at the top, below which is a license plate number composed of three Arabic letters and three Arabic digits. The different license plate is symbolic of the metamorphosis that an automobile can undergo. In a like manner, Toyota took advantage of the month of Ramadan to offer customers "wonderful surprises" in the form of dis-count sales and installment plans for various models. "This offer is valid until the end of Ramadan."[28]

It is not that women do not exist in these advertisements. In one of them, the woman is the car itself ("femina ex machina"): a Chevrolet Caprice ad states that the car is "always part of you."[29] The picture shows the car, over which the smiling heads of a "father" and "son" are visible. "In our ever-changing world, only values remain fixed and immutable. For 30 years, the beloved Chevrolet Caprice has manifested all the noble qualities you look for in a quality car. Whether you choose the excellent Caffrice LS, the luxurious Caffrice LTZ, or the lofty Caffrice SS, you will enjoy complete comfort, superb [also 'lively'] power, excellent elegance and great safety . . . just as you are accustomed to do. Because it doesn't matter if circumstances have changed, the beloved Chevrolet Caffrice always stays part of you." The man, the child, and the car become a fam-ily through the means of the woman and through the use of her. The woman becomes a tool, a machine for transporting children, for convey-ing them into life. The word *sayyarah* is feminine. Whether the man chooses the "superb," the "luxurious," or the "lofty" model, his beloved will stay with him no matter what the circumstances. It is the man who seeks and selects, from the variety of available automobiles, a "family car" that will remain such even after thirty years. But he can always switch to a newer model.

Arabism in automobile advertisements, cars as a part of the Arab family, is a theme that recurs in the context of executive cars: in the greeting *ahla[n] bi-kum* with which the Chrysler car welcomes its buyer;[30] in its "purebred" horsepower (*kuwwah hisan[an]*);[31] and in its ability to "roam the field [*maydan*, also 'battlefield'] while others stand in place."[32] "The secret of the car is in the way it confronts and overcomes challenges. Most cars quietly wait their turn, do not take initiatives, distance themselves from confrontation. But the Chrysler Stratus hastens to prove its presence as soon as it enters the field, with its powerful, commanding shape . . . It is always in the forefront ['in the chest,' *laha al-sadarah da'iman*] in terrains [*sahah*, also 'lot, field, arena'] and fields." The executive car becomes a weapon in the battle for the desert hills; it too is transported from the modern road to the open field. In the best Arab tradition, lagging behind and standing in place are something negative, a disparagement applied to one's enemies. Preserving the initiative of attack is all important; marching bravely with one's chest swelled forward has passed from the field of tribal warfare to that of modern business management.

These advertisements, in fact, present a picture similar to the phenomenon Kurpershoek discovered in his encounters with Saudi Bedouin tribes, in which he recorded traditional-style Arab Bedouin poems glorifying Western automobiles.[33] One of these poems, by a tribal poet named Abdallah al-Dindan, composed in the traditional meter -v—/-v—/-v—(*al-ramal*), contains references to showrooms exhibiting cars imported from the "dogs" (a derogatory term for those of other religions, especially Christians). Here is Kurpershoek's free translation of a passage from the poem[34]:

> 5.   O Rider of a vehicle roaring in the featureless waste,//
> Like one who is possessed by a demon,
> 6.   A car fitted with brand-new tyres,
> Selected from the dealer's showroom for forty thousand riyals
> 7.   In the early morning he sets out from the land of our brothers//
> Driving his spanking new car, a recent import from the dogs.
> 8.   The crew on board are all brash and jaunty youngsters,//
> Bold men who store in their marrow the seed of equally brave
> Ancestors.
> 9.   A vehicle that suits the dreams of a man hankering to depart,//
> One deprived of sleep by the separation from his love.
> 10.   If it is said of me, "He is not in his right mind," I swear//
> Not to give up on her, for in the end the pilgrim will reach
> Medina.
> 11.   Steering his car head-on in the wind he lets the bumper cleave
> the air//
> And does not pause until they have arrived at the loved one liv-

ing far away,
12. She whose brow shines like a polished sword
And whose conversation is sugared with honey.
13. You, fault-finders, my honour has become public property,
But they who smirch one's honour in his absence will be
forgiven.

The car thus becomes part of the Bedouin desert legacy. It mixes with poetry and its traditional meters, with wandering, nostalgia for the beloved, tribal honor, and the Arabic wealth of imagery and metaphor: the brow of the beloved as a shining sword, the meeting with her as the arrival of the pilgrim in Medina. The driver, like a camel rider, "steers his car head-on in the wind." Al-Dindan's other work contains a wide variety of traditional poetic themes: mountains, complaints of aching in the heart and eyes, abandoned camps (*atlal*), the process of poetic creation, confirmation of faith, the fate of the world, adages, expectation of rain, camel herds, love and the beloved, war poems (*razaf*), and more.[35] But if al-Dindan's car is a dream of liberation and a better life (he himself drives a tattered old van with an engine full of sand),[36] a dream woven in among his other dreams, advertisement takes these dreams and uses them for its own needs. It is quick to grasp and to exploit cultural aspirations. Advertisement too connects the car with history, but it does so for immediate, practical purposes.

Elsewhere Kurpershoek points out that:

> As the substitution of a motor car for a camel in the consolation motif suggests, the camel no longer plays a role in Bakhetaan's poetry [a name of a tribe], except when the heroic past is evoked and in a few smiles. The Saudis continue to value the camel as a herd animal supplying the kind of milk they prefer, as a symbol of prestige and their Arab roots, as a decorative element in the scenery of the desert, and as God's special gift to them. In Saudi Arabia the camel is there to stay, but I have never met a Saudi who shares any of the romantic Western nostalgia for the camel as a means of transportation.[37]

It is poetry that preserves continuity; those same poems, in the same meters and order, are turned from the camel to the car. But Geraldine Brooks's description of modern roads in the Arabian peninsula stands in contrast to the poetic dream:

> The ancient trade routes of Arabia are potholed highways now. The groaning strings of camels that Muhammad led for Khadija from coastal port to inland fortress are gone as well. Instead, trucks thud and grind from Aqaba

to Mecca through a miasma of diesel and dust. What passes for an oasis these days is a gray concrete truck stop, innocent of a palm tree or even a blade of grass.[38]

The culture of camels and wandering lives on, even though it may change its appearance and become a culture of wandering cars. Ultimately, the resultant culture is one of "narratives and poems, both contemporary and transmitted from times long gone-by."[39]

CHAPTER THREE

Sihah wa-Afiyyah: Food Ads from the *Futur* to *Hilwayat*

El-Ghonemy remarked that visitors to the Middle East "may . . . be puzzled by a conspicuously high proportion of obesity among adults. Many people seem to eat most of the time and speak of the number of loaves of bread and amount of meat consumed as a status symbol."[1]

He further points out that according to World Bank data, the average Middle Eastern family's food expenditure is approximately 40 percent of its total expenses, compared with 32 percent in other developing regions.[2] Even if his semiotic impression is exaggerated—especially considering the fact that too many people in the Middle East are much too thin due to hunger and poorness—his remarks can still shed light on the importance of analyzing food advertisements (in fact, the higher percentage of expenditure on food can be ascribed in part to the higher number of people per household, and in part to food prices that are higher in comparison to the income earned).

"Tell me what breakfast you've eaten [taken], [and] I'll tell you who you are!" proclaims a Kellogg's ad,[3] word-playing with the saying "Tell me who your friends are and I'll tell you who you are." In Arabic one "takes" breakfast, which is called *futur*, since it breaks the nocturnal fast. The text of the ad, which is accompanied by the company's smiling rooster logo, states that "Today, it is more important than ever to eat healthy, nutritious meals in order to keep our *bodies and minds* healthy and whole. And if a man may be known by his friends (*kana al-mar' yu`raf bi-man ya`ashar*), he can also be known by the most important meal of his day—breakfast, of course. It has been proven to the *ulama* that a healthy breakfast increases children's ability to learn, as well as the mental and intellectual abilities of adults. This is why Kellogg's Corn Flakes[4] conquers [*yahtall*] a very important central place on the breakfast table of anyone who *insists* on starting his day with the most intelligent [or 'shrewd,' *adhka'*] choice." The ad goes on to describe the product's ingredients, which supply a quarter of the required allowance of vitamins and other nutritious elements, half of the daily iron allowance, and a little fat, this last in order to provide energy (*taqa*). Those who need energy are men. Kellogg's is here portrayed as a friend with whom a man should keep company, or rather as being itself a male, a rooster. Kellogg's "conquers" its place on the plate, in clearly warlike language, while scientists who recommend eating the product for breakfast become in the Saudi version *ulama*, a Muslim term signifying a *religious* scholar. Therefore, the advertisement concludes, "be certain of being *a better person* when you make the choice that starts your morning!" At the bottom of the page is the slogan "[Thus] the clever [*al-shatir*] start their morning every day with Kellogg's Corn Flakes."

Another Kellogg's advertisement shows a Saudi-looking moustached man, wearing a white buttoned robe and smiling with shiny, white teeth as he awaits his serving of Kellogg's cereal and his pitcher of white milk (to which I return later in this chapter). The cereal, in this case Kellogg's All-Bran, is composed of flying bits of bran (*nakhlah al-qamh*) that are being scraped directly off a grain of wheat. The evolutionary chain of the cereal begins with a stalk of wheat. "Bran," explains the ad, "is the layer which encloses the grain of wheat, and provides us with nutritious fibers." The text, which addresses men ("add [masc.] the milk to the Kellogg's cereal"), claims that "All-Bran guarantees your health from the inside" and suggests you eat the product "in order to enjoy health from the outside" as well. The external layer of the wheat grain thus leads to internal health. This advertisement tries to convince the already convinced: the nutritious value of bran is well appreciated in Arab culture, in which many people customarily eat whole wheat bread. So even the marketing of this product is not innovative, but rather fitted to a deep-rooted tradition. Among the foodstuffs that are receding to make way for Western products, el-Ghonemy named whole-grain wheat.[5] But this example seems to demonstrate how whole-grain wheat continues to survive: the choices of which product to import, what to stress in the advertising campaign, and how to present the product in the ad are all suited to the culture.

These two advertisements characterize Kellogg's as a men's breakfast food, or as a men's breakfast in itself; but this could bring about a complete cessation in sales during the month of Ramadan, when eating and drinking are forbidden between sunrise and sunset. Therefore, the time for eating Kellogg's has to be moved earlier, to the small hours of the night. This is achieved by an advertisement titled "Blessed Ramadan" (in letters decorated by traditional calligraphic ornament). The bowl of Kellogg's is pictured against a "night" background (black with a halved crescent and twinkling stars). "Kellogg's wishes you and your family, on this dear occasion, all well-being and blessings [*kull al-khayr wal-barakah*]." Thus Kellogg's becomes a product that can also be eaten before sunrise, giving strength for the difficult day of fasting ahead. In this way, Western bran flakes are Islamicized.

Another breakfast cereal is Quaker's rye grains (*shufan*).[6] "Instant Quaker *shufan* grains [are] a healthy sort of breakfast [*wajbah iftar*], rich in vitamins and minerals, low fat and cholesterol free. It is the ideal way to start a new day full of freshness and vitality, be it at work, at school or even at home. Try [fem.] the three wonderful flavors and choose [fem.] your favorite." Here we see the difference between the men's breakfast in the Kellogg's ad (for the clever, who insist and conquer) and the breakfast for women, who prepare food for men ("at work") and children ("at school"), and then, in many cases, stay home ("even at home").

Advertisements for breakfast and other meals never show eggs, though these are eaten freely. Ads for fish, or recipes for other products that are eaten with fish, are also close to nonexistent. In the Arabian peninsula, fishing is traditionally considered an inferior profession, and selling eggs and chickens is likewise not a respectable trade.[7] The origins of this contempt may be in the nomadic desert culture (which despised seafarers and permanent settlers), but Saudi advertising, as a nomadic fantasy, preserves it still. Advertising always focuses on the glamorous.

Kellogg's and Quaker cereals are usually eaten with milk. Cow's milk is one of the most frequently advertised products in Saudi Arabia, not only as an adjunct to other foodstuffs but as a drink in itself. Thus, an advertisement by Sadefco ranks "milk for Saudi children" along with "drinks for Saudi children."[8] The importance of milk is reflected in the prominent placement of ads for it, which are occasionally found even on the inside cover of the journal.[9] In this ad, buying 12 cartons of milk (12 liters, approximately 4 gallons) entitles one to 27 free 250-cc cartons of orange juice. El-Ghonemy stated that milk, as a traditional drink, is receding in favor of "American carbonated drinks (Coca-Cola, Seven-Up,

Pepsi-Cola, and so on)."[10] But this statement seems to be inaccurate. Milk continues to be an important drink, fighting for its place in the market, and its advertising volume is much higher than that of Coca-Cola, a product to which I return.

More than other beverages, the freshness of milk is all important, especially in the hot Saudi desert sun. Al-Safi milk, "nutritious and tasty," is shown as being delivered daily right up to the threshold of a Bedouin tent by the company's milkman, who carries it in a picnic box until he hands it to the mother and her two children.[11] The woman is dressed in black, only her face exposed, while her son is in a white robe. This advertisement, from late-1990's Saudi Arabia, still maintains the historic connection between nomads and permanent settlers. Al-Safi milk is "100% fresh every day from our farms." This marketing strategy is addressed equally to urban women in Riyadh, Jiddah, Medina, or Mecca. The story of the advertisement is based on the nomad's difficulty in finding pasture for his herds and on his dependence on oasis dwellers in drought periods. As is well known, this dependence was often the source of conflicts between nomads and settlers (when Bedouins raided the settlements), as well as of an economic symbiosis in which the settlers' commodities were transported by the nomads. Bedouin culture developed a contempt for the farming culture, which was seen as inferior and unglamorous. But now, in Saudi advertisements, it is modernism that makes possible the fulfillment of the Bedouin dream: technologies of refrigeration and transportation bring fresh milk to the very entrance of the tent. The tables have been turned, the ideal realized; the Bedouin no longer has to exert himself to obtain milk. He can roam where he wants or even settle in the middle of the desert, and the milk is delivered all the way to his doorstep.

This looks like an imaginary, comic situation. The advertisement is not really suggesting that a company deliveryman will arrive at a tent in the heart of the desert in order to hand over a carton of milk. But this playful fantasy is a cultural one, founded in tradition and history. The humor and parody of the situation are based on previous knowledge. The role of the ad is "to play lightheartedly in the expansive regions of comedy [and of the desert], and playfully demonstrate the human power over spaces and times."[12]

But there is more than that here. To a large extent, the milkman, or the milk, represents the man in this story. The milkman brings to the tent the missing male element. Milk, a white liquid like semen, is essentially

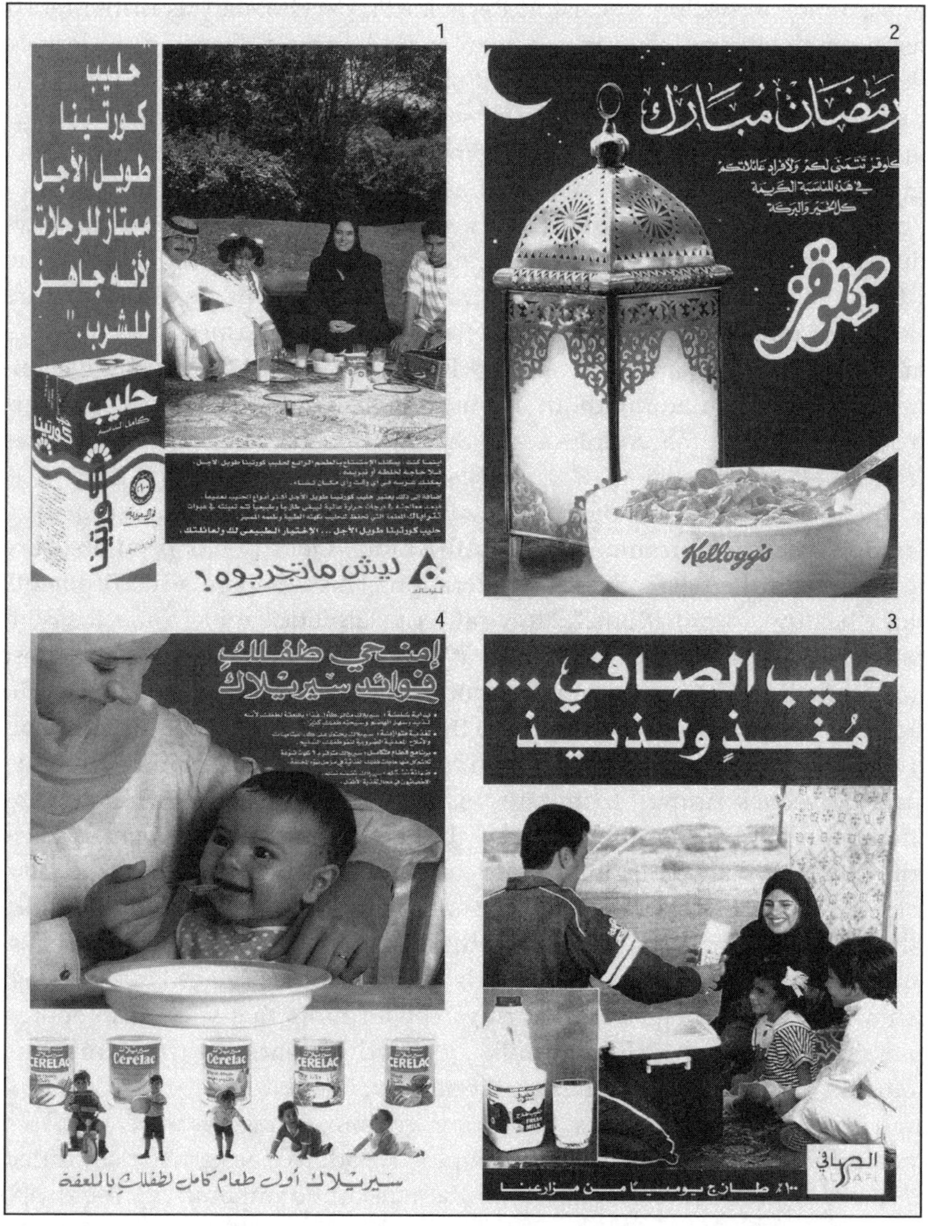

Fig.6 (1) Kurtina Milk; (2) Kellogg's - Ramadan; (3) Al-Safi Milk;
(4) Cerelac–mother and child.

masculine, according to Gaston Bachelard's psychoanalysis of matter. It is masculine even when the woman feeds her *male* offspring (in Jerusalem's colloquial Arabic, the expression *halib al-sba`*, "lion's milk," has three meanings: mother's milk, semen, and the alcoholic drink `*arak* diluted with water.) In this advertisement, it is the son who wears white, but another al-Safi ad, showing a Saudi family on a picnic in the park[13] (drinking modern milk involves a visit to "nature" and necessitates laying an Eastern rug on the ground), emphasizes the contrast between the "black" woman and the "white" man. Traditionally, in Arab culture white is superior to black. This is reflected in the differing status of white and black slaves,[14] in the flawless white *ihram* clothing worn by the pilgrim to Mecca (made without seams, which would "puncture" the perfection),[15] and in masculine versus feminine dress. This color division is continued in advertising.

The fatty whiteness of the milk raises an issue that has, in recent generations, become prominent in Saudi Arabia. Obesity has been a severe problem for the post–oil boom generation. This is where advertisements for "healthy," "nutritious," "low-fat," or "athletic" milk come in. Both modern sports and skim milk are Western imports. But even the most individualistic, goal-oriented types of modern sports can be connected to and folded back into tradition. The three sports the prophet Muhammad is said to have encouraged are individualistic ones: swimming, archery, and horseback riding[16] (compare this to medieval Europe, where swimming was slighted and neglected).[17] In one al-Safi advertisement, a glass of milk helps a young man build his muscles in a gym. This ad also stresses the contrast between white and black: on the one hand, the milk, the shirt, and the young man's teeth; on the other, his hair, beard, eyes, and pants. The man's left hand is conspicuously placed on his leg, showing a prominent wedding ring. The ad hints that success in sports, obtainable through drinking milk, can lead to marriage. Modernism is only an instrument for achieving a traditional goal.

But not all companies, reflecting consumer tastes, believe in the healthful properties of skim milk. In a Sadefco advertisement titled "Taste life" (*tadhawwuq al-hayah*, in the masculine imperative), the drops of milk create three male figures engaged in sports.[18] Athletic pursuits, bodybuilding, and realizing individual potential are male activities. One man is shown playing tennis, another is jogging, and the third is swimming. At the bottom of the page, three varieties of Saudi milk (*halib al-Sa`udiyyah*) are advertised: nonfat, low fat, and fat milk. The sports figures are created specifically from the flow of the fat milk, the stream of tradition. "Saudi milk . . . either this milk or nothing at all."

Modern sports were invented in nineteenth-century English schools as a means of control and supervision. Before sports became a tool for "forging character," they were a way to fill free time. Pupils engaged in sports were easy to control; they took out their competitive violence on each other rather than on teachers or school facilities. Bourdieu writes that sports were therefore an "extreme fiscal measure."[19] British schools in the Middle East were established under the influence of a speech by historian and politician Thomas Babington Macaulay delivered in the British Parliament in July 1833. Macaulay spoke against preventing hundreds of millions from becoming "our customers" only in order to keep them "our slaves."[20] It was at this moment in time that enlarging the market by means of exporting ideology became more important than importing cheap uneducated workforce. Colonial schools, then, and sports along with them, were created in order to produce a consumer infrastructure, to develop a market. Sports struck deep roots and today are an integral part of Saudi life and of Saudi advertisements, sustaining and developing the consumer spirit.

Milk, then, is inherently masculine. In an ad for Tawil al-Ajal, UHT milk (milk treated to have a long shelf life), the mother pours milk for her *son*.[21] Even advertisements for the national dairy industry,[22] which are intended to promote milk drinking in general and show pictures of modern Saudi women in places like hospitals and computerized workplaces, bear texts addressed to men: "Taste [masc. imperative] the most delicious taste of the best drink . . . Be [masc. imperative] certain that you [masc.] are getting your [masc.] needs from it on a daily basis." Only when there is no man in the picture can the woman wrap herself in a milk-white cloth, which leaves the absent male symbolically present. The man, too, is the one who buys the milk, as the above-mentioned sale ad for al-Rabi` milk stressed.[23] The buyer may be a husband or a chauffeur, but he is always a man. "Buy Al-Rabi` milk and get a free gift."

The "masculinity" of milk is especially striking in light of the fact that it is the female who produces milk. The traditional Middle Eastern practices of feeding newborn babies with sheep's butter for three days in order to lubricate the internal organs, followed by the two years of breastfeeding prescribed by the Koran, have diminished considerably. Breastfeeding has been supplanted by the use of bottles, starting as early as one month after birth among the wealthier classes.[24] Field studies have shown that the Gulf states consume 55 different brands of foreign-made baby food.[25] Musaiger and others have pointed out two severe health problems caused by these "harmful luxuries." The first has to do with illiterate mothers, who cannot read the expiration date on the product or the instructions for use (the amount of water to add, the maximum temperature, how to keep the bottle clean). The second is the use of polluted water in blending.[26] The advertisements for Cerelac that appear in the weekly, and are thus addressed to relatively educated women, recommend switching to the product starting from the fourth month after birth.[27] In other ads by the same company, the model who feeds the baby displays a golden wedding ring.[28] In advertising fiction, unmarried Saudi women do not feed children (in reality, unmarried sisters, for example, may live with the family and help with the children). The baby, fed from different boxes as he grows from crawling to bicycling, is a male. Sons, the ad suggests, should be fed first, even though it seems that the practice of burying daughters in famine periods no longer exists.

The food substitute market in Saudi Arabia is broad, but advertising links such products to the original food. Canderel's sugar substitute has "The taste you love / And the freshness you want."[29] Powdered milk substitutes continue to be sold mainly as a children's product,[30] and an emphasis is being put on its being "natural dehydrated milk." The Anchor company advertises the desirability of its location, New Zealand, "where the refreshing air, the pure waters and the green valleys provide an ideal environment for cattle."[31] "Because you [fem.] want your children to grow up strong and healthy, choose . . ." The slogan at the bottom of the advertisement promises that the product's "natural effectiveness is guaranteed." This powder is not marketed as a powder at all but rather as real milk, which has to be dehydrated because it is transported from New Zealand. But even in this case, there are traditional parallels: the dried milk comes to resemble dried figs.

Another milk-based children's beverage is a chocolate- or vanilla-flavored milk shake, a product that is sold in cartons. The Sadefco company stresses in an ad, as well as on the carton itself, that it is "made with Saudi milk."[32] This makes possible the slogan "The sweetness of the taste makes you feel you are flying" (*khalli al-ta'am yufarfash*). Furthermore, the drinks are called "Shake A-Choco" and "Shake A-Nilla" in English letters; in Arab transcription, *shik shuku* and *shik nilla*. That is, the English names take definite articles according to the rules of Arabic grammar: the *l* consonant of the article *al* does not appear before the 14 "sun letters." The Arabic names remain indefinite. The transformation of "vanilla" into "A-Nilla" and of the Arabic *fanila* into *nilla*, in addition to creating diminutive forms that lend the names a fairy-tale sound,[33] also brings them closer to Arab culture. Phonetically, the vanilla drink comes to resemble the Nile (al-Nil). And indeed, the advertisement shows the beverages being lifted by four magical hands out of a gushing river. Egypt is thus the gift of the "Nilla" (presumably the White Nile, since there is also a chocolate river), and the consumer lives *bayna al-naharayn*, between the two rivers.

Milk is not only a drink in its own right but is also a basic element in dairy products. The importance of the milk's freshness is high in these products, too, despite modern processing techniques. A two-part advertisement, appearing on two consecutive pages, first brings the teaser "When it was milk . . . ," with a picture of a "milk waterfall" that spurts into the ad on the next page; this advertises Pride cheese, which "was milk only minutes ago."[34] The Pride company, which makes solid yellow cheeses, foreign to Arabic culinary tradition, in Austria ("product made with pride in Austria"), states on the Arabic-language packaging that the cheese is "Saudi quality" (*jawdah sa`udiyyah*) and, in its ad, that "Brayd [Pride] is . . . fresh in the Saudi manner [*sa`udiyyan*]."[35]

In 1997, Hilwani Brothers introduced, "for the first time in Saudi markets" (thus establishing its historical place), a low-fat cheese spread.[36] The slogan for this cheese was rhymed: "The pleasure of beautiful taste / Despite the light fat" (*mut`at al-ta`am al-jamil / ragham al-dasam al-qalil*). This cheese can be enjoyed "whatever your diet" and spread "in any quantity you desire."

La Vache Qui Rit, "the laughing cow," in Arabic *jabnat al-baqrah al-dahikah*, presents Saudi children with "happy character" coloring cards, included in the package. (The text, addressed to children, is *ta`alu narsam ma`an*, "let's draw together."[37]) Mrs. Mahadumah ("nice" in spoken Arabic, "digested" in the literary language), Mr. Tafa ("additive"), and twenty-four other characters appear on the cards. The cartoon characters of the Roger Hargreaves "Mr. Men" series receive Arabic names related to food.

Western cheeses are transformed into Arabic cheeses, but original Arabic cheeses are also advertised in the weekly. Thus, for example, "Al-Mara`i's new cream cheese . . . Now with a richer, more delicious taste of lush cream."[38] Since it contains more fresh cream, it has a "strength that doesn't crumble." "Taste it today and judge for yourself." The ideal cream cheese is one that does not crumble and that can be scooped up with a fresh pita, as the accompanying photo illustrates. Another advertisement, for *Nada'* ("dew") cream cheese, mentions its "home taste" and that it is the "essence of nature."[39] Another dairy product is *zabadi*, the word meaning "yogurt" in Saudi Arabia and Egypt (*laban* in the Sha'm region; in Morocco *zabda* means butter). The yogurt produced by the al-Rabi company, whose name means "spring," is marketed in eight flavors and is "the only one with natural fruit."[40]

Zabadi is the final course of breakfast, but the other meals of the day are also prepared by the woman. In 1997, the Maggi company (transcribed *maji*; Saudi Arabic has no /g/ sound, unlike Egyptian Arabic),[41] marketing instant soup powders, organized a "Best Cook" contest, under the supervision of the Trade and Industry Department in Jiddah.[42] To participate, women were to send in a recipe making use of the company's instant soup, along with a coupon clipped from the package. The first prize was a "dream kitchen"; every participant also received a recipe book. This is more than a gimmick; advertisements of this kind attempt to construct an illusion of creative activity. It is an illusion because the possibilities of using the soup powder ultimately remain few and banal. Despite all the efforts involved, the woman always stays in the kitchen, her creations consumed almost as soon as they are made. The varieties of soup on the market stay within the bounds of familiar culture[43] and include lentil (*'adas*) soup and rye (*shufan*) soup, which are being emphasized and advertised out of all the other kinds of soups being sold. What is important is that these soups "are loved by the whole family with lunch, with dinner, or any time." In another advertisement, Maggi's instant soup is presented as ideal for preparing *bukhari* rice.[44] The suggested recipe contains, among other ingredients, mutton, pine nuts, black olives, and conventional Arabic spices (dry coriander, cardamom, cumin, black pepper, cinnamon, and *karfa*). Likewise, Quaker's soup helps a Saudi child (dressed in a white *jalabiyyah*) to prepare his homework, while his mother, out of focus and dressed in traditional veils, observes him from behind. The mother's indistinctness draws attention to the son; the whole purpose of her existence is that he should do his homework and develop.[45]

In the past, the world was divided into three food civilizations or "carbohydrate empires," based on wheat, rice, and corn. The Middle East belonged to the wheat civilization, and rice was a luxury imported from the East. Today, at least three companies advertise rice in *Sayyidati*, while bread is not advertised at all. Bread is taken for granted; imported rice still needs advertisement. But for the same reason, rice is still exotic and therefore easily marketed: be it in a traditional, cord-tied cloth bag (the Wadi Andas Company[46]) or in a modern vacuum pack (Basma[47] and Tilda[48]). Basma rice is sold in three differently colored packages (blue, red, and green—the last, the color of Saudi Arabia, becomes a primary color, replacing yellow, which bears negative associations in Arab and Islamic culture). Each package is suitable for use in different foods: *birani*, *zarbiyan*, *kabsah*, *maqlubah*, *siyadiyah*, and others, all familiar elements of Arab cuisine. *Maqlubah*, for example, is made with rice, chicken, potatoes, cauliflower, and carrots, all cooked together in a pot and then turned upside down into a large tray; hence the name of the dish, which means "overturned."

The product whose marketing is so competitive as to constitute a marketing war, perhaps the most aggressive such war in Saudi food advertising, is tomato purée. It is fascinating to observe how tomatoes, which reached the Old World following the discovery of America, blend into Arab cuisine with the aid of the al-Wafa ("oasis") and al-Sa'udiyya companies (the latter of which represents Sadefco). The very fact that tomato purée is relatively foreign to Arab cuisine causes it to be presented as a traditional product. Al-Sa'udiyyah's strategy is to publish "traditional" recipes that use the product. Every advertisement contains a quote from a real or imaginary woman in some Saudi city. The slogan accompanying these recipes is the traditional food blessing, *sihha wa-'afiyyah* (literally "health and health," an equivalent of "bon appetit"). Al-Sa'udiyyah tomato purée can be used in "mutton (*kharuf*) with green beans (*lubiyya'*)"[49] or in "*burghul* (wheat groats) soup."[50] The ingredients for the soup include chicken, thick wheat groats (*khashan*), half a spoonful of cumin, half a spoonful of dry coriander, a quarter cup of finely cut coriander, and spices: cardamom, cinnamon sticks, cloves. The spices, according to the recipe, are to be first tied in a bag or placed in a sieve and only then put into the pot. Both the ingredients and the preparation are intended to be of a traditional-classical character. Likewise, another ad for the same product suggests using tomato purée in the *iftar* meal at the end of each day during Ramadan, with the traditional blessing, "*iftar[an] hani'a[n]*."[51] Libby's ketchup, as the picture in the ad illustrates, is to be eaten with sheshlik and shish qebab.[52] We see the hand of a "father" in a traditional white *jalabiyyah*, passing the ketchup bottle to his son in a sort of intergenerational relay race (*"nawalani ketshab libiz,"* "pass me the Libby's ketchup"). Another of Libby's advertisements promoted a campaign organized by the company in partnership with the "Disney Corner" store[53]: collecting ketchup bottle tops entitled the purchaser to discounts on Disney products. The ad used the figure of Mickey Mouse, which was also imprinted on the bottle. As mentioned above, the Arab Mickey Mouse is not the same as his Western counterpart.[54] Therefore, despite the cooperation between two Western companies, intended to promote sales, and despite the Western-imported promotion method, the resultant campaign is not a Western one. This is a different Mickey Mouse, and the ketchup he advertises is for use in different sorts of food.

Not that hamburgers are nonexistent. In an advertisement by the al-Jazzar, a meat company with an appropriate traditional name (meaning "butcher"), the diverse list of products contains hamburgers as well.[55] But in addition to beef burgers, there are also chicken burgers and, especially interesting, mutton burgers (*ghanam*). That is, the very term "hamburger" widens its scope to include existing traditional elements. Zeldin points out that "fast food is neither American nor European, but a legacy of the street peddlers of the Middle and Far East."[56] Among other frozen foods—which, it is stressed, are "Saudi made" and conform to "Saudi standards" (*lil-muwasafat al-qiyasiyyah al-sa'udiyyah*)—are *"sambusak* with chicken," *"sambusak* with meat," and "beef *kaftah"* (a sort of dumpling, distinct from "beef meatballs," which are also included). The upper part of the ad shows a Saudi family (two sons, a daughter, and parents) in the course of a family dinner; the mother, her head covered, stands behind the father as he tastes the dumplings, awaiting his opinion of her creation. The text reads, "Appetizing . . . Tasty . . . Wonderful / incomparable taste . . . What is the secret?" According to this ad, the secrets of tradition and of traditional cooking are still preserved even in the industrial age. The Islamic Arab tradition allows the eating of seafood, so an advertisement for Kraft cheese is accompanied by a recipe containing crabs.

A common way for advertisers to link a food product with tradition is to associate it with the *iftar*, the supper that breaks the fast of Ramadan. Kraft advertises both its cheddar[57] and its cream cheese spread[58] as products to be eaten in this meal. The name *Kraft lil-mawa'id* (Kraft for tables) and the slogan *"ashha' al-wasafat"* ("the tastiest recipes") are registered trademarks. All three advertisements contain recipes for Ramadan in which these cheeses can be used. The first of the three ("The secret of the excellent Ramadan plate with an unforgettable taste! Pleasant *iftar*.") brings a recipe for "vegetable *masqa`ah* [a dish containing eggplants, sweet potatoes, zucchini, and ground mutton] with saffron rice."[59] The second ("Pleasant *iftar*") has a recipe for cheese-stuffed chicken breast. It recommends garnishing the dish with "asparagus, green beans, steamed rice with raisins, and *Eastern* [*sharqi*] tomato sauce." These ingredients are a mixture of foodstuffs from various periods, which all become "traditional" foods on the Ramadan table. The invention of "Eastern tomato sauce" is especially interesting: tomato sauce, as mentioned above, did not exist before tomatoes began to be imported from newly discovered America. The rice in the accompanying photograph is arranged in a half crescent (*hilal*), an Islamic symbol, and one of the most definitive symbols of the Ramadan month. Even rice, then, is converted to Islam. The *hilal* returns in all three advertisements, accompanied by such elements as a traditional copper tray, arches, a desert landscape, a wooden lattice, and an Eastern rug, all making the cheese into "a secret which lends your Ramadan delicacies an unforgettable taste" or "a wonderful, amazing taste!"

As remarked in the context of skim milk ads and of Kellogg's and Quaker's cereals, problems of obesity and high cholesterol became serious in Saudi society in the 1980s, affecting, for example, King Fahd. Therefore, advertising by many companies stresses low-fat products, and most of the men who appear in Saudi ads are quite thin. Al-Arabi oil, a vegetable oil that is "as pure as gold," emphasizes its cholesterol-free nature.[60] Likewise, the text on bottles of Afiyya oil, whose name is one-half of the traditional food blessing *sihah wa-afiyyah*, "health and health," stresses that it is good for the heart.[61] Many Arab dishes are fried or are baked with oil. Thus, Danish Luprak butter is advertised for use in frying. But "the secret of appetizing taste" is *saman*, a cooked butter mostly used in baking Arabic sweets (*hilwayat*). The Dalida company advertises *saman* as the "basic taste for delicious Arabic sweets."[62] The accompanying coupon, intended to compile marketing information and establish a consumer club, asks the reader, "Which vegetable *saman* do you [fem.] currently use?" The fact that this brand of *saman* is exported to and consumed in other Arab countries is shown by the disclaimer in the sale ad: "Valid only in the Kingdom of Saudi Arabia."

Saman brings us to sweets, including traditional *hilwayat* as well as imported chocolates, snacks, and ice creams. Sweets are a woman's way of "being an artisan"—"especially during Ramadan," as an instant pudding advertisement claims.[63] The various *hilwayat* can be served with *qishtah*, a sort of thick cream. For ten wrappers of *al-Taj* (crown) *qishtah*, along with answers to a short questionnaire, the buyer can participate in a drawing whose prizes include cars, gold ingots, discount coupons, and "various token prizes."[64] The questionnaire to be filled out and sent in is preceded by a historical account called "The Story of the Crown" (*Qissah al-Taj*):

> The story of qishtah al-Taj started in the Islamic year 1376, or the Gregorian year 1956 [actually, every Islamic year corresponds to parts of two Gregorian years, in this case 1956–57], when the first shipment reached the Kingdom through the port of Jiddah. These beginnings were a dawning morning [*sabaha[n] mushriqa[n]*] for the Saudi family, which was happy with this special *qishtah*, since become an inseparable part of it. With the passage of time, qishtah al-Taj has struck roots in the Saudi family, and with the increase in the Kingdom's population, qishtah al-Taj has been able to meet the needs of consumers and provide them with the amounts they require, at the quality they have become used to. In one year, sales of qishtah al-Taj reached more than fifty million cans, a clear sign of the position of qishtah al-Taj with all parts of the family, which becomes ever stronger with time.

Beyond the information on *qishtah* consumption in Saudi Arabia (even if the number is taken with a grain of salt, it is still only for a single company), it is interesting to observe how important it is for the importer and advertiser to relate the cream to the history of Saudi Arabia and its recent development. The import of *qishtah*, which like most Saudi importation began through the port of Jiddah, becomes a symbol of the tremendous growth the kingdom has undergone since the 1950s. Ever since the oil boom, Saudis have been swimming in cream. Crown cream is just what its name implies: it attempts to embrace all the subjects of the kingdom, all parts of the family. The company's success in meeting demand is the success of affluent Saudi society, the advertisement suggests. In order to fortify authoritarian indoctrination (the rule of the "cream" or elite) and to provide market information, the reader must answer, based on the story and on general knowledge, several multiple-choice questions: "A. Qishtah al-Taj is the first *qishtah* in Saudi Arabia since the year . . . B. In one year (last year), sales of qishtah al-Taj reached . . . J. The price of a can of qishtah al-Taj is . . . D. How do you prefer qishtah al-Taj: With honey? With jam? With *al-hilwayat* (*al-knafah, al-qata'if* . . .)? In cooking? Other (please specify) . . . [65] H. Where do you buy qishtah al-Taj? W. Complete the following sentence: The quality of qishtah al-Taj is . . . Z. In under 15 lines, list the reasons why you buy qishtah al-Taj."

An especially interesting detail to note is the alphabetical order of the questions: A (*alif*), B (*ba'*), J (*jim*), D (*dal*), H (*ha*), W (*waw*), Z (*zay*). This order parallels that of other Semitic languages, such as Hebrew, rather than the order of the letters in an Arabic dictionary (where the letters are arranged in "families" according to their shapes). This order goes back to an Arabic tradition that predates the appearance of Arabic dictionaries in the Middle Ages (a numerical arrangement of the letters, [*'abjadiyya*]). This phenomenon recurs in ad questionnaires in other fields.[66] The dates used in the advertisement are Arab-Islamic ones (sometimes accompanied by Gregorian equivalents); the importation of *qishtah* to Saudi Arabia began in the year 1386 of the *hijra*, which, it is stated, corresponds to 1956 of the Christian era ("1956 m," for *miladiyyah*; actually, as noted above, 1956–57). The last date for sending in letters is 10 Muharam 1418 *h* (for *hijrah*); the drawing will take place on 30 Dhu al-haja 1418 *h*; winners will be notified by 2 Safar 1418 *h* (7 June 1997 *m*). Knafe and Qata'if are two well-known varieties of Arabic sweets. Different elements and layers of culture are thus combined into a single "family."

Nestlé's cream also becomes "the natural companion to all your *hilwayat*."[67] Likewise, Nestlé's sweetened condensed milk becomes an ingredient in Arab sweets: "Sweetness is sweeter with Nestlé's sweetened condensed milk . . . Nestlé's sweetened condensed milk helps you prepare your appetizing, varied *hilwayat*."[68]

Sweets also include cookies and chocolates. Teashop's imported cookies (*Tishub*, in Arabic transcription) wish pilgrims to Mecca "*hajj mabrur wa-sa'i mashkur*," a pure *hajj* and an appreciated effort,"[69] linking themselves to one of Islam's five basic commandments. The Hilwani Brothers, marketing *ma'mul*, indicate on the package that the filling is "of choice Saudi dates."[70] The date-bearing palm is not just another tree in the Saudi desert; it is the tree whose shade served for protection in the oases, whose leaves were used in making roofs and for burning, and whose fruit was eaten in various forms. In modern Saudi Arabia, some date growers still give a distinctive name to each of their palms.[71]

An advertisement for Le Bonheur chocolate, a Belgian product, bears the title "Happy holiday" (*'id sa'id*).[72] The ad contains six other salutations, appropriate for various holidays and occasions: "Happy new year" (*kull am wa-antum bi-khayr*, literally, "every year you are well"); "Thank you for your pleasant hospitality" (*shukra[n] 'ala diyafatkum al-latifah*); "Congratulations on the new work contract"; "This is merely an expression of my gratitude"; "The vacation was wonderful"; "The time has come to thank you for your kindness." At the bottom of the ad is the rhetorical question, "Do you really need a reason?" Belgian chocolate thus becomes a gift to be given at various times in the course of Saudi life: a holiday, the new year, or any other occasion. Interestingly, the Swiss company Lindt advertises its chocolates with an Eastern-looking model.[73] The brown chocolates match a precious stone on a chain around the woman's neck, her brown eyes—like those of the *huriyat*, the beautiful women of paradise—and a brown beauty spot on the upper right of her chin, the Saudi version of Cindy Crawford's mole. The slogan, *"Lindur . . . ana qalbi ilayka mayal"* ("Lindur . . . I myself ['my heart'] yearn for you"), is clearly in the style of a girl's words to her beloved.

Bateel's date sweets become "Elegance . . . The woman who expresses your noble taste."[74] "Those who appreciate the special things in life know the pleasure of finding the ideal choice. When choosing a gift that expresses the taste of the giver, nothing less than the best is acceptable. Bateel. A special assortment of the best kinds of date—and a tasty chocolate made to leave the impression you desire it as a gift for yourself or for your loved ones. It truly is the ideal expression of your special personality." "When words are not enough. . . ." The slogan that ends the ad echoes a view prevalent in Eastern philosophies, which influenced the Arab and Muslim world (especially through the mediation of Sufi doctrine): that language, despite its artistic ability to build new worlds from words, cannot bring one to know the true nature of things. In this view, language is always roundabout, always "almost," always another story. There always remain things that cannot be expressed in words. And the product, it is hinted, attempts to bridge this gap, with the generous aid of advertising.

This ad, too, is accompanied by a picture of an Eastern woman, with dark eyes, finely shaped black eyebrows, and lipstick-painted mouth, wrapped in a black robe. The elegant woman is merely a supplement to the "special" male personality. She complements the correct appearance. The product in the photograph seems to be a date filled with ground coconut. The date, and especially its pit, is a clear symbol of femininity (the pit with the slit in its center visually resembles the female sexual organs), and it is here shown with a white, "masculine" filling. Arab and Muslim literature frequently refers to the date and its importance: in parables, in poetry, in medicine, and in cooking (date sugar, date wine,[75] etc.), as well as in the Koran, the Hadith, and the Sirah (biography) of the prophet Muhammad.[76] Abdallah bin Umar goes so far as to quote Muhammad as saying, "God loves him who loves the date."[77] Once again, the choice of product to import is suited to the culture.

The gift in this advertisement is conceived as one in which the giver's entire personality is reflected. Therefore, a simple, functional present will not do; the chosen gift must impress the recipient and magnify the giver. Ultimately, through a circular transaction, the gift is really to the giver. The difference in the function of chocolate as a gift in Arab culture, as illustrated in advertising, is especially fascinating. The *al-Nuqli* company, with 22 shops in Saudi Arabia, advertises its candy boxes, which alongside imported chocolates also contain mixed nuts (pistachios, almonds, walnuts) and pastries (*nukl* means "seeds, nuts, peanuts, pickles, etc., served to guests").[78] The advertisement is titled "Generation after generation, we have obtained our security thanks to our uniqueness and to the quality of our hospitality." The body of the text reads, "For many years, Arabs have been famous for their noble, beautiful hospitality and their deep-seated generosity. In order to preserve these noble traditions, later generations have wholeheartedly put their trust in the quality of *al-Nuqli* products, in order to express the sincerity of their hospitality and their genuine love for those dear to them, at every opportunity." *Al-Nuqli* candy boxes become a part of, and an addition to, Arab culture and history. Thus, the sweets are presented by the host to the guests as part of the display of hospitality and generosity, a sort of minuscule, symbolic potlatch.[79] The direction of the gift is the opposite of the customary direction in Western culture, where it is usually the guest who brings presents. Here, it is the guest who leaves the house of the host carrying the candy. The ideal of Arabism presented by the advertisement is the host, male or female (the text is in the plural and refers to Arabs), who visits one of the company's shops to prepare gifts for his or her guests in advance. Of course, this gift too is ultimately given to the host, as an honor.

An especially fascinating ad in the field of luxurious desserts was for Häagen-Dazs,[80] the ice cream with the imaginary, exotic name invented artificially as part of the advertising campaign. The ad shows a young woman who is looking at a framed picture while speaking on the telephone. She is connected to the outside world without necessarily seeing it; here, too, the connection is masked. Behind her are three other young women, who are looking at her and smiling. Two of them hold spoons with long handles. On the table are four packs of Häagen-Dazs ice cream of various flavors. The title of the ad is "Join in with pleasure" (*sharik bil-mut`ah*). This is an amazing slogan, which touches the most sensitive nerves of Saudi Arabian society, conservative and Muslim (mostly Sunni) as it is—maybe even to the extent of encouraging social transgression. The word *sharik*, in addition to its denotation of "join in, participate" (here in the masculine imperative), also refers to the act of the *sharik*, one who "joins" other gods with Allah, defying the first part of the *shahadah* that states that "there is no God beside Allah." *Shirk*, joining other gods to Allah, is one of the gravest transgressions in Islam, if not the very gravest. *Mut`ah*, "pleasure" or "delight," is also a term for the custom of "marriage of pleasure," prevalent even today in Shi'i Islam but banned in the Sunni faith. This form of marriage, which apparently originated during the first Islamic conquests, when Muslim soldiers lived for extended periods in distant frontier towns, lasts for a limited time, automatically expiring after the date specified in the marriage contract. Since this custom allows very brief marriages, men in modern Iran sometimes "marry" prostitutes in this fashion before intercourse.[81]

The advertisement does not refer explicitly to this knowledge. Presumably, the author is linking "joining in" with "pleasure" in the context of relations between a woman and a distant man. But the two terms chosen here are religiously and morally loaded. Both are perverse concepts, conflicting with the hegemonic, institutional culture (Sunni Islam): one is sanctioned by the Shi'a, the other leads to paganism. Although no man appears in the advertisement, the text is addressed to males: "Let [*di`*, masc.] the taste of Häagen-Dazs ice cream melt slowly in your mouth . . . There are few things in life for which [originally, *indahaa*, fem.] a man stops as he does for friendship and . . . for Häagen-Dazs ice cream." The man stops for "friendship," for *mut`ah*, and then moves on. This may be a man who has left his four wives (Sunni Islam, too, permits polygamy) at home and entered into a *mut`ah* marriage (perhaps as part of a long business trip), or a man who is conversing with his *mut`ah* wife when he has returned home and she is left with the memories. Many different stories can be told, but the plot of all will be based on the Saudi "forbidden," on the dolce vita of Saudi sins, the taste of cookies and cream melting in the

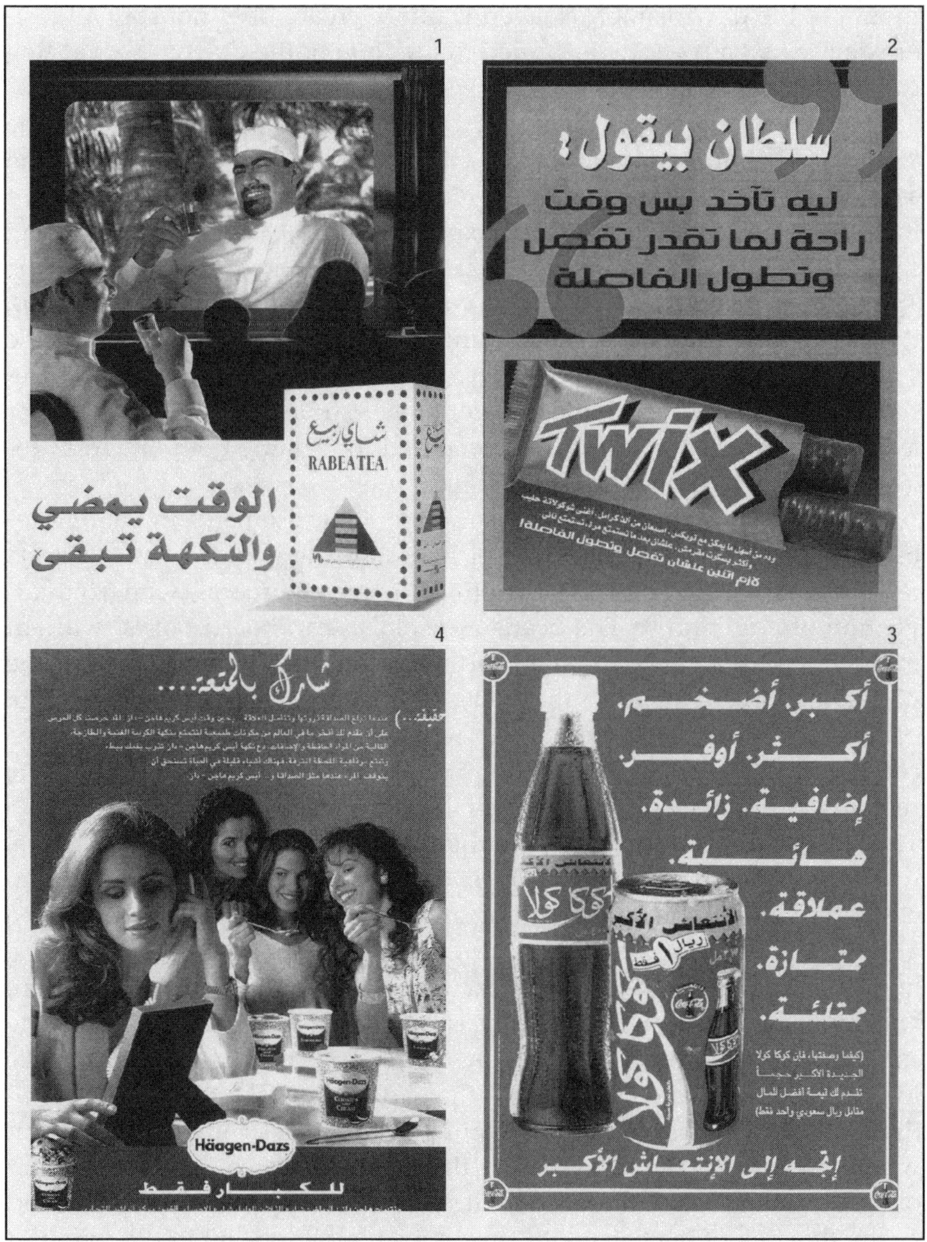

Fig.7 (1) Rabi' (Rabea) tea; (2) Twix chocolate;
(3) Coca-Cola (can and bottle); (4) Häagen-Dazs ice cream.

mouth of the daydreamer. Häagen-Dazs ice cream does not stay a Western sin; sexual adventure is "tuned to the flute of the Orient,"[82] guarding the cool secrets of the harem.

An advertisement for Twix chocolate bars features a quote from the "Sultan,"[83] whom we have met as an ancestor in the GMC ad. "Sultan says: Why just take time out when you can take a break, which will last a long time." The advertisement exploits cultural knowledge: "Sultan says" is a children's game in which one must follow the orders of the "Sultan" (as mentioned above, this was the title of the ruler in the Seljuk dynasty and later in others, including the Ottoman). Breaking apart the Twix bar, which is composed of two chocolate "fingers," comes to resemble the Sultans' "divide-and-conquer" strategy. Breaking the bar leaves one more time to rest (as compared to tackling both "fingers" together).

With desserts come hot drinks. Lipton advertisements in Saudi Arabia promote its loose tea mix, the picture showing how the "most select" tea leaves turn into "beads" of tea (in a "natural" process, with no intervention of any kind).[84] The beads are sold in cardboard boxes, without modern tea bags. Since the days of the spice trade, both the tea and the packaging have remained "the same." On the other hand, the local Rabi company permits itself to market tea in bags but stresses that "We've collected the tea in Rabi` tea bags . . . and the taste remains."[85] The taste remains in another Rabi ad as well: "Time passes, the taste remains."[86] This fascinating ad shows a mother and two children in a cinema, watching a bearded and moustached man who is wearing white (including a round white hat), smiling and sipping a cup of tea. Since there are no public cinemas or theaters in Saudi Arabia,[87] this is obviously a home theater. Behind the woman and children sits the same man, watching them and the screen; he is older, but he is still drinking the same tea and smiling. The two men, or the same man in different times, look at each other and smile across the gap of time. The woman and children are passive observers of the younger man, not seeing the older man who is looking at them. Just as in the Concord watch ads (see chapter one), the man's gaze is broader: it includes the present as well. And again, this link of tea bags with time, which also appears in the pyramid like logo of the company, makes the product a part of tradition, a part of the past.

Tea is of great importance in the Middle East. Hann, in a fascinating study, showed how tea growing in the Rize region played a significant role in what he calls "the domestication of the Turkish state."[88] He showed how tea, rather than coffee, became a mass-consumed beverage. Despite its low nutritional value, it became a product comparable to bread, in a process that started after World War I and was intensified during World War II. Ultimately, he writes, the success of tea (a drink of Eastern origin) lessened the Westernization of consumption habits and contributed especially to blocking the spread of alcoholic drinks. Moreover, tea became a symbol of national pride: while Kurds prefer tea smuggled from Syria, Iraq, or Iran, Turkish workers in Saudi Arabia are proud of Turkish tea.[89]

In Saudi Arabia, a country governed by the Shari'a, with the Wahhabi interpretation, alcoholic beverages cannot be advertised (though they are smuggled into the country and consumed privately). Their social role is filled by pseudoalcoholic beverages. The Saudi drink "Taste of a Meeting" (*ta'am al-liqa'*) is modeled after the English product Vimto (made in Manchester),[90] whose label stresses that it is alcohol-free. Importation adapts itself to cultural-social-political limitations. The spectrum of imported and domestic products is bound by local concepts.

As with tea, only a small percentage of coffee advertising takes place in weekly journals. Such advertising is expensive, and many of the marketed coffee brands do not make their way onto the high-quality chromo pages. One international corporation that attempts to penetrate the Saudi and Arab market via *Sayyidati* is Nestlé, manufacturer of Nescafé. It, too, exploits local culture and tradition to sell its imported product, whether through the traditional New Year's blessing, *"Kull 'am wa-antum bi-khayr"* ("Be well every year"), accompanied by "Season's Greetings from *Niskafe*,"[91] or through the use of classical terms to describe coffee beans: *ajwad anwa' al-qahawah*, "choice coffee varieties."[92]

Advertisements for traditional drinks seem to compete with imported Western beverages such as Coca-Cola, Sprite, Seven-Up, and the like. But here, too, it is crucial to realize that Saudi "Coca-Cola" is not the same as American "Coca-Cola." The very identity of Coca-Cola as a powerful symbol of the American consumer culture causes Saudi advertisers to be extremely cautious. Saudi ads for Coca-Cola are among the most conservative, modest advertising pages in a magazine. One such advertisement simply pictures a bottle and a can of the drink, side by side.[93] The text employs an almost banal repetition of adjectives: "Bigger [*akbar*]. Huger [*adham*]. More [*akthar*]. More abundant [*awfar*]. Additional [*idafiyyah*]. Extra [*za'idah*]. Tremendous [*ha'ilah*]. Gigantic [*amlaqah*]. Excellent [*mumtazah*]. Full [*mumtali'a*]." Beneath the superlatives, enclosed in parentheses, is the comment, "No matter how you describe it, the new, largest Coca-Cola gives you more for your money, for one *Saudi riyal*" (my italics). The transition to a product sold in Saudi riyals requires a different kind of advertising as well. The use of a simple ad, containing only adjectives, shows an understanding of tradition and of the appropriate discourse. The simplicity serves to deify the product in the style of Arab-Muslim rhetorical tradition, with its repetition and synonyms. The list of adjectives becomes the "beautiful names" (*al-asma' al-husana*) of Coca-Cola. Likewise, another Coca-Cola ad shows a girl in a modest black suit, holding up a huge can of the beverage in front of the camera.[94] The text reads, "Words are [or: speech is, *kalam*] lengthened with the free extra amount." The use of "words" is just as important as the images, which are chosen minimalistically and selectively.

The Coca-Cola Company also markets its Sprite product in Saudi Arabia.[95] In this case, too, the advertisement is graphically very simple. A box in the upper left-hand corner shows a young man in a desert region, scratching his head, behind him a broken-down car. The lower right-hand corner shows a can of Sprite. Between the two is a field of uniform color, sliced diagonally by a "river" of a different color. The text, in the middle of the picture from top to bottom, tells a story called "When my car broke down": "When my car broke down in / A deserted spot, I had / No choice but / To walk. The distance was / Great, my thirst was worsening because of / The heat of the sun and the severe / Humidity. Finally I reached / A junction, and this time / I had two options. / A sign guided me to / A garage / For cars, and another / To a general store. Here there came over / My thought [or "imagination"] the shape of a carbonated drink tasting of / Pure, refreshing, safe lemon. / . . . The car can wait. / Walk [*sayir*, here in the meaning of: "make it disappear"] your thirst with Sprite."

What we have here is desert poetry, in short lines, telling in words (the picture supplies only the context) the story of an automobile breakdown in the middle of the desert. The oasis crossing the difficult terrain, where one can quench one's thirst, is the gushing river of Sprite. The poem takes the landscape into account: when the words meet the surging waves of Sprite, the words bypass the waves and are not written on them. When modern civilization, the car, fails, one returns to tradition: to walking. The word *taqatu'* ("junction" or "crossing") appears exactly when the words reach the channel of the Sprite river, and suddenly there are two options, one on each side of it: the car, or a can of Sprite; fast-paced modern life, which ultimately breaks down, or the serenity of quenching one's thirst on the other side of the ravine. As soon as you have crossed the river, be it only in words, your imagination is taken over by the taste of "pure, refreshing, safe lemon." "Lemon-lime" becomes authentic lemon. The gushing water of the oasis mixes with carbon dioxide and artificial flavoring. The transition from one side of the ravine to the other is a return from the state to the tribe; tribal conflicts over water sources still take place in modern Saudi Arabia.[96] Compared to modern life, such conflicts are romantic, imaginary, "serene." The commercial success of carbonated beverages, a fascinating psychological-physiological phenomenon even in its Western version (why do these airy bubbles, and the noise produced in opening or pouring, so captivate us?), here takes on a somewhat different significance. Sprite, with its surging bubbles, becomes a sort of conch that still holds the sound of gushing water in an oasis (a rare phenomenon in itself). Water in the desert is so rare that that of the Zamzam stream in Mecca was made sacred (the Saudi national airline used to serve Safa water, which, though packaged by the French Evian company, is associated in legend with this stream), and Muhammad permitted the faithful to purify themselves in sand before praying (*tayammum*). Sprite thus becomes a metonymy for wandering waters in the modern oasis, for an impossible general store in the heart of the desert. The bubbles become reflections.

To summarize, imported foods undergo transformations of various extents. They take on the flavor of the local culture and mingle with local products in the pages of the weekly. From breakfast to the Ramadan supper, these foods are cooked in the pressure cooker of culture, absorbing spices from different periods. Ultimately, every nation stamps its seal on its food, and accepts change only if it can hide the change from itself, by stamping every innovation with its seal as well.

CHAPTER FOUR

Ughmuri Ahasisaki: Cosmetics and Personal Care Products

The importance of cosmetics and perfumes, *mustahdarat al-tajmil wa-l-ʿutur,* is strikingly evident throughout the many issues of *Sayyidati.* Based on the number of pages devoted to cosmetics and perfumes in the pages of this periodical, they are unquestionably the number one advertising field in *Sayyidati.* The weekly also publishes a cosmetics guide, "The Arab Woman's Guide to Health, Elegance, and Beauty," orderable in 1996 for US $12.[1] The dollar price stresses the fact that the guide—and the weekly—are also for sale outside Saudi Arabia; the exchange rate of riyal to dollar, as pointed out earlier, is constant. The use of dollars also grants the weekly the prestige of being a foreign, imported magazine. In this chapter, I examine the contemporary Saudi ideal of beauty, as reflected in advertising. In keeping with the general thesis of this book, I will also show how this ideal of beauty is dependent on previous knowledge.

"Do you like my hair?" asks an advertisement for an Ivari product that claims to protect against hair loss. The ad shows a black-haired woman with abundant, wavy hair. The chair she sits on, the table behind her, the white marble statue on the table, and the picture on the wall are all in rococo style. This style, a late development of the baroque, often occurs in ads as a symbol of wealth and luxury. This eighteenth-century ornamental fashion, originating in the France of Louis XV and Louis XVI, is still considered an ideal of beauty and opulence in twentieth-century Saudi Arabia. The preference for rococo over all other European designs is not surprising, given that this genre was strongly influenced by arabesque art[2]; the ornate rococo style was inspired by distinctively Islamic-Arabic artistic traditions. The luxury that, in this and other advertisements, serves as a metaphor for luxuriant hair is thus an Arabic-Islamic luxury in European garb, Arab ornamentation returning after a tour of Europe. It is interesting to note that when "Europe" is imported in advertising, it is the Europe of a different period. This is true in architecture as well; the famous Dolmabahçe palace of the Ottoman Sultans, built in Istanbul in the nineteenth century as a modern replacement for the Topkapı Palace, is in the style of the seventeenth century. Even in the nineteenth century the concept of European splendor was an anachronistic one. In Egypt, this style is called "Louis-Farouk," a sort of French-Egyptian hybrid.[3] European luxury in the form of baroque and rococo ornamentation continues to serve as an ideal of beauty in today's Saudi Arabia, affecting the design of houses and the concept of the modern luxury house. This may explain the ease with which Yardley's "Baroque" perfume is marketed in Saudi Arabia.[4]

Abundance of hair contrasts with the stark, bald desert; indeed, baldness is a desert, suggests an Organics shampoo ad that sets off a young woman's flowing hair against the background of a sandy terrain.[5] Another company's ad describes hair loss with the adjective *ghazir* (copious, profuse), which usually characterizes falling rain.[6] The expectation of pouring rains in the heart of the desert region survives, the battle between agriculture and wasteland continues, the modern field being Saudi scalps. Likewise, a Clairol shampoo ad stresses that the product is "a special mixture of natural plants and herbs."[7] The "natural" plants found in the desert are quite different from the unspecified ones used in the shampoo; the reference to natural plants gives the product historical status, respectability, and credence.

In Saudi advertisements, the ideal hair color for a female is black, which may be smooth or wavy but not curled. Thus a Pantène advertisement pairs the slogan "Feel the health in your hair" with a photograph of a young woman passing her hand through her smooth, black hair.[8] Similar models appear in ads for Silvikrin ("Let your hair breathe"),[9] Sunsilk ("The promise of natural beauty"),[10] and Artist(e).[11] The last of these found an interesting method of expressing the smoothness and waviness of hair: the A in the company's name is transliterated into Arabic as *alif mamdudah*, rather than ordinary *alif*. The wavy form and graphic expansiveness of the symbol are a visual illustration of wavy hair. "The crown of beauty waves [*yatamawwaj*, to undulate, roll like a wave, or be wave-formed] with delicacy and beauty," states an ad for Nihar, a coconut hair oil.[12] Most of the area of the ad shows the black, wavy-smooth hair of the model. The desired smoothness is that of silk: an article placed across from a shampoo ad describes ways of attaining "silky hair."[13] An advertisement for Daniel Galvin products promises to make the buyer's hair "delicate and silky."[14] Shampoo is thus associated with the prestige of silk, despite the fact that silk is regarded negatively as a luxury item in orthodox Wahhabi doctrine (especially for men who are not supposed to wear silk until the Day of Judgment [*yawm al-din*]. In Islamic eschatologic literature, one of the first signs of the end of history is the appearance of men wearing silk. Men should not be too delicate while within the ordinary course of history.)

Curly hair can be made smooth using Glatt, a product of the cosmetics company Schwarzkopf & Henkel.[15] The curly-haired woman with an "Eastern" appearance begins to smile when her hair becomes smoothed, but the product itself changes as well: the package, which carries Arabic text as well as Latin transcription, says only "Schwarzkopf," without the name "Henkel."[16] In the post–Gulf War 1990s, the name of the American commander of Operation Desert Storm is familiar and linked with success in Saudi "knowledge." This seems a probable association for a Saudi reader faced with this name, especially in the context of achieving victory in difficult terrain, that of curly hair. But one doubts that the product would be successful in Iraq.

The natural hair color of Arab women, as is prominently visible in advertising, is black. A Pantène ad contains a diagram illustrating how a pro-vitamin enters a hair; the hair is shown in black, the chemical substances in white.[17] On the other hand, where dyeing and fantasies are concerned, all women want to be blonde. Walter Armbrust wrote about Egyptian television commercials featuring blonde models, whose voices are overdubbed with the ("black") voices of Egyptian women,[18] creating a new "black-blonde" or "Eastern blonde" hybrid. Elsewhere, I have shown the part played by Princess Diana's blonde hair in her becoming an Egyptian cultural heroine.[19] Blonde represents the exotic, the other, the unfamiliar, the exciting. Turning one's hair blonde (in any way: by dyeing, by sexual conquest, by fantasy) signifies overcoming "black" destiny and is a victory over the blonde, colonialist states of the North (Europe). Thus, an advertisement by Kadus shows the sixty-three colors and hues that the company markets. Twenty-three of these, more than a third, are various kinds of *ashqar* (blonde). Among the blonde hues are several that a Western observer would not call blonde at all: for example, "dark blonde" (*ashqar ghamiq*), "dark gray blonde" (*ashqar ramadi ghamiq*), "dark copper blonde" (*ashqar ghamiq nuhasi*), and others that bear little similarity to Western "blondes." This blonde is different, broader, more tolerant, and hospitable.

Other interesting colors in this ad are those of the "sandy" (*ramali*) family, which resemble desert sand; a color "like natural rose" (*khashab al-ward al-tabi'i*); the "copper" (*nahasi*) family of colors; and the color of *yaquti*, a precious stone that we previously encountered in watch advertisements (see chapter one). These colors represent materials indigenous to Arab culture and tradition. The forbidden dark wine red (*akhmar nabidhi ghamiq*) and the bold purple (*banafsaji*) are relegated to the bottom of the list. It should be remembered that women's hair in Saudi Arabia is not exposed but rather is gathered in a *khimar*, *abayyah*, or other traditional item of clothing. Dyed, well-groomed hair is reserved for the immediate family; the blonde woman is actually the husband's fantasy, just as, in many advertisements, the *mahjubah*, the woman dressed in a *hijab*, is a gift-wrapped present to the husband.

Another hair dye company, V05, blesses the buyer's hair with *sihha wa-'afiyah* ("to your health"), the words of the traditional food blessing.[20] The blessing, then, is transferred to another field, from food to cosmetics; it is the use of tradition that is important. The text of the advertisement starts by stating, "Companies from all over the world are competing to gain entry to *our* markets in the Gulf region." From the very beginning, this international company makes itself a part of the Gulf, observing with concern the "foreign" competitors attempting to invade the region. After lengthy explanations, the ad ends with the Arab proverb, "Talk stays talk until experience confirms it," and then, "So try it [the product] and don't forget us in [your] 'personal prayer' [*du'a'*, also "wish," "appeal"]." The product thus becomes part of the cycle of Saudi life, just like prayer. The foreign commercial company has become a national-religious zealot. An advertisement for Clairol hair dyes shows that the imported packages, with their photos of Western women, were left unchanged for the Saudi Arabian market (replacing them would have cost time and money), but the ad itself shows a young black-haired woman of Eastern appearance, with the text, "Because natural color gives you a feeling of security and beauty."[21]

Though possibly not as genetic-natural as black dye, the use of henna is common and maybe even "traditional." But the product can just as well be imported from France.[22] Here, once again, the choice of an imported product is suited to the culture that imports it. "After inconvenience and difficulties in applying henna, there is now an easy, simple solution. Madam, within minutes your hair can acquire color, sheen, and nourishment, and all this takes no more than minutes with French henna dyes." This henna comes in nine colors and hues, "for all hair colors."

But not all hair is to be groomed. A woman's body must remain smooth and hairless. The depilation a married woman should perform every twenty days is a *sunnah* (a strongly recommended tradition, although not an obligation). According to certain Islamic traditions, men too should remove their body hair every forty days.[23] *Sayyidati* advertises hair creams and lotions, as well as electric hair removers. A hair removal cream that, in English, is for use on the face and bikini line becomes in Arabic "for the face and personal areas"[24]; the bikini disappears. Nair cream is sold in "rose perfume" and "lemon perfume" varieties and leaves skin "soft as silk"[25]; Immac cream features exactly the same scents.[26] A Philips hair remover called Satin*elle* likewise promises to leave skin "soft as silk."[27] Roses and silk, two items traditionally used to arouse excitement and passion in the Arabian deserts, continue to serve the same function. The satin in the French name Satin*elle* (*zaytuni* in Arabic— from zaytun (olive)—possibly because of the fabric's smooth, shiny, "oily" side), named after the medieval Chinese port from which the textile was exported to Europe (which was described by Marco Polo in the thirteenth century as one of China's largest ports and is usually identified with Tsinkiang),[28] becomes pure silk (*harir*) in the Arabic version (satin is composed of natural cotton; the shine is achieved by using large skips of wraps over wefts)—there are no mistakes, only Freudian-cultural errors. The use of the rose, from all flowers, contains a religious allusion: the rose is known as the favorite flower of the prophet Muhammad (Muhammedi is a reference to a perfumed rose, and various Islamic rulers had their portraits taken while holding a rose). A facial cream promises a "velvety" touch.[29] In this way, too, female skin always remains wrapped in some sort of a cloth.

The skin of the face, revealed and revealing, is known in Arabic as *sahifat al-wajh* ("the newspaper of the face," though the word *sahifah* existed with various meanings before the invention of newspapers). Since a woman's face is the only part of her body that is not covered (apart from the hands, which we encountered in the watch advertisements), *Sayyidati* advertises a wide variety of facial creams, lotions, and the like. Furthermore, the exposed skin of the face becomes a metonymy for the rest of the body's skin, which remains covered. The skin around the eyes is an especially important part of the facial skin (which in turn is an important part of the body's skin). The area of the eyes stays exposed even in the strictest masks. "For your eyes, let time stop," declares a Givenchy ad.[30] The Qazaz, one of Saudi Arabia's leading importers of cosmetics, chose to place an ad for Elizabeth Arden facial cream across from an article titled "How People Look at the Divorcee"; in the photograph accompanying the article, the divorcée's face is blurred.[31] The advertisement confronts the divorcée with "Sleeping Beauty" (*al-jamal al-na'im*), a cream "which acts while you sleep, all night, for fresher, younger skin." Beauty is necessarily a quality of the fresh, young, passive princess saved by the Saudi prince; a divorcée cannot possibly have a beautiful face. Although many women's families today insert a clause into the marriage contract permitting the woman to demand a divorce, the Hanbali *madhhab* ("school of law," one of the four legal streams in Sunni Islam), prevailing in Saudi Arabia, makes it almost impossible for a woman to break the marriage tie without her husband's consent.[32] The face of the divorcée, the woman who dared to rebel and take responsibility for her life, is blurred and erased.

A woman is defined by her skin type—"normal," "dry," or "sensitive." Accordingly, a Nivea ad shows three models of Saudi appearance. The three look extremely similar (black hair, pearl earrings, white blouse, skirt), the sole difference being their "skin type." Especially interesting is the design of the Arabic-language cream bottles: the bottle for "normal" skin cream has a white body and black "hair" (a black cap); the "dry" variety is black with a white cap; and the "sensitive" cream is albino, both the bottle and the cap being white. Readers who desire details about Avon skin products must fill out a form that accompanies the company's advertisement and send it in to its Jiddah offices. The name to be filled in is that of the *rabb al-usrah*, "the father of the family."[33] He is also the one who gives his son the "gentle caress" in a Nivea body lotion ad featuring a "father and son" (not a father and daughter, a mother and son, or a mother and daughter).[34]

A Vaseline Intensive Care body lotion advertisement also exploits the gap between the actual and the desired, between social reality and many women's unfulfilled dreams.[35] The ad takes up three left-hand pages (on the first two a vertical half-page, on the third an entire page). On the first page, it begins by showing a delicate feminine hand, underneath which is the question "Where are you?" (There are no vowel marks, so the second-person form might be masculine or feminine.) On the second page is a picture of a bottle of body lotion; above it is the text, "I am here for you" (*li-ajliki*, the pronoun is marked with *kasra* to indicate the feminine), below it, "To shield, tend, and nourish your skin." The third and last page unites the woman's hand with the bottle of lotion, and the text, which is in quotation marks, reads, "I need you . . . to take care of my skin . . . In our country's cruel climate, your skin needs someone to protect it, take care of it, and shield it, so it can preserve its pleasantness, delicacy, and freshness . . . My faith in Fazalin . . . has never been shaken, and my skin knows no other way to delicacy and freshness since I came to know Fazalin." This three-part advertisement accompanied a story on "husbands' violence" (*'unf al-azwaj*). The photographs in the article show women with blurred faces, and a picture of a man about to hit a woman who is covering her face. The analogy between the ad and the story is clear: the solution for the grave problem of violence against women ("our country's cruel climate" refers to more than just the harsh desert sun) is using Vaseline body lotion, a lotion that behaves like a real man, gentle and considerate. Every woman "needs it," and as soon as she comes to know it, she gives thanks for her good fortune and observes monogamy in cosmetics; from then on, she knows no other skin cream.

A woman's facial skin is the only area of her body that is regularly exposed to sunlight. Therefore, we find no advertisements for suntan lotion but only for various sorts of protective facial creams.[36] Ultraviolet rays fall into two categories, designated by the first two letters of the Arabic alphabet, *alif* and *ba*.[37] Facial skin can be protected from harmful desert dust by the use of Bioré face stickers.[38]

Dettol, in an advertisement for one of its soaps, shows a man sitting on a living room sofa embracing a boy and a girl, one on each side.[39] The girl is playing with dolls, the boy with electronic games. The boy is clearly the elder, somewhat older than the girl. The text of the ad reads, "They refresh themselves cleanly and enjoy themselves healthily." The body of the ad tells the woman reader (there is no woman in the picture itself, but the text is phrased in the feminine imperative) about the advantages of purchasing the soap for her children and her husband. The woman is only an instrument (for pregnancy, for buying soap, for taking the picture) that makes possible the father's relationship with his children.

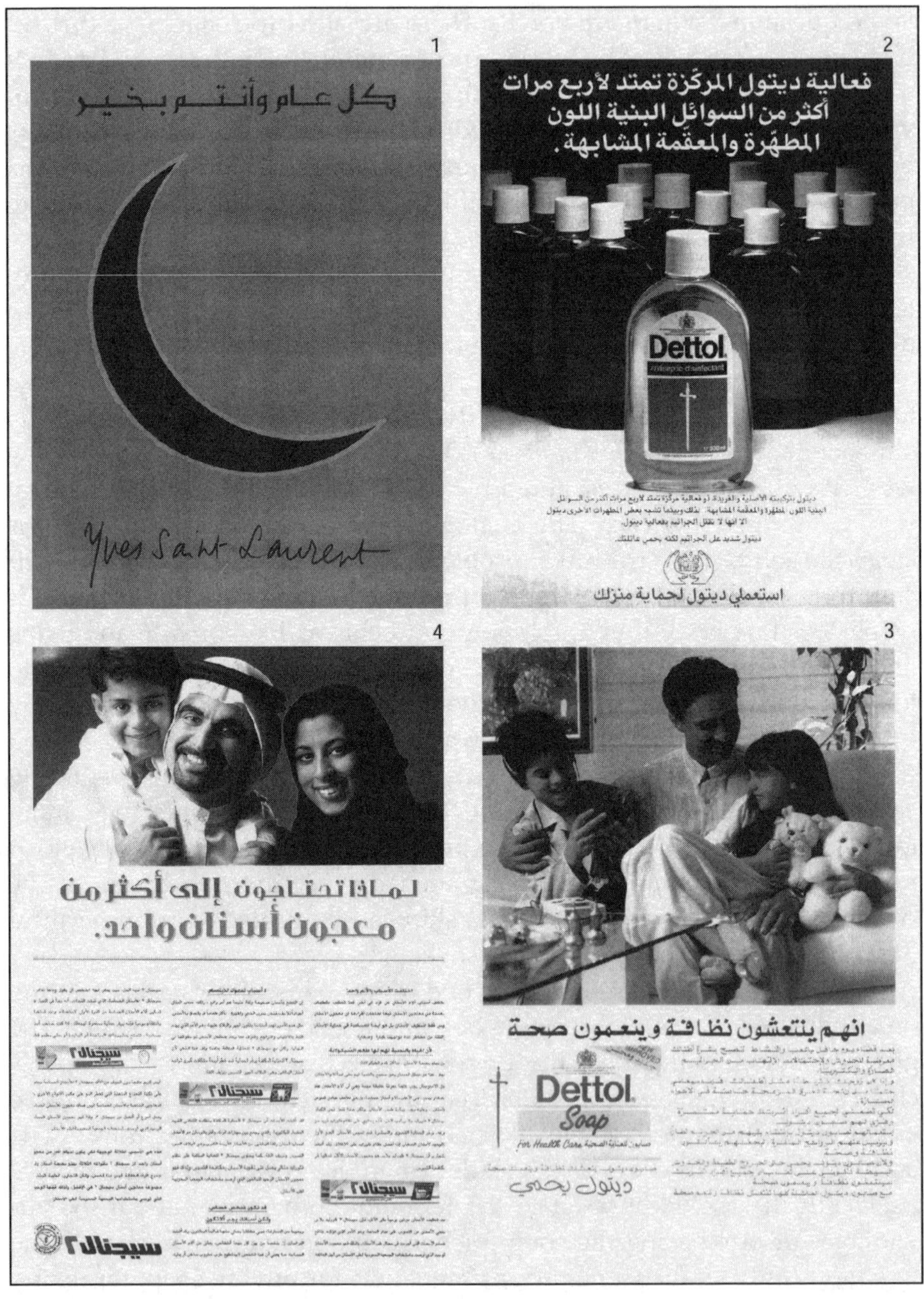

Fig.8 (1) Yves Saint-Laurent; (2) Dettol–antiseptic disinfectant; (3) Dettol soap; (4) Signal 6 toothpaste.

Athar al-Hakim, an Egyptian movie and television actress, advertises Lux soap.[40] Lux advertisements in the United States decades ago featured film stars, including Rachel Welch. The use of an Egyptian celebrity in a Saudi ad is not surprising, since Egypt is the largest media exporter to other Arab states; its film and television industry is without a doubt the most developed in the Arab world. Celebrities promoting soap recur in ads for Dove, which feature Suzan Nur,[41] Rima Karkafi,[42] and others.

Decleor published an advertisement for plant-based skin care products for men and women,[43] "One drop lasts all day." The ad exploits the necessity to economize liquids, implanted in desert culture (an ad for a Grohe faucet, with a single knob and a rotary head, stresses that it "helps conserve water"[44]). The Arabic translation of the names of the plants used "Arabizes" the product further: the ingredients include *zayt al-marimiyyah*, sage oil, made of an herb with long grayish-green leaves, used in traditional Arab medicine in tea to cure stomachache; *zayt badhr al-baqdunas*, parsley seed oil, often used in traditional cooking and medicine; geranium, whose Arab name (*ibra al-ra'i*, "shepherd's staff") is indicated in parentheses; and a plant known as *has al-ban* or alternatively *iklil al-jabal* (both names are cited), used in traditional medicine for treating kidney stones. "Decleor products are used in the kingdom's most prestigious beauty shows," says the ad. In a like fashion, an aloe vera based hair removal product from Immac becomes a "sabra (*sabar*) compound."[45] The ad imparts some historical data: "Natural sabra has been used in skin care for centuries because of its caressing, moisturizing qualities."

Clinique constructs an ad for its Turnaround face lotion around traditional Arab blessings, *ahla[n]* (hello) and *wida'a[n]* (goodbye)[46]: the first to greet the new lotion "in case we haven't met," the second to bid farewell to lines, wrinkles, and other skin problems. "So . . . if your skin embarrasses you, say hello to [*rahibi bi-*] Turnaround and say goodbye [*wida'an*] to skin problems." The verb *rahhaba (bi-)* retains its Arabic preposition even when accompanying the English product name.

The problem of perspiration and body odor, *'araq*, which lends its name to the pungent liquor, is especially severe in the desert. But in Saudi Arabia, deodorants are nonalcoholic. "Perspiration odors? Deo Sauber . . . the only one which rids you of them for the whole week with a single use"[47]: an alcohol-free product. This deodorant promises to "remove perspiration odor" for an entire week, as opposed to others that are only effective for twenty-four hours. The advertisement shows seven smiling youths engaged in various activities, one for each day of the week. But the Saudi week is different from that of the product's home country: it begins on Saturday; work ends on Wednesday; on Thursday, the man can help the woman prepare food or simply watch her; and Friday is the happy day of rest, known as *al-jum'ah,* after the term for the Friday mosque that "gathers" the believers (*jama'ah*). The deodorant, then, adapts to a different kind of week. Likewise, an Elizabeth Arden face cream yields first results within six days,[48] so women can look better on the *al-jum'ah.*

Like other products, cosmetics are marketed on a larger scale during holiday periods. "On holidays and special occasions, all your hopes come true with beauty."[49] If you "dream of being the most attractive," "devote yourself to Clarince makeup—pleasure [again: *mut'ah*], glitter, color . . . Everything you need in order to be noticed."[50] The sexual devotion to Clarince makeup is expressed in Islamic terminology: *istaslama* is also one who has devoted him- or herself to Islam (which means "devotion"). The Body Shop chain promoted "a Ramadan display presented by *Dhi Budi Shub* to its respected [*al-kiram*] customers during the dear [*al-karim*] month of Ramadan and the holiday of *'id al-fitr al-mubarak* [the blessed holiday of breaking the fast]"[51]; the following year, it offered a cosmetics basket as a "Ramadan gift," for 99 Saudi riyals.[52] The Western sales technique of reducing the price by one unit to make it appear cheaper (99 rather than 100) here combines with the traditional mystic significance of the number 99 (the 99 beautiful names of Allah, a multiple of 33 in the *misbahah* rosary, etc.).

A double-page advertisement by Yves Saint-Laurent dedicates all its space to the traditional New Year's blessing *"Kull am wa-antum bi-khayr"*; the traditional wooden lattice, which we have encountered in other ads, is here constructed of the firm's initials, YSL, and is placed behind the perfume bottles.[53] The following year, the same greeting is accompanied by a half crescent, all on a green background; the color green symbolizes Islam and is also the background for the Arabic text on the Saudi flag.[54] According to Islamic tradition, the flag of the prophet Muhammad and the robe of 'Ali, the fourth caliph, were both green. Arabic contains many words for various hues of green; due to the color's religious significance, some believers do not pray when standing on a green *sajadah* (prayer mat). Since green stands for the Islamic faith, many mosques, palaces, private houses, and tribal symbols, as well as the flags of some Muslim states, are green; this also serves to ward off the evil eye.[55]

"If San Luran" also "wishes you well, *sayyidati* (my lady), for the holidays, and presents you and the ladies of the Middle East, for the first time and before the women of the rest of the world, with its new perfume . . . which is captivating [*al-akhadh*, also 'gripping,' 'amazing']."[56] The first marketing experiment for the new perfume, called *In Love Again*, thus becomes a gesture of honor, and the guinea pigs, the mini-mice, become a group of women fortunate enough to precede the rest of the world.

The ideal lips are those painted with deep red lipstick. Lipstick advertisements do not feature other colors besides red.[57] In fact, the Arabic name of lipstick literally means "red for the lips" (*ahmar al-shafah*). The preferred red is a brilliant one; "Woman's love of brilliance knows no bounds," states an ad for Givenchy lipstick.[58] Lipstick as a phallic symbol, shown just before being rubbed against a woman's lips, recurs in many ads.[59] This is another opportunity to print and advertise sex in a society that seemingly[60] does not permit explicit expressions of sexuality, a way of publishing sexuality "without" sexuality.

Beyond the lips lies another important field of cosmetics and hygiene advertising, the mouth and teeth. Dettol's mouthwash fights bacteria: "Nothing beats Ditul for guarding your home and family from harmful bacteria," announces an ad showing a picture of the bottle.[61] The design on the label is a white sword on a green background. The text at the bottom of the ad indicates that the sword symbol is a trademark ('*alamah tijariyyah*). Another advertisement for the same product compares it with its rivals: "The concentrated action of Ditul is four times as strong as similar, brown-colored cleaning and purifying liquids."[62] The fight against bacteria is a real one, perhaps one in the warlike Wahhabi tradition and that of the bold wars of the *ayam al-arab*; it is to be waged with the help of the color green and a bellicose vocabulary.

Sijnal 2 toothpaste published a two-page advertisement explaining "why you need more than one toothpaste."[63] The picture shows a "father" dressed in a white *jalabiyyah* and a white *kaffiyah*, fastened with a black '*aqal*, under which a traditional headdress is just visible. His beard and moustache are well groomed, his eyebrows thick. On his right is his "wife," dressed in black, her lips contoured with a makeup pencil. The man holds a child on his back, on the side away from the woman; the child too is all in white. The "son" is not placed between the two "parents"; he clings to the father. For a one-child family, the ideal is a male son. The light in the picture comes from the man's side, while the woman is in the shadow. This is "life with the taste of chocolate," as the text suggests: an ideal, tartar-free (*tasawus al-asnan*) life. This is "the only toothpaste recommended by the Saudi Dental Association"; the association's logo, containing a map of Saudi Arabia, appears next to the picture.

Perfumes are also adapted to the target culture. They constitute such an important portion of cosmetics products that the journal *Sayyidati* itself manufactures and markets a perfume bearing its own name[64] (also available in a "*Sayyidati* Gold" version[65]). Gold recurs in many advertisements unrelated to jewelry; it often appears as a prize in promotional drawings and sales, and many ads compare their product to gold. In Saudi Arabia one can even buy a perfume that contains drops of pure gold.[66] "Black gold"—oil—is translated into traditional gold. The use of gold and the prestige associated with it have a long history, as I show briefly in the next chapter.[67]

"*Ughmuri Ahasisaki*" ["cover your (fem.) senses/emotions"], advises an ad for Marbert's Scarf perfume.[68] The picture shows a bottle of perfume with its body wrapped in a scarf and its head bearing a sort of white coif. The ad plays the game of sexual seduction in accordance with social rules: the verb *ghamara* means both "cover" and "flood, wash"; *ghamr* is both "deep water" and "burning"; *ghumira 'alayhi* means "faint, lose consciousness"; *mughamarah* means "gamble, adventure." The play of opposites, the confronting of concealment with revelation, fire with water, adventure with restraint, the sanctioned with the forbidden, serve to promise a swoon of ecstasy while conforming with cultural rules. The bottle is described in Islamic dress, while sexuality is achieved by verbal means. In like fashion, Vicky Tiel's Sirène perfume is also pictured covered with cloth, only the head exposed.[69]

Van Cleef and Arpels's Miss Arpels perfume is a "good [*shadha{n}*], pungent smell of a perfume inside ('in the heart of') a diamond." "Pungency" is not repulsive—on the contrary, it is attractive and seductive. The diamond-shaped bottle is shown in front of a framed mirror, which reflects (on the other side of the room) a white shuttered door; the door opens onto a wide porch with an Eastern ornamented balustrade, behind which (in the garden) are palm trees. The simple procedure of transcribing the name of the perfume into Arabic, Mis Arbelz, creates the complexity of the ad and the connection between the picture and the perfume. *Massa al-mar'a* means "come to a woman, have intercourse with a woman"; *massaha 'ila* means "bring (a woman) to (some state)"; *mass* (which appears in the slogan and implicitly in the shape of the bottle) is "diamond"; *hajah masa* means "urgent need"; and *qarabah masa* is "immediate kinship." The reader of the ad cannot see what is taking place in the room itself, which seems to be a private room on the second floor of a Saudi luxury house. All that is visible are the palms outside, the trees that symbolize desert enchantment and Eastern seduction. The light is that of high noon; the rest of the house's occupants have perhaps gone out. The reader sees no one, only the perfume bottle; but he knows there is a room that contains a young woman (a "Miss"), who can be felt, come to, brought to some state; that the diamond can be touched.

Rasasi's perfume collection does not disturb the imagined realities of Saudi life, either. Among the five imported perfumes is Blue Lady; in the ad, the bottle, with wide shoulders and slim waist, casts a shadow on the wall behind it in the form of a woman.[70] Fantasy becomes reality through the means of the traditional *karagöz*, or shadow theater. Likewise, the perfumes Chastity and Secret both bear unintrusive, even culturally appropriate names. Surprisingly, of the five perfumes it is Romance that makes the least exciting impression in the advertisement. The lack of sexuality becomes a source of intense passion.

In a similar fashion, Kesling's C'est Magique comes in bottles designed to suit Saudi social reality: the bottle of men's perfume is in the form of a taut spring, the sprayer protruding upwards; the women's bottle is a bent-in spring in which the sprayer is hidden[71]—an internal spring designed to contain the masculine one. The same company advertises its Sinaï perfume, named after the Egyptian desert region, which borders on Saudi Arabia and is historically linked to it. The bottle wears two smooth, round, "golden" earrings, one on each side, in traditional Bedouin fashion.[72] The desert also plays a central role in advertisements for Givenchy's Organza ("Inside me, something of eternity"[73]) and Christian Dior's men's perfume Dune.[74] The heat of the desert is also suitable for marketing Kenzo's Parfum d'été: the order of the months in the advertisement is "*Yanayir* [January], *Fibrayir* [February], *Yulyu* [July], *Yulyu, Yulyu* . . ." And indeed—aside from two months of winter, the Saudi year is a long July.[75] "One day, heat will cover the world," says an apocalyptic ad for Anaïs Anaïs[76]; it is "Eastern" heat that will conquer the world. Divina, from a company called Swissarabian, was created when "the imagination and magic of the Orient, the sweet smell of the rose, the

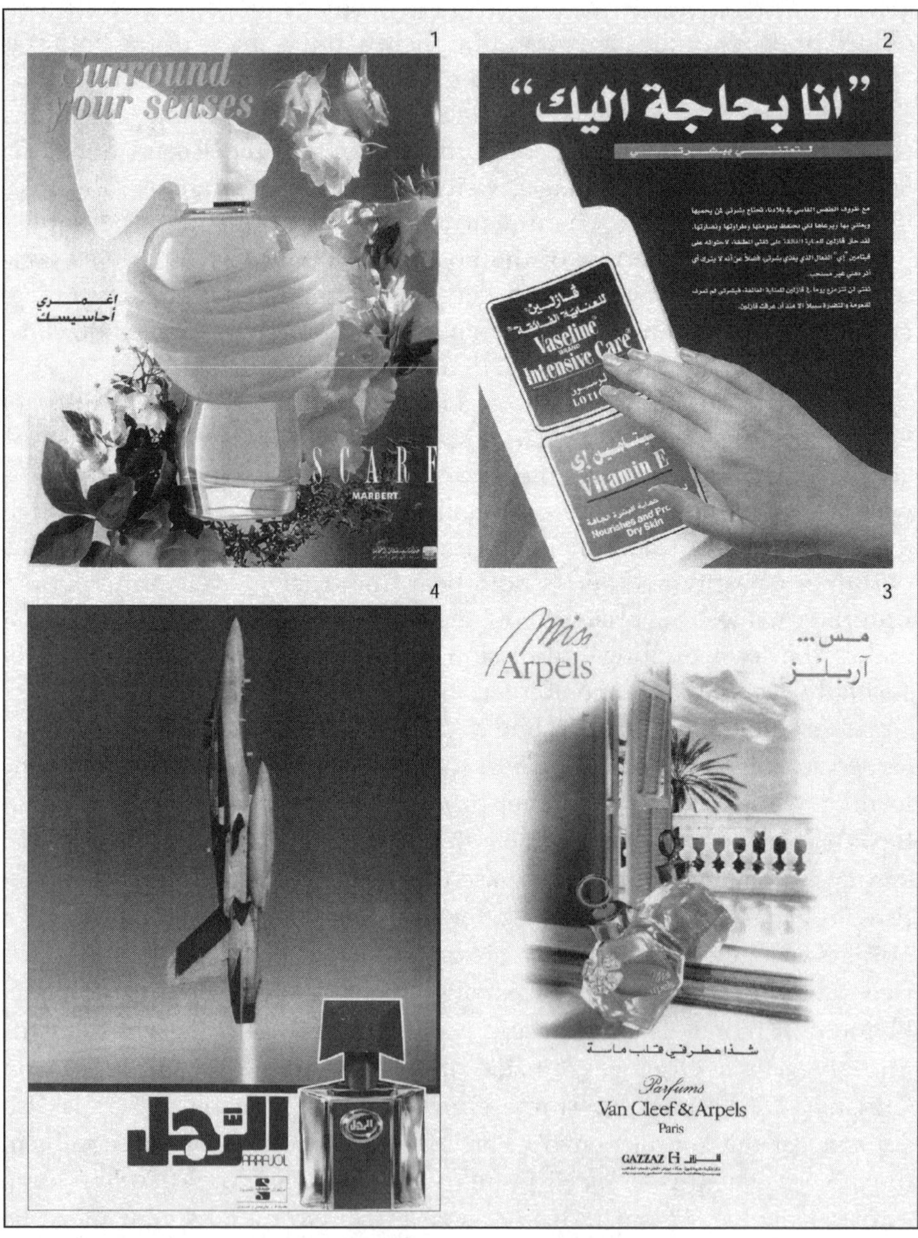

Fig.9 (1) Scarf perfume, Marbet; (2) Vaseline Intensive Care; (3) Miss Arpels
perfume, Van Cleef & Arpels; (4) Arrajol (Al-Rajul) perfume.

scent of fruit, were gathered together and became a life-content which cannot be resisted."[77] Traditional Oriental imagery still stands proud in 1990's Saudi Arabia. Carita marketed a perfume bottle with a sort of hookah pipe connected to the sprayer ("breathe the perfume of beauty").[78] The Oriental life is the true Dolce Vita, as a Christian Dior perfume is named[79]: a life dramatically different from that of the West.

Rasasi's Jewel perfume is placed on a map of Asia, precisely covering Saudi Arabia and the Arab states: the diamond in the crown of the East.[80] In the English-language map, the Indian Ocean is called the Arab Sea. The points of the compass change too, southeast becoming north. The "Arab" diamond changes the world order, and neglected directions now become desirable.

Women's perfumes are not necessarily intended for women; often they are meant for men, those who will buy them as gifts and will receive them back as scents. "So . . . ?" is "a special perfume with an independent personality."[81] An ad for independence requires a blonde Western model; her shirt sleeves have clearly been artificially lengthened, and her stomach and legs have been similarly hidden. Independence has been limited, but the very idea of seeking it led to the use of a Western model. For Saudi models, autonomy remains a dream. Even bold, perfumed fantasies stay decent and properly dressed.[82] Furthermore, it is the perfume (*atar*, a masculine noun) that gains independence; only through a relationship with it can a woman strive for her own independence. In advertisements, most of the messages that refer to freedom and independence are left in English. The slogan for Tommy Girl perfume, "A Declaration of Independence," was left unchanged.[83] The slogan "Forever Changing, Forever the Same," for Alfred Sung's Forever, was modified slightly into *"Da'ima[n] mutajaddidah . . . wa-thabitah ila al-abad"* ("Always renewing . . . and eternally stable").[84] Complete "change," dissociating oneself from the existent, becomes "renewal" within the bounds of reality.

Sometimes cosmetics and perfumes are not sufficient for feeling good; readers are then referred to plastic surgery. The Anaheim Image Medical Center in Los Angeles published an ad in *Sayyidati*, suggesting that "When you visit Disneyland in Anaheim-Los Angeles, don't forget to visit the Anaheim Medical Center for Beautification and Laser Treatment."[85] A variety of operations are performed at the center by Dr. Husein Suleiman. Even in Los Angeles, surgery is carried out by an Arab doctor, who retains a connection to the world of his origin. In another ad, placed across from a poem by a Moroccan reader titled "That's What I Want," Dr. Bashar al-Badhra from the *Al-Nakhil* ("date") Center in Filastin (Palestine) Square in Jiddah proposes various cosmetic operations including correction of "African and Chinese noses."[86]

The field of hygiene contains more than glamorous perfumes and cosmetics, however; it also comprises the treatment and removal of bodily excretions. Of course, this subject too becomes glamorous and dreamlike. An advertisement for Private's protective pads ("health" bandages, *sihiyyah*) shows a woman wearing a white *khimar*, sitting on an imaginary flower ("The feeling of natural cotton all through the seasons").[87] The slogan of the Kotex ("Kutiks") company's hygienic bandages is "She understands my needs," or simply "She understands," accompanied by a trademark symbol (*tatafahham*™).[88] The series of advertisements shows women of Arabic appearance; only their smiling faces are visible. "Kutiks understands that the most important thing a woman needs is protection (*al-himayah*); Kutiks also understands that a woman yearns for perfect serenity. The Kutiks hygienic bandage collection offers you what you want: maximum protection . . . the feeling of perfect serenity . . . For the protection you need and the serenity you desire / Kutiks understands." A woman stays "protected" also, or especially, during pubescence. The trademark of "understanding" is an adaptation to cultural knowledge.

The Arabic for toilet paper is *waraq hammam*, "bathhouse paper"; the bathroom is also sometimes called *hammam*. The bathhouse tradition apparently entered Arab culture via Greece and Rome, and was intensively developed. So important were bathhouses that their number constitutes one of the indices of the Muslim empire's economic prosperity: the decrease in the number of *hammamat* in the Abbasid Empire was the clearest indicator of its decline.[89] In the twentieth century, modern building styles have significantly reduced the number of public *hammamat*. Toilet paper and the home bathroom preserve an ancient tradition, a tradition to which Kleenex links its toilet paper.[90] The use of toilet paper, of course, is a modern custom. This paper is "more delicate, stronger, longer . . . Gives value to your money . . . Don't settle for less than Kleenex." Public restrooms can also educate women about their social role: women's restrooms in Saudi Arabia are marked with an image of a fully covered head.[91] The sign of the woman is her covering. Men's restrooms are marked with a *kaffiyah*, held by a black *aqal*—a powerful symbol of manhood and masculinity.

Women's cosmetics products in Saudi Arabia are ultimately intended for the man; they serve to beautify his bride. In tribal Bedouin culture, and even more so in strict Wahhabi-Hanbali Islam, to be unmarried is a flaw.[92] Marriage represents success in life. Therefore, a large number of ads show a scene of a bride preparing for her wedding. "The joy of the bride is completed by choosing . . . Batshi," declares an advertisement for a cosmetics and gifts shop.[93] A Wella shampoo ad features a girl with full, lush hair, wearing a bridal gown.[94] Johnson & Johnson published an ad titled *"uqbal al-ayizin"* ("next, those who need it"), a common blessing said to unmarried wedding guests or relatives. The entire ad is a conversation between two sisters, one of whom is getting married[95]:

> *"Ma sha' Allah* (what God will), Shima', how beautiful you were on your wedding day!"

> "Thanks to you, the best sister in the world . . . Do you remember how embarrassed I was about the dress, the hairdo, the makeup, designing *al-kushah*, the henna party, the wedding and the guest list, and . . . my glasses?"

> After describing the advantages of the contact lenses that are being advertised, the ad ends humorously:

> "Who knows, maybe soon you'll be using Johnson & Johnson products for your children!"

> "`A'isha! Drink your coffee!"

The "best sister in the world" is named A'isha, like the beloved, young, mischievous wife of the prophet Muhammad. Alongside the description of the traditional wedding, accompanied by a cup of coffee and a sisterly conversation, is a picture of the bride (in a white dress with ornaments in the bodice, white gloves of embroidered lace, a wreath, and a turned-up bridal veil) and her "sister" (in a similar dress, but without gloves or wreath). The ultimate point of getting married, after the money has changed hands, is to give birth to children who will take part in the cultural-consumerist community.

One must keep in mind that a Saudi wedding is, in many cases, a deal between men. For comparison with the feminine dialogue above, here is Geraldine Brooks's description of a characteristic traditional dialogue between the father of the bride and the groom, a few days before the wedding[96]:

"I give you my daughter, _______, the mature virgin, for marriage according to the laws of God and his Prophet."

"I take your daughter, _______, the mature virgin, for marriage according to the laws of God and his Prophet."

"Do you accept my daughter?"

"I have accepted her."

"God bless you with her."

"I hope to Allah that she will indeed prove a blessing."

After this dialogue, all present repeat the *fatihah*, and the marriage is finalized when the father and the groom sign the marriage contract. The dowry has, of course, been previously settled upon. Marriage is a financial pact. In 1993, a religious advisor for the *Saudi Gazette* wrote to one woman reader that as soon as she was married, her husband's word would become law for her.[97] Women can only smile and hope to give birth quickly to a male son, thus proving themselves to be a blessing. Therefore, in this ad too the man is present, though unseen. He is present behind all the ads for cosmetics and beauty products discussed in this chapter. He is always "there."

CHAPTER FIVE

Home and Away: Electronics, Leisure, and Recreation

This chapter deals with the concepts of "home" and "away," their combination and their boundaries. We begin by analyzing advertisements for kitchen appliances intended to facilitate daily tasks; examining ways of filling free time, always on the increase due to the use of technology; and then looking at recreational activities outside the home—tours and trips outside Saudi Arabia and the Arab world. Finally, we will look at advertisements that have to do with fulfilling commercial fantasies both at home and away, including ads for women's banking in Saudi Arabia. By linking these issues, I intend to illustrate how "the home" expands into public space, how culture is like a tortoise shell that one cannot leave behind, as it defines both "home" and "away."

To start with daily life, kitchen appliances all undergo a metamorphosis. Kenwood's mixer (*khalat*) can be used, as an as for it shows, to make hummus salad, tabula salad, *kubbah*, and other fried dishes (for making the dough stuffing).[1] The Moulinex meat grinder is explicitly labeled as featuring an additional part meant especially for preparing *kubbah* (with appropriate pictures).[2] Moulinex's Minipro vegetable chopper becomes "The new *muluhiyyah* chopper from Moulinex."[3] *Muluhiyyah* is a bush whose green leaves, after being chopped, are used to make a dish with the same name, which can be eaten alone or with rice. "For many years," the ad points out, "the housewife has suffered from chopping *muluhiyyah* in the traditional fashion, in order to serve the family's preferred dish. Every time she tried chopping *muluhiyyah* with a new machine, she did not get the [desired] result or the delicious taste. Today, Moulinex has created a *muluhiyyah* chopper especially for this purpose. This small, handy [*muluhiyyah*] chopper chops *muluhiyyah* in the preferred fashion while preserving its natural elements." The chopper, originally created for completely different reasons and for preparing quite different foods, becomes one specially designated for making a traditional Arab dish. It was made "especially for this purpose." The sound *mu* at the beginning of the name Moulinex is connected with the same sound at the beginning of the word *muluhiyyah*. This dish, so closely identified with Arabism—probably one reason why al-Hakim bi-Imru'llah (996–1021), the well-known Fatimi ruler and founder of the Druze religion, forbade his subjects to eat it—becomes identified with a Western electronic appliance (thus transforming the appliance).

Braun's blender also facilitates "chopping and slicing plants [*a'shab*]"[4]—though, just as in the advertisement for cosmetics discussed earlier, it does not specify which plants. Philips's kitchen appliances ("*ma'a[n] li-hayah afdal*," "together to a better life") all become devices for preparing the Ramadan meal: "Your *iftar* table [the *iftar* is the meal that breaks the Ramadan fast after sunset] in the blessed month of Ramadan, *dawma[n] amirah* ['always built, full,' a traditional Muslim blessing] with Filibs products."[5] The slogan, printed on a green background, is accompanied by a picture of a minaret with a half-crescent on its spire, in front of which is another structure crowned by another half-crescent (the mosque and its minaret?). In another ad, Philips wishes the reader a "blessed Ramadan with Filibs"; the picture shows a large tray full of rice, kebab, and shishlik and, before it, a plate of hummus and beans.[6] Even U.S.-made aluminum foil is advertised during Ramadan as ideal "for covering the contents [of dishes] in storage" (across from an article on "Ramadan dishes from Saudi Arabia, Egypt, and Morocco").[7]

Tefal's grinder becomes "the modern technique for the traditional taste [*al-nukhah al-taqlidiyyah*] . . . for grinding anything from coffee and cardamom to spices, *al-maksurat* [a variety of nuts such as walnuts, pistachios, almonds, and peanuts] and sugar cubes."[8] A refrigerator from LG Electronics is shown full of products by companies we encountered in the chapter on food, such as *al-Rabi* juices.[9] General Electric refrigerators are sold with the aid of diamonds and traditional rings.[10] Moulinex vacuum cleaners are advertised as good for vacuuming prayer mats (*sujad*).[11] Coral laundry soap is so effective that it is "as if you were doing the laundry by hand," and is good for washing *'abayyat* (the plural of *'abayyah*).[12] All these examples show once again the extent to which all advertising is culture dependent.

An ad for Falcon's electric appliances brings us back to the desert.[13] The ad shows, lined up against a desert background, a refrigerator, a freezer, a washing machine, a dryer, an oven, a microwave, a vacuum cleaner, and a mineral-water cooler. Above the appliance hovers a falcon, like a mythological phoenix. The trained falcon recurs often as a traditional symbol of beauty, speed, and loyalty. Falconry is the most characteristic local sport, one that existed long before the arrival of European ball games, and seems to be encouraged in recent years as a sort of national pastime.

The desert and the falcon—both familiar and well-recognized symbols of the Arab culture, as observed in the ads for watches in chapter one—often appear together in ads for mobile phones, as the falcon is a symbol of mobility while the desert is a place where one is likely to need a cellular phone. In an ad for Ericsson's mobile phones ("the wonders of performance"), the falcon "is an incarnation of permanent superiority."[14] In another such ad, an Ericsson phone declares, "We wish you a happy day"; the phone is pictured on the roof of a field vehicle (the modern camel) in the heart of the desert, next to the car keys. The driver has apparently gone out for a trek, or stopped to rest, and it is the cellular phone that allows him to communicate. In the background is another Jeep; thanks to technology, the ancient desert roads are teeming with life again. Technology is a return to tradition. The cellular phone makes it possible to lead a modern life even in real, traditional regions, in the middle of the desert. It is also through technology, through cellular phones and Jeeps, that one can return to one's origins.

As shown in earlier chapters, it may be valuable to also examine what is *not* advertised. I found no ads for sewing machines. In contrast to the many ads for kitchen appliances and the pride women take in preparing food, clothes in Saudi Arabia are now bought ready-made. In the period studied, *Sayyidati* also published no advertisements for personal computers and related products. Likewise, there are no ads for cameras (though film is advertised in the context of vacations; see below).

In the field of home retail, even "the American home goods houses" (stores that unite American furniture and home appliance manufacturers in Jiddah, Riyadh, and Medina) offer 30 percent discounts for Ramadan.[15] The ads do not show the actual furniture, but they do teach us something about Saudi cities: the stores are located, of course, on streets that bear characteristically Muslim or Arabic names. The *Asam Nas* shopping, for example, which houses the IDdesign warehouse, is not far from al-Falaq Square, named after a surah of the Koran. Because Arabic and Muslim street names are common in many Middle Eastern cities, giving the street name in the ad provides a common link among markets throughout the Middle East. It is important to note the location of central business districts (CBDs), again, not necessarily as a Western influence, but as a continuation of the bazaar tradition.

The arrows on the map accompanying the ad show that, in Saudi Arabia, one drives on the right. An interesting fact is that the perfectly straight streets shown on the map are not merely the fantasy of a quick commercial sketch. The streets in Riyadh were carefully planned, with the aid of petrodollars. In fact, construction of infrastructure, especially sewage, electricity, and sometimes roads, often precedes that of the houses. In Riyadh, infrastructure waits for residents.

Leisure is an important element in the culture of any consumer society and is thus of great interest to advertisers. The definition of leisure is, of course, problematic. All time that can be filled is "free time," and all action (even when unrewarded) is "work" or "activity." A possible criterion might be the "dream" nature of the activity. Watching television is a more dreamlike activity than ironing or cooking. Smoking during work is a short "dream break" (which is dependent on culture and marketing), an invasion of fantasy into everyday life. Sex, of course, is the most problematic activity of all. As a Saudi joke goes, an Englishman, asked whether sex is work or pleasure, answers, "a bit of both"; a Frenchman says, "pleasure, naturally"; and a Saudi Arabian answers, "of course it's pleasure—we leave the work to foreigners." The use of sex as a fantasy of "free time" and "pleasure" has been encountered in perfume advertisements. It was there that women were allowed a smell of sex as a masculine fantasy. Here, too, in ads for leisure activities, women can only have fragrances. For Saudi men, sex is a leisure activity; but for women, whose livelihood depends on their availability for sex, on their reproductive capabilities, sex is a work activity.

Sexual-philosophical quandaries aside, the most obvious modern options for filling an ever-growing amount of free time are radio and television. The veteran Radio Monte Carlo station still advertises its broadcasts, but ads for communication technologies in Saudi Arabia also include satellite broadcasting. The possibility of receiving satellite broadcasts in Saudi Arabia is not self-evident: it entails bypassing the authorities' control over broadcasts. Satellite stations are received in many Gulf states: the Showtime corporation has branches in Saudi Arabia, Oman, the United Arab Emirates, Kuwait, and Bahrein.[16] Among the channels included in the package is the documentary channel Discovery, as well as a special channel, Style, dedicated to programs on baby care and child rearing; its slogan is "Your [fem.] baby is a world of secrets! Discover it with Style."[17] Among the satellite stations, the one that most obviously corresponds to Saudi social values is emphasized: the one that stresses the link between a mother and her baby. Indeed, the satellite company published an advertisement showing a trained falcon, wearing a special metal hat and standing on a leather glove that it grips with its talons; the slogan reads, "Do you still strive to see the best?"[18] The falcon is pictured against a background of orange desert and hazy palm trees. Only the small print discloses that the package also includes the Movie Channel, MTV, and other typically Western channels. The local audience is reached through the falcon and through mothers, whose purpose is to raise their children. The ART (Arab Radio Television) broadcasting company published an ad calling on potential advertisers to use its services, "the shortest way to any Arab's heart."[19] The station promises advertisers that their message will reach "the greatest number of viewers, who follow interesting programs such as that featuring Hamdi Qandil, *Ya Halah* ['hello' in stylish spoken Arabic], [programs about] Islam and social problems, the information bank . . . [and more]." These programs are intended for "the prestigious [*al-raqiyyah*] family" and are chosen to suit "every part of the family." Another program, which ART advertised in a special ad, is *Suhun wa-Funun* ("plates and arts"; a play on words that indicates a wide variety of foods, much like the expression *"al-junun funun,"* "the varieties of madness are many"). This program was broadcast every day during the month of Ramadan to enable housewives to prepare diverse dishes for the *iftar* meal.[20]

Another, more traditional way of filling free time is smoking. As noted above, smoking is a way of introducing a form of "leisure" into work and daily chores, a sort of small-scale, marginal recreation that is synchronized with performing tasks, a virtual connection of pleasure with duty. Among ads for Winston ("deep-rooted American taste"),[21] Marlboro (showing a cowboy on a horse under a raging waterfall),[22] and other Western companies, one also finds ads for al-Majlis cigarettes. This brand features an "American" tobacco blend with an "Eastern taste," and is "made in Switzerland." The *majlis*, the tribal men's council in which all members are equal and decisions are made by wide consensus, was a social institution of great importance and remains a significant element of tribal democracy.[23] In rural areas of modern Saudi Arabia, men still gather at the imam's house for a meal after prayer on Friday.[24] Women convey questions and requests to the imam through their husbands, not directly.[25] An advertisement for cigarettes shows six men in white *jalabiyyat*; three of them wear white headdresses, one a red and white checkered headdress, and two are bare-headed.[26] All have moustaches, and two also sport beards. They are sitting Eastern-style, legs crossed and folded, on Persian rugs and cushions. The men are in the course of a lively conversation; between them are cups of black coffee and, in the middle, a pack of al-Majlis cigarettes. The divan is obviously one designed for such events in an Eastern luxury house. The text tells the story of the scene: "One of them said . . . 'there's nothing better than Lebanese food!' That was the beginning of the end . . ." Another man prefers Italian food, another French, a third "traditional Saudi" cooking, a fourth Chinese food. "Maybe it would have been better not to broach the subject at all . . . But one man thought he could connect them all." What connects all the men is al-Majlis. "So the next time you invite your friends for dinner, try offering them al-Majlis . . . without noting the nationality of the food you serve." Thus, al-Majlis cigarettes realize the dream of pan-Arabism, of the single origin common to all Arabs.

Another advertisement for the same brand[27] shows another *majlis* meeting: "One of them said . . . '*Ya shabbab*, I've decided to get married!' The poor man! With one of them trying to frighten him with the idea that he would soon become a father, another reminding him he would be questioned every time he came home late, and two others expressing their opinions freely . . . he really didn't know if he had made the correct decision or not. But he was sure he was right when he started [smoking] the special new Majlis cigarette . . . So the next time you get together, try al-Majlis and enjoy your laughter as you picture him being questioned by his wife." The humorous situations of arguments over a meal or male banter about marriage are all part of the male atmosphere of the *majlis*. It is a sort of exclusive men's club within Arab culture. The decisions taken also do not go against social norms; ultimately, the man knows that getting married is the right decision. He conforms to tradition. Jealous friends are a convention as well, also designed to suit custom. In accordance with tradition, al-Majlis also advertises narghile (hookah) tobacco

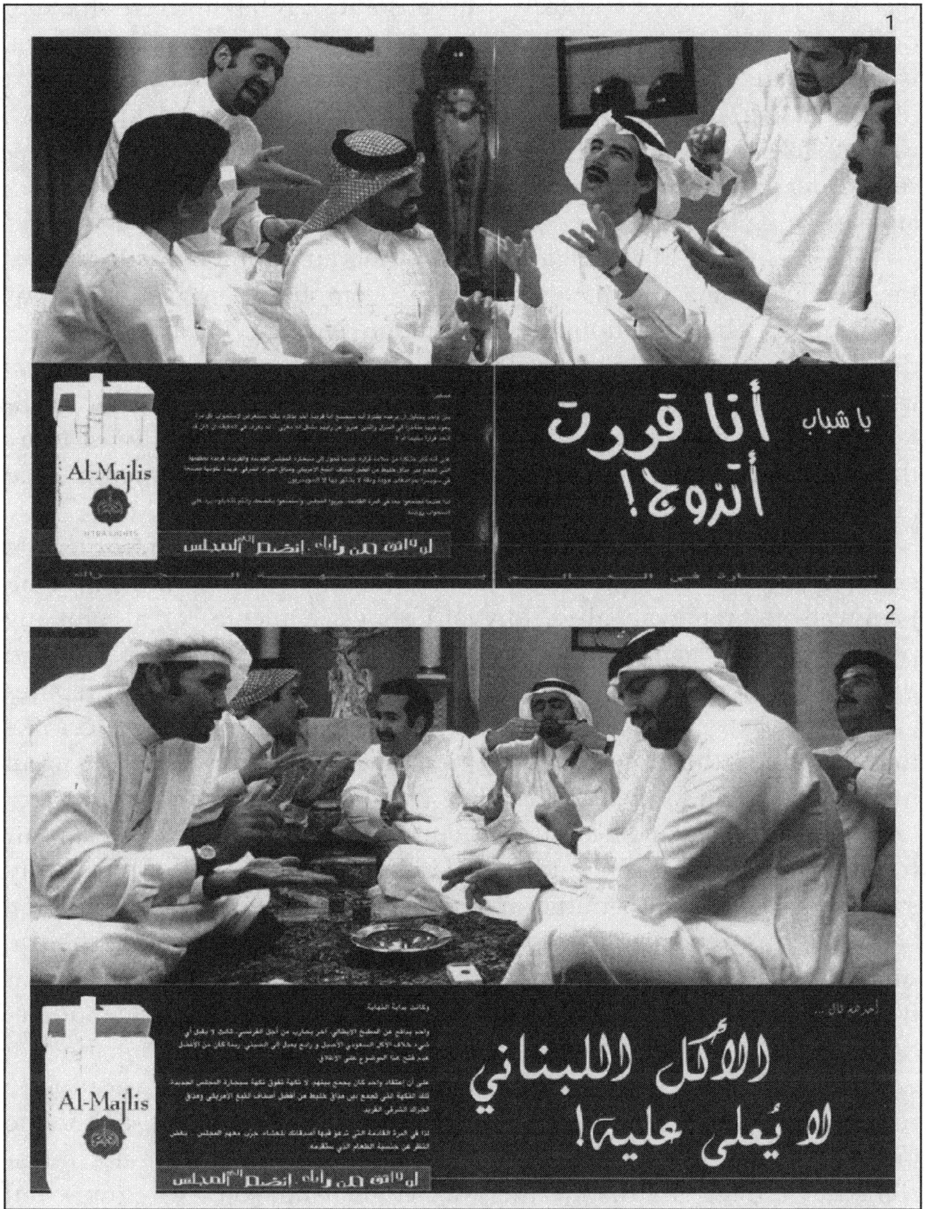

Fig.10 (1) Al-Majlis cigarettes ("I've decided to get married!");
(2) Al-Majlis cigarettes ("nothing better than Lebanese food!").

(*ma'sal*), "a question of taste."[28] The absolute prohibition on smoking declared by Abd al-Wahhab, founder of the predominant Wahhabi sect, is not implemented. While the prohibition of alcohol is strictly adhered to in advertising and commerce (though alcohol is consumed in private), that of smoking is neglected, and advertisements for tobacco and cigarettes are published prominently (evidence suggests that some even smoke during the hajj).

The ads for al-Majlis cigarettes illustrate an additional cultural element reflected in advertising: the "Arab" emphasis on gesture, show, and timing. This pseudofictional situation is a glorification of melodrama; facial expressions are deliberately exaggerated. This is not an amateurish advertisement, as it might appear to Western eyes, but a different fashion of expressing emotions and describing situations. More than a snapshot, this is a sort of gestural pantomime, implanted in Arabism.

Vacations and trips abroad are another important element of leisure culture. An advertisement for Saudi Arabian Airlines (al-Khutut al-Jawiyyah al-Arabiyyah al-Sa'udiyyah) shows a picture of a company plane, childishly hand-painted in pastels. The slogan is, "Even children prefer flying with us."[29] For child passengers, the company prepares "tasty *hilwayat* . . . a sketchbook and colored pens . . . so they feel like they never left the atmosphere of the home." The purpose is "to grant mothers peace and quiet, so that they can have the opportunity for perfect rest and for taking pleasure in our appetizing meals, served in our traditional Saudi style." "Saudi Arabian Airlines: our style of hospitality stems from the heart of tradition in order to reach every heart" (*li-yatal kull qalb*, "to extend to all hearts," a formal literary expression). The tradition of Arab hospitality is emphasized in other company ads as well.[30] Be it in drinking the traditional cup of coffee, or in the mother-child relationship, home-style hospitality continues during the flight. In fact, a woman never breaks free of the bonds of home. There is no vacation to release her from cultural fetters. Moreover, the man too is present on the journey, for Saudi women of any age must be able to show a document signed by a male guardian (father, uncle, husband, son, even grandson) allowing them to travel. This includes even short journeys within Saudi Arabia.[31] Women are under constant supervision.

Culture also designs airplanes in Saudi society; when the planes were repainted, the company's new logo was designed to contain a palm tree, two swords, and a half-crescent: "our new colors, from the essence of our noble country." "Every new day, Saudi Arabia leads [*tusayyir*, the word for leading a camel] its journeys to the four corners of the world, carrying all our glory, our pride in development, and the face of our shining kingdom. As our country's ambassadors to the world, we are renewing our form as an international airline in order best to guarantee our high expectations and our golden heritage . . . We are honored to serve you [*na`atazz bi-khidmatikum*],"[32] the ad ends, with a traditional blessing. In another advertisement, the company promises "an atmosphere of Arab generosity and hospitality . . . [including flights to] 25 cities within the kingdom."[33]

But it seems that innovations, "pride in development," and the use of modern technologies do not clash with the fact that Saudi Arabian Airlines employs only foreign women as flight attendants[34]; Saudi women may not fly unaccompanied or come into contact with men.

There is a wide variety of leisure destinations. Dubai offers a holiday in the style of the *Thousand and One Nights*: "1001 convincing reasons to visit . . . and here are some of the best: Dubai gives you much: interesting shopping opportunities, ideal family offers, excellent hotels and restaurants, beautiful gardens and beaches . . . Let Dubai welcome you [*turahhibu bikum*]."[35] The text is accompanied by a picture of a beach and hotels, in a traditionally ornamented frame, and pictures showing horseback riding (men only) and motorboating (men only), a jewelry shop (a man and a woman), and a traditional divan (two men dressed in white). In another ad, Dubai offers "the world's largest duty free shopping center," where one can even buy a car.[36] The reader is also informed of a new Marks & Spencer store that adapts itself to the nocturnal shopping sprees of Ramadan: its opening hours for the month are Saturday to Thursday, 10 a.m.–1 p.m., and 6 p.m.–1 a.m., and Friday, 6 p.m.–1 a.m. During Ramadan, then, the store is open daily until one in the morning! (The afternoon break, from about 1 p.m. till evening, is common throughout the year in Saudi Arabia and the other Gulf states due to the extreme heat.[37])

Bahrein offers, "in this month" (May 1997),[38] a musical concert (the category of music is symbolized by an `ud) in the Gilgamesh Hall (named after the ancient Babylonian mythological figure) of the Hilton Hotel; races; an "Egyptian exhibition" of products from that country; a cruise in the traditional boat known as *banush*; "the sixth heritage festival, extended due to the interest shown by citizens and visitors . . . which includes an exhibit of Arab equestrian activities and professions . . . in addition to yearly exhibitions in the heritage village in the garden of the Bahrein National Museum"; recreation and entertainment in the *Ayn-Adhari* or "stream of virgins" garden, reminiscent of the life of the *shahid* in paradise; water sports; the *al-Arin* nature reserve (whose name, signifying literally "lion's den," is also used to mean "woman"); and more. "Al-Bahrein: the island of the glowing smile" is a vacation from Saudi Arabia, where men and women may not go to amusement parks or go ice-skating together, as there are separate opening hours for each sex.[39]

For those who desire trips to more distant destinations in the Middle East, Royal Air Morocco (*al-Khutut al-Malikiyyah al-Maghribiyyah*) offers flights to Morocco that are "your passport to the best family vacation."[40] Here, too, the family is stressed: it is present even when one is on vacation. Another advertisement shows a Saudi family (father, mother, son, daughter) gazing at a Moroccan landscape; the text quotes an Arab proverb, "One who has seen is not like one who has heard" (*laysa man ra'a kaman sami'a*). An ad for Turkey emphasizes the link between East and West as well as the *hilwayat* common to the Turks and the readers of *Sayyidati*[41]; an "invitation to visit India" in the fiftieth year of its independence describes elephants carrying a sort of *mihmal*, the camel-back canopy used by Muslims in the hajj procession for transporting the cover of the Ka'ba (the *kiswah*) away from the center of authority.[42] The prophet Muhammad exploited the surprise felt by Muslims on encountering the exotic elephant as a means of exalting the power of God.[43] Al-Khatib al-Baghdadi (1002–1071) knew to tell about elephants decorated with peacock colored silks in the court of the Abbasid caliph al-Muqtadir (for the reception of the Byzantine ambassador in 917).[44] "India" is therefore identified by an animal that is no longer foreign to Islamic culture but is still considered exotic. The exoticism of the Indian elephant distinguishes it from the camel, a distinction that cannot be found in Western advertising. In Saudi Arabia the camel is "us" and the elephant is the "other." Western advertising, on the other hand, mixes the two together within the menagerie of exoticism and the wild zoo of otherness.

The *Emirates lil-'utulat* (Emirates for Vacations) company offers guided tours of Europe and Australia.[45] British Airways, in a fascinating ad, offers European trips.[46] The ad shows a "mother" taking a picture of her "husband" and two "sons" at the gate of a castle, which is carved with European heraldic symbols. The head and shoulders of the man, originally a European in a black suit, have been replaced with those of a

Saudi man with a moustache and white *jalabiyyah*. This creates a sort of rough hybrid, with a Western suit and Saudi head and shoulders. The Saudi man, overtly and with no attempt at obscuring the fact, takes the place of the Western man and enters the heart of the European fortress. This European ad, which describes a "family" vacation and is therefore appropriate for Saudi advertising, was chosen from the airline's ad collection and cosmetically retouched.

Sales campaigns also exploit vacations: the purchase of Kodak film entitles the buyer to a coupon, where, by filling in the names of the capitals of the United Arab Emirates and Malaysia, one can win airplane tickets to those destinations.[47] The required knowledge is Arabic-Islamic. An ad for Sony's handheld video cameras, which can be taken on trips "around the world," places the Pyramids and the Sphinx centrally among the world's most important sites.[48]

Other advertisements are intended to promote foreign and domestic tourism in Saudi Arabia. An ad for a "tourist palm village" (*qaryat al-nakhil al-siyahiyyah*) on the coast at Jiddah offers apartments for rent on a weekly basis, including yacht anchorage.[49] An ad selling apartments in Medina quotes a *"hadith sharif"*: "He who has a root in Medina should cling to it; he who does not should strike a root there, be it even a short one" (prices start at 1,140,960 riyals, or $304,662 at the fixed exchange rate).[50] The apartment building is deliberately photographed from an angle in which it is partly obscured by the great Medina mosque, which houses the tomb of Muhammad. An advertisement addressed to "the people of Mecca al-Mukarramah ['the honorable,' the title of Islam's holiest city], its visitors, and the *mu'tamarin* [those undertaking the '*umrah*, a pilgrimage outside the hajj period]" calls on them to visit the *al-Hijaz* market (named after the area of the Arabian peninsula that was the source of Islam), whose construction "has been completed with Allah's help [*bi-'awn Allah*]" not far from Zamzam Square (the name of the famous stream near the Kabah).

Barring their husbands' support, do women have independent sources of funding for vacations and shopping? Some women are part of the workforce (the Saudi cable company, the country's largest industrial conglomerate, proposed the construction of a women-only factory, in which all workers up to the chairperson would be women),[51] but in addition, women receive an inheritance according to Koranic law: one-half of what their brothers receive. In post–oil boom Saudi Arabia, even this half can reach considerable amounts. Though women in Islam are allowed control over their own money, this control was theoretical in Saudi Arabia until 1980, as they were not permitted to enter banks for fear of their encountering men. In 1980 the first women's banks opened; all employees in such banks are women, and a guard at the entrance denies admittance to men.[52] Separate banks necessitate separate advertisements and financial services; women have their own special credit cards (*al-'asriyyah*) and are called upon to open accounts for their children. Advertisements for banks stress their safety deposit services. Safety deposit boxes are crucial for women, for storing jewelry or gold as well as marriage contracts—the two possessions that guarantee a woman's financial future in the event of a divorce.

This is also one of the most obvious reasons why many advertisers place an emphasis on gold. Prizes in sales campaigns are often pure gold: "half a kilogram of gold,"[53] "win gold in boxes" (gold pieces in Anchor's dehydrated milk cartons).[54] A watch collection by Consul is named "Golden Bay."[55] The *al-Yamamah* commercial market is "a name linked with gold"[56]; Patek Philippe advertises its "Golden Ellipse" watch[57]; and when *Sayyidati* entered the perfume business, it marketed a perfume called "*Sayyidati* Gold."[58]

The use of the precious metal gold as a metaphor for wealth and splendor is rooted in ancient traditions, in the Islamic world as well as in the West. When Hunanin, librarian to the caliph al-Ma'mun (813–833), retired, he received an amount of gold equal to the weight of all the books he had translated.[59] *Sayyidati* ads, characteristic representatives of modern literature, feature various kinds of "gold": "yellow gold" (the ordinary variety), "white gold,"[60] oil that is "pure as gold,"[61] and, of course, in the background is the "black gold" that makes it possible to acquire all the rest. But the main point is that in modern Saudi Arabia, gold is more than an abstract metaphor; it is concretely distributed. Moreover, it serves as a financial guarantee for women in monetary difficulties, despite the existence of a modern Islamic banking system.[62] When the husband performs the "golden section" (*sectio aurea*), so to speak, the woman is left with the gold she kept in a bank safe.

Money kept in banks may also be used to fulfill one of Islam's five basic commandments: charity. One of the most interesting phenomena in *Sayyidati* is the appearance of ads for charitable institutions, especially those focusing on children. Charity too becomes a product to be advertised; even the *Waqf* (different kinds of public endowments) enjoys public relations.

Society and culture are ubiquitous, from the transformation of kitchen appliances, through the filling of leisure time by watching television or taking vacations, to the modus operandi of financial institutions and possible future events within and beyond the family. Culture encloses individuals in an omnipresent spider web from which they cannot escape, not even on a trip to Europe. Ultimately, cultural baggage cannot be cast off.

The Calligraphic Ad: Pens, Writing, and Grammar

Among the advertisements in *Sayyidati* is a considerable number of ads for pens: a Parker pen against a desert background ("Imagination has no boundaries"),[1] a Mont Blanc pen in the Ramses II (*Ramsis al-Thani*) series photographed against a papyrus with hieroglyphics,[2] even a Christian Dior pen.[3] A fascinating Mont Blanc advertisement shows, on the right, the pen in an inkstand, black against a white background. On the left-hand side of the ad, Arabic words, printed in white, form the image of the pen and inkstand on a black background.[4] The world of this advertisement is created by words, by calligraphic writing.

The profusion of ads for pens and "writing" in *Sayyidati* is not surprising. Islam confronts Socrates, "he who does not write,"[5] with Muhammad, "he who does not read." Reading and writing are temporal activities that require effort; myths, on the other hand, are extratemporal. But it is to the magic of the myth, to the miracle of "reading" on the night of *al-Qadr*,[6] and to the prohibition of statues and masks (influenced by Judaism), that the sanctity of words and letters in Islam owes its development; with it came extensive study of the arts of calligraphy (*khatt*) and arabesques, and of the science of linguistics.[7] Arabic writing, probably first attested in graffiti writing on the wall of the Rama shrine in Sinai (A.D. 300),[8] received tremendous impetus from the appearance of Islam.[9] This chapter therefore deals with the words in advertisements, the grammar that connects them as well as their visual form.

The history found in Saudi advertising is a history of superlatives, positive adjectives, modifiers: "wonderful," "glorious," "unique," "amazing." In the preceding chapters, we encountered a startling number of adjectives. This fact is understandable given that Western advertising also employs adjectives frequently; appellations, that is, pseudo-moral mythological pronouncements, are difficult to contest. It is interesting that Arabic possesses an additional linguistic mechanism that is exploited to promote products: the superlative. In contrast to languages that express the superlative analytically ("most beautiful"), Arabic possesses an *af'al* inflection, equivalent to the English suffix -est. But a consonant inflection feels "stronger" and "more real" than an "artificial" addition to an existing word. The fact that almost any adjective can be intensified by inflection enables the conveyance of a more powerful advertising message. A single preexistent word is always more natural, more primitive, than a two-word combination; the latter seems more artificial, more contrived, compared with products described as *ajmal* (most beautiful), *ahsan* (best), or *adhka* (most intelligent). The use of single-word superlatives reduces the arbitrary nature of the advertising message.

Another important fact is that in Arabic, the verb precedes the noun; put otherwise, in a verbal clause, the predicate precedes the subject. To use a Saudi slogan: "*Indama la takafi (1) al-kalimat (2)*" means "When words (2) are not enough (1)."[10] This fact lends the product "motion" and "activity" as soon as it is described. From the first encounter with it, it is doing something, changing, acting. The product immediately enters the Arabic's system of ten verbal inflections, which enable the same root to be conjugated with different meanings.

A common technique for stressing the noun (the "product") in modern Arabic is the use of *mubtada*, a noun-first sentence pattern, as in an advertisement for Shiseido facial cream: "*Al-jamal la ya'raf hududa[n]*" (Beauty knows no boundaries). Beauty, the facial cream, is emphasized here by a special, exotic linguistic construction (normative Arabic would require the verb to appear first). In the case of Japanese facial cream, this is possible and desirable. The grammatical choice sharpens the message. The fact that Arabic normally makes no distinction between present and future tense in verbs also aids advertisers to construct their fantasies: future desires are fulfilled immediately with the present purchase of the product. Like most modern writers, no advertiser uses the *sin al-mustaqbal*, the /s/ morpheme that distinguishes future from present; the possibility of distinction between the tenses remains archaic. This tense vagueness is a commercial blessing.

Another grammatical point illustrated in the same sentence is the "nonhuman plural," which Arabic treats as a feminine singular ("the beautiful [fem. sing.] dresses"; "the precise [fem. sing.] watches"). Ultimately, the kingdom of advertising comprises all inanimate objects, and these are all feminine: the female is an object in the system of objects.

In this context, it is of course important to keep in mind that Arabic words have gender. This is not the place for a linguistic discussion of which words are "feminine" or "masculine" in Arabic and why. For our purposes, a noteworthy phenomenon, which we have encountered several times, is that advertisements addressed to women may be written in the masculine (such as the Häagen-Dazs ad, among others). Many "women's" ads are ultimately intended for men, because of the restrictions and prohibitions to which women are subjected. Women sometimes serve as mere agents for male purchases. On the other hand, there is also the interesting phenomenon of deliberate spelling mistakes meant to distinguish masculine from feminine. When writing without vowel marks, certain verbal forms do not show gender, for instance the second-person-singular past tense (both genders end with the letter *t*, with the vowel *a* for the masculine, marked with a *fathah*, and *i* for the feminine, marked with a *kasra*). An ad for Artist(e) shampoo, whose added (e) makes it marketable to both men and women (in French, that is), chose as its slogan the sentence, "The best you've used for the health of your hair." The word for "used" is spelled *isti`malti*, ending with the letter *ya*. This is a deliberate misspelling, intended to emphasize the final /i/ sound (the only option left to the reader is to interpret the final vowel mark as a *kasra*), making the verb necessarily feminine.[11]

Arabic advertisements often employ wordplay, puns, and alliterations to smooth their message: "At first you may think that the *Afalun* car is just [*mujarad*] another new automobile, but as soon as [*mujarad*] you get to know its qualities . . ." This ad plays upon the double meaning of the word *mujarrad*.[12] Another instance: "*Krim akthar. Sha`r aqall. Nafs al-si`r*" ("More cream. Less hair. The same price.").[13] Here, the similarity of *shi`r* and *si`r* is exploited to create a catchy sales slogan; likewise in the pun "*al-`ilamiyyah al-alamiyyah*," "world research."[14]

Repetition, too, can be considered a form of cultural wordplay. In Arabic, as in other Semitic languages, repetition is seen positively: saying the same thing in several different ways or with several synonymous words shows linguistic wealth and precision of thought, while elucidat-

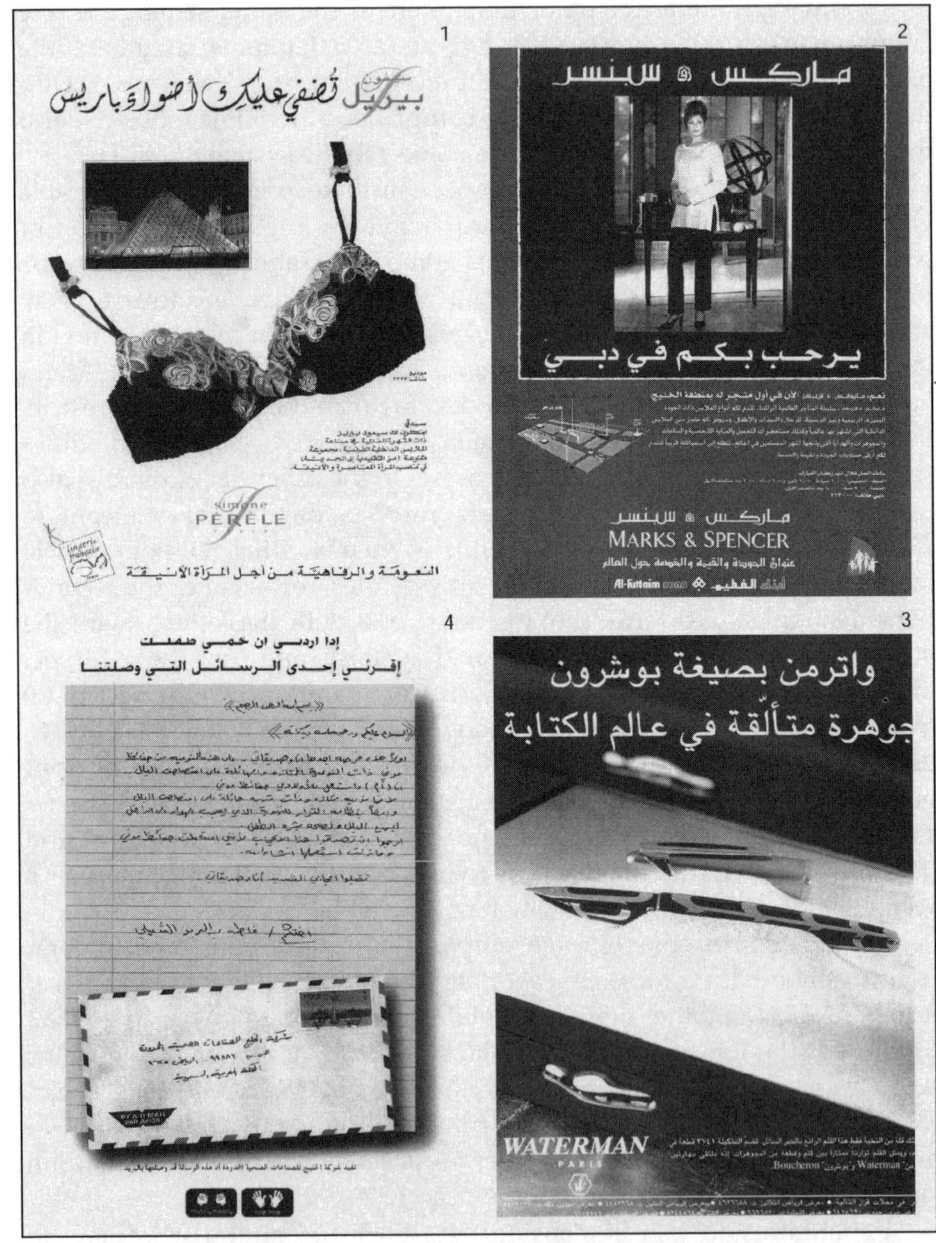

Fig.11 (1) Simone Pérèle, Paris; (2) Marks & Spencer;
(3) Waterman, Paris; (4) Shirkat al-Halij lil-Sana'at.

ing the message and making use of the magic of the language. This phenomenon exists in speech and literature, as well as in Islamic traditions
(such as the Sufi *dhikr*) and in Islamic pedagogy, whose main method
was repetition[15] (one cannot become a *hafiz al-qur'an* without learning by
rote[16]); for advertising, it is a godsend. Perma shampoo makes hair
lami'a[n] wa-baraqa[n], "glittering and shiny," giving it *al-lama'an wa-l-
bariq*, "glow and glow."[17] Likewise, a double-page ad for Sijnal 2 toothpaste constantly repeats the same text in synonymous words,[18] and the
slogan for al-Majlis pipe tobacco is "A question of taste and taste"
(*Dhawq wa-madhaq*), two equivalent terms.[19]

Most advertisements are in literary Arabic, but some include text in
the spoken language, in the Saudi or Egyptian dialect. Literary Arabic
enables advertisers to reach a broader audience; spoken Arabic, on the
other hand, makes the product alive, current, real. Thus the slogan in an
al-Safi milk ad is *"Leysh ma tajribuhu!"* ("Why shouldn't you drink it!").[20]
Though the sentence is a question, it ends with an exclamation mark.
This simple procedure makes the question a rhetorical one, even an answer. The reverse question mark of Arabic (corresponding to the right-to-
left direction of the script) is also used in advertisements. Another slogan
in spoken Arabic is Sadefco's: "Saudi milk . . . This milk or nothing"
(*"Halib al-sa'udiyyah . . . Kidda al-halib wa-la balash"*).[21] The words *kidda* and
balash exist in the spoken Arabic dialects of Saudi Arabia and Egypt.
Kidda also appears in a quote from star Egyptian actress 'Athar al-Hakim:
"It is very important that every one of us should take care of her skin;
because of this [*ashan kiddah*] I use Lux."[22] The conjunction of the words
'ashan and *kiddah*, found in Egyptian Arabic (which, naturally, is the dialect spoken by al-Hakim), makes the quote "genuine." A Twix advertisement uses the spoken language copiously and consciously[23]; *"Sultan
biqul"*—*biqul* is spoken Arabic for "says"; *"ley ta'akhud bas"* ("why do you
take only")—all three words are in spoken Arabic, and the *dh* of the literary language appears as a *d*, as in some dialects. *"li-annam ithnayn alshan
tafsal"* ("because they are two so that you [can] separate [them]"): *li-'anam*
is spoken Arabic for "because they are" (*li-annom* in the literary language), *alshan* spoken Arabic for "so that." This is an advertisement for a
snack, a young, fast-paced, playful product, so it is in the spoken language.

Arabic can be written with or without vowel marks. Text in advertisements usually do not mark vowels, even when the same word can be

read in more than one way. Multiple meanings and possibilities of interpretation are useful to advertisers, just as homonyms are (for example, *sa`ah* is both "hour" and "clock" or "watch"). In this way every word, like the broom of the sorcerer's apprentice, contains within it different possibilities for bifurcation. But vowel marks are sometimes used to distinguish masculine and feminine: "Nestlé's sweetened condensed milk helps you [*yusa`iduki*] prepare . . ."[24] Here the letter *kaf* has a *kasrah* vowel mark, making it clear that preparing sweets is a task for women only. Often the lack of vocalization creates deliberate ambiguity: the word spelled *k(a)rim* can be read either as "generous, noble" or as "cream."[25]

Arabic possesses consonants that do not occur in European languages (and vice versa); European languages possess vowels that do not occur in Arabic. Thus, for example, the word *perpetual* becomes *berbetual*.[26] The Corum watch company is Curum[27] in Arabic, while Kellogg's becomes Kaluqz.[28] Pride becomes Brayd,[29] Maggi Maji[30]; Egyptian dialect does possess a hard /g/ sound, but most others do not. The word "ketchup" (originally Indonesian-Melanesian) becomes *katshab*, and the Libby's company is Libiz—the English possessive *s* unites with the name in Arabic to form a single word.[31] In Arabic, the Western /s/ sound can be interpreted as two different phonemes. Sunsilk shampoo thus becomes *œansilk (sansilk)*,[32] the /s/ being transcribed once as *œ* and once as *s*, lending the product an added "complexity"; of course, the choice of *k* also has an alternative in the emphatic *q*. The Belgian company Le Bonheur becomes Labunir in Arabic: the French masculine *le* becomes *la* since literary Arabic lacks an /e/ vowel.[33] Of course, the literal signification of words like *pride* or *bonheur* is completely lost in such transcriptions. As for the two "new" Arabic letters, invented to signify consonants nonexistent in Arabic, their use is rare but occasionally encountered: the name Avalon is transcribed as Afalun, with three dots over the *fa* (as over the letter *fa*), to express the sound /v/.[34] Dove shampoo is similarly treated.[35] But Orlane's Extrait Vital moisturizer becomes Akstariya Fital.[36] The choice of a particular Arabic consonant sometimes conveys a message, as in the case where the letter *A* was transcribed as *alif mamdudah*, whose wavy shape was appropriate for the shampoo advertisement, though an ordinary *alif* could have been used as well.[37]

Likewise, the letter *â* in the French word *âge* was also transcribed as *alif mamdudah*,[38] a choice presumably influenced by the circumflex. The use of *alif mamdudah* to transcribe the letter *a* is especially common in names of perfumes and cosmetic companies such as Elizabeth Arden and

Arpels.[39] The prestige, uniqueness, and splendor of these products cause the use of a special, ornate *alif*, a rarer, more stylized letter. This phenomenon sometimes recurs when transcription calls for a decision whether to use the *huruf al-mad*, the letters that signify both consonants and vowels and are referred to as "expansion letters" in Arabic.

When product names pass from a European language to Arabic, not only do they lose their denotation, but two-word names are often compressed into one word, to make them catchier. Bio Depiless body cream becomes Biyudiblis[40]; reduction, as of two words into one, serves to strengthen myths and exalt them, turns them into a holistic truth, into a more fundamental truth, into a divine oneness. Transcribing foreign words rather than translating them sometimes produces amusing neologisms, as when "stainless steel" becomes *ala stinlas stil*, "which is not stainless steel": the double negative, one English and one Arabic, seems to leave the steel stained[41] (this unintentional mistake demonstrates the road a foreign name passes, how it loses its meaning and becoming incomprehensible even to the translation agent himself). A clothing detergent called Fid Fad became Fidfad (spelled without vowel marks), which means "wide" in Arabic.[42] The choice of transcribing the *d* sound with the letter *dad* (rather than *dal*) enables a punning slogan: "Fidfad, *li-malabis fidfidah taltasaq*" ("Fidfad, for wide clothes which do not stick"). This transformation demonstrates interesting phenomena from the other side of the linguistic continuum: the assignment of cultural meaning to a neutral word through the process of translation. After "cleaning" the symbol by means of reducing its meaning to the "zero degree", the translation is a choice of meaning formation.

The opposite phenomenon, of transcribing Arabic words into English, also exists: the al-Rabi' ("spring") company also writes its name in English, "Al-Rabie."[43] The use of English sometimes provides a modern flavor, a needed foreignness, an urge for success. Arabic grammar may be "bent" to obey English rules: the Halwani Bros. company, as it spells its name in English, is in Arabic *Hilwani Ikhwan* (rather than *Ikhwan Hilwani*).[44] On the other hand, the English name may also "obey" the rules of Arabic grammar, as in the case of the "Shake A-Choco" and "Shake A-Nilla" drinks described previously[45]; the *l* of the definite article *al* does not appear before the "sun letters."

An interesting phenomenon is the use of French in advertising. Whereas English represents modernity, French has symbolized prestige ever since Ottoman days. The "prestigious aroma" of French occasionally leads Saudi advertisers to retain French words or expressions in ads translated into Arabic and even place them in original Arabic-language ads. For example, the sentence *"Maître Chocolaterie Suisse depuis 1845,"* in an ad for the Lindt chocolate company, is left unchanged and untranslated.[46] Likewise, Givenchy's makeup collection for autumn-winter 1997–98 is still called *Féé d'Hiver*, as well as *Sahrah al-Shita'*.[47] An advertisement for Champs-Elysées perfume contains a two-line sentence in French: *"La vie est plus belle / Quand on l'écrit soi-même"* ("Life is more beautiful when one writes it oneself").[48] The sentence is not relevant to anything, but it is in French. "Frenchness" is also exploited by sophisticated visual means: an ad for bras by Simon Pérèle (Paris) shows the 3333 model pictured against the glass pyramids of the Louvre.[49] French and Egyptian are combined in the breast-shaped pyramids.

To turn to punctuation: Saudi advertising makes extensive use of ellipses (. . .). This mark serves to express suspense and emphasis. "A wonderful and . . . amazing taste!"[50] "When words are not enough . . ."[51] Just like the technique of repetition, the *alif mamdudah*, and the avoidance of vowel marks, this style of punctuation leaves much to the imagination. In many ads, emphasis is achieved by underlining a word or phrase, a method more usual in handwriting than in advanced graphic technology.[52] Manual calligraphy continues, outlasting the monopoly of the scribes (*waraqin*).

In the preface, I compared advertising to poetry. An interesting element of Saudi advertising is rhyme, which of course serves to make the slogan catchier. Thus al-'Arabi oil: *"biyahali al-qali* ["leaves fried food *or* frying"] *muqarmash min barah wa-tari wa-ladhidh min jawah* ["crispy on the outside, soft and tasty on the inside"; a partial rhyme]."[53] Teashop's cookies wish the reader *"hajj mabrur wa-sa'i mashkur"*;[54] Halwani Bros. cookies are more poetic still: *"abwah jadidah bi-hubah wahidah / munasibah lil-awlad wa-mufidah."*[55] Wella shampoo proposes, *"Ikhtari ma huwa farid. wa-iktashafi nafsaki min jadid"* ("Choose what is special. And discover yourself anew").[56] Interestingly, as in poetry, the rhyme does not have to be perfect; the above advertisement poems contain several kinds of rhyme. Furthermore, one can construct a sort of graphic rhyme, a correspondence between final letters of similar shape, such as final *ya* and *alif maksurah*. Formally, the only difference between the two symbols is the diacritical mark, two dots, which appears under the *ya*. This sort of graphic rhyme appears in a Rabi' tea ad: *"al-waqt yamdi / wal-nukhah tabqa.*"[57] Phonetically, there is no rhyme here (*i* versus *a*), but the "graphic rhyme" catches the reader's eye. In this way, rhyming is preserved in the transition from oral to written culture, though its character may change.

I have noted the importance of writing in Muslim culture and the monopoly of the scribes or *waraqin.*[58] Sezgin, in his history of Arabic writing, catalogues more than 1.5 million manuscripts written by Muslims over four and a half centuries.[59] Calligraphy and arabesque, arts developed in a culture that forbade representation of the human figure, brought about a glorification and deification of the Arabic script. Advertising provides many opportunities for Arabic calligraphy. Due to calligraphic experience and to the cursive, ornate Arabic script,[60] one of the advertiser's tasks is to design an attractive logo for client companies, using various forms of writing: sometimes the modern Arabic script is used, while other ads revert to a curlicued, embellished type of script, such as an ad for Oetker's caramel syrup.[61] On a bottle of Libby's ketchup, the name of the Disney company (Dizni in transcription) becomes an ornamental design in which the diacritical dots—on three letters—the *ya*, the *zay*, and the *nun*—resemble pairs of eyes, matching those of Mickey Mouse, who appears above the logo.[62] "New York," the name of a Chrysler model, becomes a sort of decorative frame, bounding the ad from above and below.[63] The name Givenchy becomes in Arabic Jifanshi, the letter *fa* bearing three dots (representing the sound /v/, as noted above).[64] The six-letter word creates a set of graphic parallels: between the shapes of the initial *jim* and the final *ya*; between the first *ya* and the *nun* (both are "tooth-shaped" letters); and between the triple-dotted *fa* and the *shin* (which also has three dots). In the Kotex (Kutiks) company's logo, the two dots over the *ta* are positioned vertically (:) rather than horizontally (‥).[65] Arabic calligraphy is also present in an ad for Kleenex toilet paper, *waraq hammam.*[66] Each of the three words in the slogan, "*An`am, amtan, atwal*" ("More delicate, stronger, longer"), is designed functionally: the first is in a thin ("delicate") font, the second in a thick ("strong") one, and the third is lengthened, exploiting the possibility of extending the line that connects the letters *ta* and *waw* (this was the only available way of lengthening the word, since the letters *alif* and *waw* do not connect forward). Also, the letters in the upper half of the ad, which contains only two lines ("*waraq hammam*" and "*Klinaks*"), appear to be formed of toilet paper, which trails past the words on both sides. The name of the al-`Isa company, which markets electronic appliances, is written in fiery letters in an ad for heaters,[67] and in icy ones in a refrigerator ad.[68] In an ad for Dubai's duty-free shopping center ("The world's leading free market"), the letter `yn in the word `alam ("world") is designed in the shape of a globe, with the Arabian peninsula at its center.[69] All the possibilities of Arabic calligraphy are utilized.

In some cases, following calligraphic tradition, the text is accompanied by ornaments that resemble diacritics or vowel marks but have no significance beyond embellishment.[70] Also, in accordance with tradition, the same words are sometimes repeated in different fonts or sizes. The motif repetition characteristic of Arabic art—as well as of Arabic advertisement, as I have shown in the discussion of the use of synonymous adjectives—is also expressed in the reiteration of graphical and ornamental themes.[71] Repetition with variation is a useful technique for making a trade name familiar. But this is more than a simplistic importation of Western marketing methods: the device of reiterating the same message over and over is rooted deeply in Arabic culture.

The Arabization of products also involves the use of various symbols: letters, numbers, "reverse" (i.e., Arabic) question marks. An ad for a new Marks & Spencer store in Dubai invented a new "Arabic" character: The ampersand, in the Arabic transcription, becomes an ornate, calligraphic *waw* (Marks wa Sbansar).[72] In Arabic, the conjunction *wa* ("and") is written with the following word, not as an independent character. Here we see the invention of a new symbol, influenced by English and by the importance of the ampersand in the company's name and in its public identification. The Arabs now have their own "&."

When names of Western products and companies are written, they can often be difficult to understand. Such names are sometimes designed as a sort of calligraphic ornament, or *tughrah*, of the product (an example is the Rama watch advertisement discussed previously). Western names in Arabic transcription can be almost unrecognizable. This problem may actually constitute an advantage for the product: the typographical ambiguity (just like the verbal ambiguity discussed above) facilitates its association with the target culture. Thus, for example, in the above-mentioned advertisement for Miss Arpels perfume, transcribed as Mis Arbalz,[73] the delicate young lady of the English version becomes a harsh imperative in Arabic. One difficulty is where and whether the letters are to be divided in reading: "Ted Lapidus" becomes Tidlabidus, creating a new hybridic brand name[74]; similarly, the name "Champs-Elysées" is transcribed Shanzilizya.[75] Here, too, the compression of two words into one makes the name catchier, easier for a foreign ear to accept.

The entire Arabic language, then, with its various layers and different historical periods, is exploited in Arabizing commercial products. Grammatical constructions, calligraphic knowledge, and cultural preferences all combine to furnish inanimate objects with new identities, to appropriate and localize them. The entire Arabic dictionary—the symbolic compendium of many generations—is enlisted for the task, with the deliberate retention of ambiguities and shades that allow Arab readers to interpret an advertisement, fill in what it omits, and elaborate it according to their own previous knowledge. A dictionary always marks the mental horizons of a given culture; and grammatical rules, like policemen, always give some sense of order. They team to translate commercial products, place them in their dependable hierarchy, and regulate the markets like an enthusiastic *muhtasib*. The many translators used for this process have a continuing interest in preserving the Babylonian Tower, which might not be efficient enough from the international economics point of view but is definitely good for local businesses. Language is the greatest tariff of them all.

Hybridic Arabism

Advertising, the visual art of capitalism, is, in essence, a vehicle for cultural production, a machine that creates culture. Advertisers take products and services, strip them of any cultural overlay, then attach them to well-known historical symbols. The more easily the symbols are recognized, the faster and smoother the process of cultural production (in fact, this is the reason why the mechanism of advertising is *the* "field of cultural production," to use Bourdieu's famous term). Advertising seeks to find the common denominator of a given society, its most redundant mental images, its essential myths—and rewrite this palimpsest called product. It is this process that extracts the essence of culture, time and again, and serves it to the table of the cultural reader, to the plate of most members of the specific culture, as a sweet confiture.

The metalanguage of advertising transcends individual cultures. It is the medium of all mediums, the metamedium that enables the export and import of all other mediums, the medium that "camelizes" a car, "Islamisizes" clocks and time, and "Arabisizes" cartons of milk. It is here, each time a name or a slogan is attached to a product, that another cultural universe is born. Each ad is a new quantic separation, presenting a parallel universe, a new cultural system.

This constant separation of economies, through their aesthetics, is deeply rooted in the political separations of our world. Cultures, and cultural wars, are fueled by the process of cultural interpretation embedded within advertising. Advertising produces new outfits, new "fronts" (to use a Goffmanian term),[1] for existing products/bodies to wear. These outfits are a mere reorganization, a patchwork, of earlier textiles. This process enlivens culture and keeps it relevant. The whole process turns culture into a vivid, glamorous entity by distributing and insinuating its archaic, ragged meanings between the latest shining products. By doing that, advertising stimulates cultures—and the gaps between cultures. By preserving and developing the unique *Denkstil* ("thought style") and *Denkkolective* ("thought collective") of each culture (two key terms in Ludwik Fleck's thinking),[2] advertising always comes back to haunt (and to hunt) us, taking the form of one global conflict or another. It is this irrational separation, this tower of Babel, this Darwinistic taxonomization into different species that nurtures the diversity of humanity by developing its richness while at the same time engendering the fiercest wars over symbols.

It is tempting to blame the advertisers themselves, or the global corporations behind them, for the resulting battles. Yes, certainly, they profit by adjusting their products each time anew, manipulating symbols and, in the process, widening the cultural gaps. They control the "bridges" between cultures—the products—giving the illusion that those products can bridge the unbridgeable. This process, though, is larger than cynical corporations, and beyond individual cynicism; it is the gist of the culture-building mechanism. Whether the producers of a given campaign intend it or not, each ad expands the specific culture by producing new meanings from what is old and familiar. Each advertisement markets a whole new world.

"The ads are by far the best part of any magazine or newspaper," observed Marshall McLuhan back in 1964. "More pain and thought, more wit and art, go into the making of an ad than into any prose feature of press and magazine. Ads are news. What is wrong with them is that they are always good news. In order to balance off the effect and to sell good news, it is necessary to have a lot of bad news."[3]

We can now understand the dichotomy of good/bad even better: the cultural wars are just the other side of the advertising process, the page next to the luminous ad. In every newspaper, in every news report, we have the dreamlike islands of commercial breaks. The ugly and ruthless help to sell the illusion of a heavenly happiness, and each one of them is, in fact, just a mirror-image of the other. This absolute happiness, our warm cultural happiness as we always knew it, is accented by the harsh news from the outside, from other places. Global conflicts are the political outcome of the economic aesthetics of divisions and separations.

"Nevertheless, and in spite of many differences in detail," wrote Edward Hall in 1976, "anthropologists do agree on three characteristics of culture: it is not innate, but learned; the various facets of culture are interrelated—you touch a culture in one place and everything else is affected; it is shared and in effect defines the boundaries of different groups."[4]

These three features of culture are exactly where advertisers find their bread and butter. If we are to reorganize Hall's claim (to "advertise" it), we could say that the advertising process takes "shared" components from "various facets of culture," mounts them on products (thus, "interrelating" them), "[re]defines the boundaries of a given group," and educates the cultural public, making culture *look* as though it were "innate."

The Middle East is part of this *global advertisation*, a term which might be coined in order to stress the aesthetics and material culture of marketing and global economics. Throughout this book we have seen numerous examples of this mechanism. Clocks, cars, washing machines, food processors, ice cream—all experience a process of transformation, of "returning home," of "becoming one of us."

In his book on wealth and poverty in the Middle East, el-Ghonemy writes:

> There is sufficient evidence of a shift away from traditional products which meet the taste and demand of large sections of the population, particularly the poor, towards modern, expensive items consumed in affluent societies and designed according to Western tastes, using Western raw materials and a labour-capital relationship. These products include baby food, bread, soap and synthetic detergents, household appliances and footwear.[5]

In this study, I have shown that when Western products are imported to Saudi Arabia, they undergo a social metamorphosis; that is, they are "culturalized," "traditionalized," "localized," and adapted to social reality, in this case Saudi-Arabic-Islamic reality. One of the functions of advertising is precisely this: to start with a product created for certain tastes, for a certain social reality, and stress the elements in it that may be appropriate for a different culture. Of course, the importing culture is also invaded by all the accompanying Western elements of the product, but in many cases these are neutralized and made inconspicuous by blurring and lack of emphasis. They cannot affect the social situation; therefore, the medium (the product) is not necessarily the message, but a palimpsest that can be wiped clean and written on anew. The combination of existent technology and cultural knowledge or material culture creates new products. In this way, a Swiss watch comes to represent periods of Arab-Muslim history; Philips's kitchen appliances turn into tools for preparing Ramadan meals or *muluhiyyah*; a four-wheel-drive vehicle becomes an inseparable part of the Arab family; a children's vanilla drink is transformed into a "Nilla" or Nile drink; a foreign hair-dye company masquerades as a domestic firm; a cellular telephone is equated with an Arabian falcon; and so on, limited only by the imagination of the advertiser. For every Western product, an Arab biography and a private history are fabricated, showing where it has come from and where it is going. Furthermore, this study has shown that advertising channels are utilized not only by importers but by domestic manufacturers of "traditional" products as well—who, so to speak, store old wine in new bottles. Traditional pipe tobacco, *zabadi*, milk for drinking—these too are products to be advertised on full-color chromo pages. Of course, these products do not depend on complex technology and are necessarily not based on modern scientific knowledge, but this very fact requires us to stress that they exist, and continue to exist, in a technological environment.

Another conclusion of this study is that when Western products are advertised, they are primarily those that do not conflict with the cultural values and knowledge at the base of the importing society. Alcoholic drinks, of course, are not advertised, nor is immodest clothing (although they might be consumed privately, away from the eyes of the hegemonic culture). Even in the case of perfumes, the primary imports are products whose "heads" are veiled, and which preach "secrecy" or "chastity." Likewise, marketing and sales techniques are modified to suit the culture; in Saudi Arabia, a price of 99 riyals is not merely a reduced form of 100 but possesses age-old historical significance. And prizes in sales contests are often gold, even gold bars, due to that metal's cultural importance.

This study has touched on many layers of Saudi social and family life, including the status of women. Saudi women, as Simone de Beauvoir might have said, are made, not born. They are educated into the Saudi story. Advertisements play a part in this education. Consider, for instance, the remarkably prominent masculinity found in the ads of what is primarily a women's weekly. While *Sayyidati* strives to be a magazine for the entire Arab family, the presence of men in many of the ads is surprising. Even when he is not visible in the ad, the man is always standing guard, overseeing the woman's actions. Women are always covered, always concealed by something: a veil, a partition, a wall, a mask of makeup. The marketing of the (women) weekly as a "family" weekly corresponds to the fact that at no stage in their lives do Saudi women exist without their "family." They are defined by their changing role in the family, according to their age or marital status. This is why ads directed at men can appear in a women's magazine without offending male honor. Moreover, even in advertisements that do not show men (such as the Häagen-Dazs ad), or in those for women's beauty products (creams, perfumes, and so on), men are always present in spirit. When a child is pictured with parents, the child will be male; when two children are shown, the boy will be older than the girl. Just as Saudi women do not visit shopping malls without a male escort,[6] they must be accompanied by men when roaming the virtual bazaar of magazine ads.

It must be remembered that *Sayyidati*, and therefore this study, does not address all classes of Saudi society. The magazine's primary audiences are the upper and especially middle classes; the boundary line is, first and foremost, literacy (though the skill of "skimming" may sometimes be sufficient). But new technologies, and the association of these technologies with previous knowledge and existent material culture, trickle down in a long-term historical process through the literate classes to other social strata. Again, it should be noted that advertisements attempt to construct a social ideal, a goal of education; to draw conclusions about real life from data drawn from ideals must be done cautiously and judiciously.

The reader of this study might observe that the phenomena and concepts described by the study likewise exist in the West. There is a critical difference, though. Identical phenomena may be associated in the West and in Saudi Arabia with very different social knowledge. For instance, the West too still employs the "elder son" motif. But in Saudi Arabia, the use of this motif (and all use is dependent on time and place) relates to a stricter social knowledge. The occurrence of some phenomenon in the West, in a similar but different manner, does not reduce its authenticity in the Saudi social experience. The newly created advertising medley does not distinguish "local" from "foreign." It creates a new connection, which becomes local in an ad hoc, contingent fashion.

The most striking example of the link between products and existing knowledge is the use of Ramadan in advertising. In almost all areas Ramadan seemed to be the most potent promotion device of all and the consumption peak of the year (somewhat like Christmas in the United States). Almost every kind of product is marketed aggressively during Ramadan: cosmetics, food, cars—everything sells. The religious self-restraint of the fast and other holiday customs builds up an energy that, in conjunction with the rise in leisure time, the custom of gift shopping, the profusion of public events and traveling, translates into a consumerist shopping spree. As early as the first centuries of Islam, institutional theologians condemned the phenomenon of licentious abandon on Ramadan nights after the breaking of the fast. Similarly today, hedonism and ostentatious consumerism skyrocket during Ramadan; *Sayyidati* undergoes a sudden growth in this month, page counts increasing to accommodate the greater number of advertisements.

The connection between Muslim religious practice and trade is not surprising. Islam was born in a traders' city; its prophet was a merchant, as was his wife; its greatest philosopher, al-Ghazali (died 1111), wrote that "markets are the tables of God"; the first book in praise of trade was written by a Muslim (Ja'fr ibn Ali al-Dimashki's twelfth-century *The Beauty of Trade*)[7]; the market and the mosque were intimately connected in Islamic cities. The relationship of Islam and commerce continues to this day.

The extensive use of Ramadan and other Islamic symbols (that is, of "Islam") necessitates an additional caveat, in the context of the preface's emphasis on "Arabism." As I mentioned in the preface, there exist other cultural currents, other influences. We must accept "some infinite maybe which will leave no stone or fact standing,"[8] be content with the approximately certain and the certainly approximate. After all, Arabism and Islam are closely related, and the spread of Islam also disseminated some of the values of Arabism. Islam challenged the values of Arabism, then integrated them into a system of religious propagation, marketing, and advertisement. Still, if a single most prominent cultural current is to be identified, I would choose "Arabism," with all its symbols and customs. But (there is always a "but") the identity of advertisements is much more complex: they are at once Arabic, Saudi, Islamic, Western. The practice and manifestations of Islam in Saudi Arabia are first and foremost Arabic; the opening hours of stores during Ramadan have a great deal to do with the weather conditions of the Arabian peninsula. This Arabism, however, is also predominantly Islamic-Wahhabi, as can be seen, for example, in the status of women. The *turath*, the heritage, that appears in advertisements is a multilayered, archaeological one, full of affinities and contrasts.

Saudi advertising also reflects tribal values; these values are at the base of its lexicon of images. Just as Saudi Arabia is a tribal state, just as over seventy years of central rule have been unable to efface the legacy of centuries of tribalism,[9] advertising too returns to and makes use of the tribe. It exploits the "ancestor" of the tribe, genealogical dynasties, the tribal council (*al-majlis*), the values of *muruwah* (manhood), tribal poetry, and much more. Once a product is integrated into the tribe, '*asabiyyah* or tribal solidarity applies to it as well. Lancaster showed how the Saudi state's attempt to inculcate Rawala Bedouins with the values of permanent settlement in place of those of the nomadic lifestyle concluded with the abandonment of theoretical studies in favor of practical "tribal" exercises (such as military drills).[10] Advertising learned the lesson of this failure and flips it: it provides the nomadic ethos even to urban dwellers.

In the course of history, the deserts of the Middle East have proven fertile ground for new religions. The advertising religion too is readily accepted here, though with certain adaptive modifications. The advertised product is exalted, worshiped, deified, precisely due to its presence in trivial, everyday cultural situations: the fact that it is foreign to such situations, that it sticks out, underscores its uniqueness. The product lowers itself to the level of the common people, of everyday life, a descent that makes clear that this is not its natural place. As a camouflage for the "sacrilege" of conversion to pagan consumerism, as a disguise for the *shirk* (the sin of placing other gods beside Allah), nostalgia and historical sentimentalism are nurtured.

The Arab, Islamic, Wahhabi, Saudi, and also the Western worldviews are necessarily superficial. When the party is over, all that is left is the unbearable lightness of social manipulation. The logic of advertising is a modal logic, one of possible rather than actual worlds. Advertising pretends to be a carnival; to blur the binary distinctions man-woman, present-nonpresent, child-adult, East-West; to enable one to "read" an alternative reality. But since it depends on the use of power, on the hierarchy of control over means, on the prescribed roles of seller and buyer, it retains, behind its million-riyal smile, all the traces of the hegemonic culture.

Western companies that export products to Saudi Arabia are those willing to play the game by Saudi rules. When an ad shows a woman with bare arms, or one in an "indecent" posture, she will always be a Western woman, or a tourist observing an alien world. For the Saudi woman reader, such pictures remain an unfulfilled fantasy. So even when an alternative reality is presented, it is no more than a dream; or perhaps even an antigenic vaccine against the possibility of cultural revolution, a sort of guided imagination exercise meant to release pressure. Here we see "all the world's dreams." The blending together of all times and places into a single finely chopped *muluhiyyah* makes meaningful political activity directed toward change all but impossible. Change and political activity cannot exist without difference, without motion. But advertising is a frozen moment, a dream. Even when it offers a "solution," that is, when it presents the picture of a different world, it shows only the final outcome, never the path that leads to it. Without this path, without rational debate, the gates of heaven remain hidden, though heaven itself is painted in bold brushstrokes. The way to the perfect final outcome remains necessarily impossible. It is the illusory freedom offered by advertising that leaves the reader, especially the woman reader, politically impotent. There is no political freedom here, as a pseudo-objective, radical fatalism hovers over everything. The golden cage, the *qafs*, once again prevents the princes, and the princesses, from overthrowing the sultan.

Keith Michael Baker writes:

> En toute société, la politique dépend de l'existence de représentations culturelles qui définissent les relations entre acteurs politiques, permettant de ce fait à des individus et à des groupes d'élever des revendications les uns contre les autres et contre le corps entier. [11]

But the political relationships in advertising are predefined. The air of advertising is congested with the inevitability of culture. Even the choice between fashions and tastes takes place within the permitted spectrum of variety. The cheap seduction of consumer products hides social codes defining gender relations, intergenerational relations, punishment and atonement, folk beliefs, and more. Readers become part of the *ahl al-dhikr*, "family of those who remember," and of the *ahl al-taqlid*, "family of tradition" (or alternatively "of imitation").

It is for this purpose that advertising makes tradition hyperrealistic, thus emptying it of any real content. All it creates is a disappearing act of tradition. It reconstructs a tradition that is "more social than social," a tradition for the masses. The mass media are an ecstasy of tradition, a mirror reflecting it (to return to the Concord watch ad). The response to imported Western products is not a forsaking of old values but an excess of traditional determinism; Arabism as a circus. Cultural inertia is strengthened by a history composed of a collection of frozen historical moments, a banal history of an Arabism that is realer than real, an exaggeration of Arabism—not the history of advertising, but advertising as history. In the words of the Jahili poet Labid ibn Rabi`, "Their signs are worn out, like the inscriptions their rocks have preserved."[12] Myths, in their reduced, refined state, continue to haunt Arab culture, which becomes a hostage, a convincing argument for extortion, a provocation, an insurance policy, a colossal mummy.

In this sense, the culture can be seen as Westernized, not in the modern sense but rather in the sense of baroque theatricality (I have stressed the importance of the baroque and rococo styles). This is an "Eastern" Westernism. To call it a Saudi social pornography, a prostitution of Arabism wrapped in colorful cellophane, would be simplistic. This is an Arabism that changes according to its changing position, like the symbol accompanying the letter *alif* whose form depends on the following vowel. In this sense, advertising is integrated into a social laboratory that is rebuilding Arabism, for the mass media is, after all, the primary means of truly collective cultural consumption. This Arabism is like a shop one can enter to try on clothes; one can choose not to buy, but one cannot really negotiate.

This is the secret of advertising, fashion, gambling, of all the lewd systems that break apart moral energies and liberate immoral energies, those that feed gaily on the signs of things alone, in defiance of their truth. In this, they go back to magical and archaic energies that have always gambled on the omnipotence of thought against the power of the real world, immoral energy that shatters meaning, that traverses facts, representations, and traditional values and electrifies societies blocked in their Platonic images.[13]

The interplay of Western products and Arab-Muslim culture, and the encounter of local products with Western marketing techniques and with the need to compete with imports, creates new products that are neither completely Western nor completely Arabic. The meat grinder, after all, does not change, and the knowledge necessary for its design and creation remains the same, but it now grinds different meat for different products. This grinder will never be used for pork, at least not in the open market of the ads, in their aesthetical museum. This grinder's fate has destined it to grind mutton for Ramadan mincemeat. In this way, Marx's economic theories mix with Weber's sociocultural theories, without the possibility of determining for sure which came first, economic or cultural processes (as noted, sometimes "cultural importation" filters out products that are inappropriate for the culture). Either way, it is advertising that both designs and reflects this combination.

I have referred several times to the work of Baudrillard, whose ideas are both illuminating and fruitful. But ultimately, his pessimism is to be avoided; just as human beings are not mere hunks of flesh and electrical impulses, culture is more than a collection of recycled quotations. The new configurations of these quotations, new connections between them, the occasional flicker of an innovation—these are the manifestations of culture, and presumably always have been. Simulation too gradually becomes real, imagination gradually turns into recognition. Every generation reorganizes its simulation and markets it. Reediting can bring about alterations that fundamentally change the world of the readers. History is turned off and on (*wird gelichtet und wird genichtet*) time and again, but like the world itself, it retains a curious sort of cultural continuity. "If all the conditions have changed, it is as if all creation has been replaced from its foundations, and the entire world has altered; as though it is a new creation, a new growth, a renewed world," wrote Abd al-Rahman Ibn Khaldun (1332–1406). But not all conditions change; the present and future always show traces of the past. When people feel the world is changing too fast, they discover that the old possessions are still there in the bottom drawer; they take them out and try them on again. The clothes of culture are a patchwork quilt. The past does not become passé.

Therefore, the underlying subject of this study, which deals with the myths and symbols of advertising, is contemporary Saudi historiography. Advertising links different goals and different agendas, blends them together, overturns them and makes them into a new sort of *maqlubah* (an Arabian dish prepared in this blending and overturning manner). The transition from product to brand, from what is manufactured to what is purchased by consumers, creates culture; advertising yields the "added value." This transition is not necessarily intelligible to the consumer and, in its deeper layers, maybe not even to the advertiser (despite sophistication and market analyses). In the words of anthropologist Margaret Mead,

> Cultural understanding of the sort discussed in this Manual can be achieved only within a frame of reference that recognizes the internal consistency of the premises of each human culture and also recognizes that much of this consistency is unconscious: that is, is not available to the average member of culture.[14]

Baudrillard would claim that in the encounter of Westernism and Arabism, the contribution of the former is not necessarily the products themselves, but the transformation of everything, including Arabism, into metaphors and images, into a semiological system.[15] Structurally speaking consumption is not merely the purchase of products, of pleasure and of release for impulses. It is a system of signs, a communications system, a morality, an ideological value system, a social logic. But Arabism was a semiological system well before its encounter with the West. It was a communications system with a social logic even before this "encounter." The idea of using *urf* and *adah*, the "known" and the "customary," that is, the rituals of each society and culture that Islam came upon, was imprinted long before the encounter. It goes without saying that Arab images are not a Western import, but neither is the idea of using them. True, Saudi advertising, like its Western counterpart, is an escape from reality, a mental *hijrah* from "present" to "glorious future" that will resurrect the "illustrious past" (in this sense, Saudi advertising is fundamentalist). But it is crucial to realize that the idea of the "land of heart's desire," detached from the present, is not an import from the America of L. Frank Baum[16]; Arab poetry, for example, is a broad country of desires. And as with any religion, the advertiser does not require an actual revelation, but only the possibility of one: the *khalifah* (caliph, "substitute") of the period, the messiah, the vanishing imam, whose appearance is deliberately put off in every generation anew. This future, this nostalgic dream, this recycled hope, yearns for a different order than the one aspired to by Western advertising.

Notes

Introduction: Toward a Semiotic Analysis
of Advertising in Saudi Arabia

1. Already in the nineteenth-century Ottoman Empire, this process did not bring about the Westernizing or abandonment of the old and the familiar; see Elisabeth Frierson, "Cheap and Easy: The Creation of Consumer Culture in Late Ottoman Society," in Donald Quataert, *Consumption Studies and the History of the Ottoman Empire, 1550–1922, An Introduction* (Albany, N.Y.: State University of New York, 2000), pp. 243–260 (Hereinafter: Quataert - *Consumption*).

2. I do not see any difference between the two sides of the distinction Quataert tries to suggest ("cultural issues" vs. "political ideology"), but agree with him that "societies have constructed social values around goods for centuries and not only in Europe" (Quataert - *Consumption*, pp. 11–12).

3. Daniel Lerner, *The Passing of Traditional Society: Modernizing the Middle East* (Glencoe: The Free Press [1958], 1963).

4. Marshall McLuhan, *The Medium Is the Message* (Harmondsworth, Middlesex: Penguin Books, 1967). See also his *Understanding Media* (London: Routledge & Kegan, 1967).

5. See the discussion of "modernization" and "dependency" approaches in the context of Middle East communications studies in Annabelle Srebreny-Muhammadi and Ali Muhammadi, *Small Media, Big Revolution: Communication, Culture and the Iranian Revolution* (London: University of Minnesota Press, 1994), pp. 4–9.

6. Marshall McLuhan, *The Global Village* (New York: Oxford University Press, 1989).

7. Edward W. Said, *Orientalism* (New York: Pantheon Books, 1978); id., *Covering Islam: How the Media and the Experts Determine How We See the Rest of the World* (London and Melbourne: Routledge & Kegan Paul, 1981). See also Talal Asad, *The Idea of an Anthropology of Islam*, Center for Contemporary Arab Studies, Occasional Papers Series (Washington: Georgetown University, 1986), p. 14; Lila Abu-Lughud, "Zones of Theory in the Anthropology of the Arab World," *Annual Review of Anthropology*, 18 (1989), pp. 267–306.

8. See explanation of the idea in Nick Stevenson, *Understanding Media Cultures: Social Theory and Mass Communication* (London: Sage, 1995), p. 52 (Hereinafter: Stevenson - *Understanding*).

9. Michel Foucault, *Discipline and Punish*, trans. Alan Sheridan (New York: Pantheon, 1977), pp. 184–186.

10. Eric Hobsbaum, "Introduction: Inventing Traditions," in Eric Hobsbaum and Terence Ranger (eds.), *The Invention of Tradition* (Cambridge: Cambridge University Press, 1983), pp. 1–14.

11. Gregory Starrett, *Putting Islam to Work: Education, Politics and Religious Transformation in Egypt* (Los Angeles: University of California Press, 1998) (Hereinafter: Starrett - *Putting Islam*).

12. See Nico Stehr, *Knowledge Societies* (London: Sage, 1994), p. 10 (Hereinafter: Stehr - *Knowledge*).

13. Jean Baudrillard, *The Transparency of Evil: Essays on Extreme Phenomena*, trans. James Benedict (London and New York: Verso, 1993), p. 23 (Hereinafter: Baudrillard – *Evil*).

14. Jean-François Lyotard, *The Postmodern Condition: A Report on Knowledge* (Minneapolis: University of Minnesota Press, 1984), pp. 4–5. See also Stehr: "A very important point, however, is that knowledge can be objectified; that is, the intellectual appropriation of things, facts and rules can be established symbolically, so that in the future in order to know, it is no longer necessary to get into contact with the things themselves but only with their symbolic representations" (Stehr - *Knowledge*, pp. 13–14).

15. Baudrillard - *Evil*, p. 9.

16. See Stevenson - *Understanding*, p. 52. See also Baudrillard on "canceling symbolic value": Jean Baudrillard, *L'Echange Symbolique et la Mort* (Paris: Gallimard, 1976).

17. Baudrillard - *Evil*, pp. 7–8, 12: "Communication is more social than the social itself: it is hyper-relational, sociality overactivated by social techniques."

18. Jean Baudrillard, *The Consumer Society: Myth & Structure* (London: Sage, [1970] 1998), p. 27

19. Baudrillard - *Evil*, p. 17.

20. Baudrillard - *Evil*, p. 6.

21. See David Gurevitch, *Postmodernism: Tarbut ve-Sifrut be-Sof ha-Me'ah ha-Esrim* (Tel Aviv: Dvir, 1997), p. 57.

22. J. Van Velsen, "The Extended-Case Method and Situational Analysis " in Arnold Leonard Epstein (ed.), *The Craft of Social Anthropology* (London: Tavistock Publications, 1967), pp. 129–153 (Hereinafter: Van Velsen).

23. Walter Benjamin, "Thesis on History," in *Illuminations* (New York: Harcourt, Brace and World, 1968), pp. 255–266.

24. The term "trace" is from Jacques Derrida. A trace is the "presenceless presence" of a text that is no longer "there." See Jacques Derrida, *Of Grammatology*, trans. Gayatri Chakravorty-Spivak (Baltimore and London: Johns Hopkins University Press, 1976), p. 90.

25. See Peter W. Edbury and John Gordon Rowe, *William of Tyre: Historian of the Latin East* (Cambridge: Cambridge University Press, 1988), pp. 54–56.

26. David S. Landes, "What Room for Accident in History? Explaining Big Changes by Small Events," *Economic History Review*, 157, 4 (1994), pp. 637–656.

27. Marc Bloch, *The Historian's Craft*, trans. Peter Putnam (New York: Vintage Books, 1953), pp. 20, 43–47.

28. François Bédarida, "The Modern Historian's Dilemma: Conflicting Pressures from Science and Society," *Economic History Review* 150, 3 (1987), pp. 335–348.

29. Clifford Geertz, *The Interpretation of Cultures: Selected Essays* (New York: Basic Books, 1973) (Hereinafter: Geertz - *Interpretation*).

30. Joyce Appleby, Lynn Hunt, and Margaret Jacob, *Telling the Truth About History* (New York: Norton, 1994).

31. Marc Poster, *Cultural History and Postmodernity* (New York: Columbia University Press, 1997), p. 8 (Hereinafter: Poster - *Cultural*); Roger Chartier, *Cultural History: Between Practices and Postmodernity*, trans. Lydia Cochrane (London: Polity, 1988), p. 37.

32. Poster - *Cultural*, p. 10.

33. Marcel Danesi, *Interpreting Advertisement: A Semiotic Guide*. Ottawa: Legas, 1995), p. 15 (Hereinafter: Danesi).

34. Ibid.

35. I use the term "modern printing" because techniques of xylography (wood engraving) originating in the Far East existed before Gutenberg.

36. Gillian Dyer, *Advertising as Communication* (London: Routledge, 1982), pp. 16–17.

37. Danesi, pp. 16–17.

38. Yosef Drori, "'Igeret ha-Bsorah al Kibush Yerushlayim," *Katedrah*, Hotza'at Yad Yitzhak ben Tsvi, 46 (December 1987), pp. 7–12.

39. Khalil al-Azam Jamal al-Din al-Qasimi, *Qamus al-Sina`at al-Sha'miyyah*, 2 vols. (Paris: Mouton & Co., 1960), profession no. 399.

40. Cf. Allen Douglas and Fedwa Malti-Douglas, *Arab Comic Strips: Politics of an Emerging Mass Culture* (Indianapolis: Indiana University Press, 1994), p. 3 (Hereinafter: Douglas and Malti-Douglas).

41. Among the reasons for this delay were the monopoly of the scribes (*waraqin*), low literacy, the differences between literary and spoken Arabic, lack of raw materials, the concentration of printing in the hands of the authorities, the preference of lithographic to typographic printing (possibly due to the cursive nature of the Arab script and the fact that letters appear differently according to their position in the word), and more. See Khalil Sabat, *Ta'rikh al-Taba`ah fi al-Sharq al-Arabi*, vol. 2 (Misr: Dar al-Ma`arif, 1966); F. Robinson, "Technology and Religious Change: Islam and the Impact of Print," *Modern Asian Studies*, 27 (1993), pp. 229–251.

42. As in the case of Muhammad Ali in Egypt. See Panayiotis J. Vatikiotis, *The History of Modern Egypt: From Muhammad Ali to Mubarak* (Baltimore: Johns Hopkins University Press, 1991).

43. See the table summarizing the development of Arab journalism between 1800 and 1877 in Abd al-Rahim Ghalib, *Mi'ah Am min Ta'rikh al-Sahafah Lisan al-Hal* (Beirut: Jarus Press, 1988), pp. 142–148.

44. Danesi, p. 19.

45. G. C. Woodward, *Presentation and Influence in American Life* (Waveland: Prospect Heights, 1988), p. 192.

46. James Webb Young, *How to Become an Advertising Man* (New York: API, 1963), p. 7.

47. Danesi, p. 19.

48. Amoz Oz, *Kol ha-Tiqvot: Mahshavot al Zehut Yisra'elit* (Jerusalem: Keter, 1998), p. 191.

49. Umberto Eco, "Towards a Semiotic Inquiry into the Television Message" (1965), reprinted in *Working Papers in Cultural Studies*, no. 3 (Birmingham University Center for Contemporary Cultural Studies, Autumn 1972), pp. 103–121.

50. John Fiske, *Introduction to Communication Studies*, 2nd ed. (London and New York: Routledge, 1990), pp. 10–16 (Hereinafter: Fiske - *Introduction*).

51. Ibid., p. 57.

52. David Sless, *In Search of Semiotics* (London: Croom Helm, 1986), pp. 63–64 (Hereinafter: Sless). Compare also Edward Buscombe, "Ideas of Authorship," *Screen*, vol. 14, no. 3 (1973), p. 77: "The author is constituted only in language and a language is by definition social, beyond the particular individuality."

53. See discussion of the ideas of I. A. Richards in Fiske - *Introduction*, p. 26.

54. Sless, p. 118.

55. Stuart Hall, "Encoding and Decoding in the Television Message," in S. Hall, et al. (eds.), *Culture, Media, Language* (London: Hutchinson, 1980).

56. Compare Stuart Hall, "Culture, The Media and the 'Ideological Effect,'" in James Curan, et al. (eds.), *Mass Communication and Society* (London: Edward Arnold, 1977), pp. 315–348. See also Edward S. Herman and Noam Chomsky, *Manufacturing Consent: The Political Economy of the Mass Media* (London: Vintage, 1994), pp. 1–35.

57. Just as in the Middle East, any other product of culture, including popular culture, is political; e.g., comics. See Douglas and Malti-Douglas, p. 1.

58. See Danesi, p. 97. Compare also Edward G. Browne, *The Press and Poetry of Modern Persia* (Los Angeles: Kalimat Press, 1983).

59. John Fiske and John Hartley, *Reading Television* (London: Methuen, 1978).

60. Anwar Chenje, "Arabic: Its Significance and Place in Arab-Muslim Society," *Middle East Journal* 19 (1965), p. 450.

61. Shmuel More, *Ha-Ilan ve-ha-Anaf* (Jerusalem: Magnes, 1997).

62. Le'a Glazman, "Ezrach Kama'stan ve-Hofesh ha-Nviha: He'arot ve-Hirhurim be-Shulei Dmuto vi-Ytitsirato shel ha-Mashorer Nizar Qabani (1923–1998)." *Itun 77* 228 (February 1999), pp. 25–26 (Hereinafter: Glazman).

63. Re'uven Snir, "ha-Sifrut ha-Arvit ba-Me'ah ha-Esrim: Model Histori-Funktsionali-Dinami." *ha-Mizrah ha-Hadash*, 36 (1994).

64. Glazman, p. 26. She points out that doubtless "Qabani's tremendous popularity was a result not necessarily of the inherent value of his work, but largely of its catchiness and marketability, often verging on commercialization and at the expense of good taste."

65. John Fiske, *Reading the Popular* (London and New York: Routledge, 1989), p. 2 (Hereinafter: Fiske - *Popular*).

66. For a definition of "discourse," see Michel Foucault, *The Archeology of Knowledge and the Discourse of Languages*, trans. Sheridan Smith (New York: Harper & Row, 1976), pp. 215–220.

67. Fiske - *Introduction*, p. 2.

68. Claude Elwood Shannon and Warren Weaver, *The Mathematical Theory of Communication* (Urbana: University of Illinois Press, 1949).

69. Harold Lasswell, "The Structure and Function of Communication in Society," in L. Bryson (ed.), *The Communication of Ideas* (New York: Jewish Theological Seminary of America, Institute for Religious and Social Studies, 1948), pp. 37–51.

70. Rachel Halfi, "Semyotika Hi," in Zisi Stavi (ed.), *66 Meshorerim–Mivhar Hamishim Shnot Shirah Ivrit Hadasha* (Israel: Yedi'ot Ahronot, 1996), p. 313. My translation.

71. Emmanuel Kant claimed that all experience is a combination of previous concepts and new information, and that pure reason, unfounded on previously existent concepts, is impossible (see his *Critique of Pure Reason*). Ernst Gombrich showed that interpreting a picture in a certain way depends on the previous experience of the observer; see his *Art and Illusion* (London: Phaidon Press, 1968).

72. Umberto Eco, *A Theory of Semiotics* (London: Macmillan, 1976), p. 7.

73. For example, Charles Peirce's connection between object, sign, and interpretant, the last being the mental concept created both by the sign and by the user's experience with the object. See Charles Sanders Peirce, *Collected Papers* (Cambridge: Harvard University Press, 1958); J. Jay Zaman, "Peirce Theory of Signs," in Thomas Sebeok (ed.), *A Perfusion of Signs* (Bloomington: Indiana University Press, 1977), pp. 22–39. Also compare linguist Ferdinand de Saussure's distinction between signifier and signified, and between various sorts of signs: icon, index, symbol, etc. See Ferdinand de Saussure, *Course in General Linguistics* (Glasgow: Fotana & Collins, 1974) (Hereinafter: Saussure).

74. For example, paradigm and syntagm; digital and analog codes; presentative and representative codes; nonverbal communication codes; elaborated and restricted codes; broadcast and narrowcast codes; arbitrary codes; aesthetic codes; denotation and connotation; myths; metaphor and metonymy; etc. See the basic summary in Fiske - *Introduction*.

75. Quoted in Van Velsen, p. 136.

76. Peter L. Berger and Thomas Luckmann, *The Social Construction of Reality* (London: Penguin Books, 1967) (Hereinafter: Berger and Luckmann). See also John R. Searle, *The Construction of Social Reality* (New York: Free Press, 1995).

77. The basis of these ideas is the same as that of Karl Marx's thoughts on "ideology" and "false consciousness," the latter of which was developed by Friedrich Nietzsche. See *The Genealogy of Morality* and *The Will to Power*.

78. Karl Mannheim, *Essays on the Sociology of Knowledge* (London: Routledge & Kegan Paul, 1964).

79. See George William Grace, *The Linguistic Construction of Reality* (London: Croom Helm, 1987). On the relationship between linguistics and anthropology, see Ruth Benedict, *Patterns of Culture* (New York: Houghton Mifflin, 1934); Ruth Benedict, *The Chrysanthemum and the Sword: Patterns of Japanese Culture* (Boston: Houghton Mifflin, [1946] 1989).

80. Aharon Shabtai, *Ahavah* (Tel Aviv: Am Oved, 1987), p. 86. Danesi adds that symbols "allow us, figuratively speaking, to carry the world around us in our heads" (Danesi, p. 14). According to Saussure, "Language exists in the form of a sum of impressions deposited in the brain of each member of a community, almost like a dictionary of which identical copies have been distributed to each individual. Language exists in each individual, yet it is common to all" (Saussure, p. 19). The idea that language and reality are congruent, or at least closely related, has a long history, predating Wittgenstein. This notion, of course, has also been echoed in literature. George Orwell, for example, in his afterword to *Nineteen Eighty-Four*, wrote that the logic behind "Newspeak," the reformed version of English purged of meanings that might conflict with the state ideology, was to make all other forms of thought impossible. The connection between language and reality was also expressed by the well-known Arab philosopher 'Ibn-Rushd. There are, of course, views that hold that seditious, oppositionary, "carnivalistic" reading is also possible; but opposition only exists within a given reality and as a dialogue with it.

81. Berger and Luckmann, pp. 66–83.

82. Fridrich Engles, *The Origin of Family, Private Property and the State* (New York: International Publishers, 1973).

83. Maurice Halbwachs, *On Collective Memory* (Chicago: University of Chicago Press, [1968] 1992).

84. Benedict Anderson, *Imagined Communities*, rev. ed. (London and New York: Verso, 1991), pp. 5–7.

85. Gary Hoppenstand, *In Search of the Paper Tiger* (Bowling Green, Ohio: Bowling Green State University Popular Press, 1987), p. 11.

86. See *The CIA Worldfact Book* (2003). See also Gad Gilbar, *Kalkalat ha-Mizrah ha-Tichon ba-Et ha-Hadashah* (Tel Aviv: Misrad ha-Bitahon, 1990), pp. 74–137; Binyamin Shvedran, *Neft Ha-Mizrah Ha-Tichon: Brachah ve-Iyum* (Tel Aviv: Am Oved, 1975), pp. 177–235.

87. Saudi Arabia, Ministry of Planning, *The Third Development Plan 1980–1985*, (Riyadh: 1981); id., *Summary of Saudi Arabian Third Five Year Development Plan*, 2nd ed. (Riyadh: 1985); id., *Fourth Development Plan 1985–1990* (Riyadh: 1986); id., *Fifth Development Plan 1990–1995* (Riyadh: 1990); Donald M. Moliver and Paul J. Abbondante, *The Economy of Saudi Arabia* (New York: Preager, 1980), pp. 98–112;

Ateiyiah S. Al-Rowaithy, *The Effectiveness of the Saudi Arabian Government's Program to Modernize Saudi Society Through the Development of a Non-Oil Industrial Sector*, Unpublished Ph.D. thesis (Claremont, CA: Claremont Graduate School, 1986); H. G. Habelton, "The Saudi Arabian Petrochemical Industry: Its Rationale and Effectiveness," in Tim Niblock (ed.), *State, Society and Economy in Saudi Arabia* (London: Croom Helm, 1982), pp. 235–277.

88. In 1997 total profits were estimated at 164 billion riyal (of which some 129.5 billion were oil profits). Total expenditure was estimated at 181 billion riyal. The riyal's exchange rate against the dollar is a constant, fixed in June 1986 as 3.745 riyal to US $1. See *The Europa World Yearbook 1998* (London: Europa Publications Limited, 1998), vol. 2, p. 2933 (Hereinafter: *Europa-1998*).

89. *Europa-1998*, p. 2943.

90. See "Mifrats: Kovets Yediot Tashtit Kalkala Vetikshoret," *Hatsav*, May 4, 1996, p. 2.

91. As early as the 1970s and 1980s, a consumer society with high purchasing power was developing in Saudi Arabia. See, for instance, Laron Jensen, "Widespread Affluence Makes Arabian Peninsula a Prime Market for U.S. Home and Leisure Products," *Business America*; 6 (April 1983), pp. 20–24.

92. See, for instance, J. S. Birks and C. A. Sinclair, "The Domestic Political Economy of Development in Saudi Arabia," in Tim Niblock (ed.), *State, Society and Economy in Saudi Arabia* (London: Croom Helm, 1982), pp. 198–213.

93. Yousef A. Uthaimeen, *The Welfare State in Saudi Arabia: Structure, Dynamics and Function*, unpublished Ph.D. Thesis (Cairo: The American University, 1986); Delvin A. Roy, "Saudi Arabian Education: Development Policy," *Middle Eastern Studies* 28, 3 (1992), pp. 477–508.

94. The literature on foreign workers in Saudi Arabia is extensive. See Robert E. Looney, "Patterns of Human Resource Development in Saudi Arabia," *Middle Eastern Studies*, 24, no. 4 (1991), pp. 668–678; id., "Structural Change in the Arabian Gulf: Impact of the Foreign Workers," *Population Bulletin of ESCWA* 37 (December 1990), pp. 129–172; Peter W. Woodward, *Oil and Labor in the Middle East: Saudi Arabia and the Oil Boom* (New York: Preager, 1988); Nazli Choucry, "Asian in the Arab World: Labor Migration and Public Policy," *Middle Eastern Studies* 27, 2 (1986), pp. 252–273; Tayseer Abdel Jaber, "Inter Arab Labor Movements: Problems and Prospects," in Said El-Naggar (ed.), *Economic Development of the Arab Countries* (Washington, D.C.: IMF, 1993), pp. 252–273; Baquer Salman Al-Najjar, "Population Policies in the Countries of the Gulf Cooperation Council: Politics and Society," *Immigration & Minorities*, 27, no. 2 (1986), pp. 252–273; J. S. Birks, I. J. Secombe, and C. A. Sinclair, "Labor Migration in the Arab Gulf States: Patterns and Prospects." *International Migration* 26 (1988), pp. 267–286; Nader Fergany, "Manpower Problems and Projections in the Gulf," in M. S. El-Azhary (ed.), *The Impact of Oil Revenues on Arab Gulf Development* (London: Croom Helm, 1984), pp. 155–169; Bashir Dabla, "Migration and Its Sociological Impact in Saudi Arabia and Kuwait," *Population Bulletin of ESCWA* ,29 (December 1986), pp. 77–92.

95. On the Shi'i minority in Saudi Arabia, see, for instance, Jacob Goldberg, "The Shi'i Minority in Saudi Arabia," in Juan R. I. Cole and Nikki R. Keddie (eds.), *Shi'ism and Social Protest* (New Haven and London: Yale University Press, 1986), pp. 230–246.

96. Derek Hopwood, "The Ideological Basis: Ibn Abd Al-Wahhab's Muslim Revivalism," in Tim Niblock (ed.), *State, Society and Economy in Saudi Arabia* (London: Croom Helm, 1982), pp. 23–35. See especially what he calls the "Arabian Background to Wahhabism," pp. 25–28. Also James Buch, "Secular and Religious Opposition in Saudi Arabia," in Tim Niblock (ed.), *State, Society and Economy in Saudi Arabia* (London: Croom Helm, 1982), pp. 106–124.

97. The idea of "regional diffusion" describes phenomena (e.g., biological mutations, ideas, clothing fashions, technologies, etc.) that are "born" in a certain place and diffused through a larger region. See Carl Sauer, *Agricultural Origins and Dispersals* (New York: American Geographical Society, 1952).

98. *Stratigraphic change* is a process in which the system passes from a single stable state, through a period of divergence, to another stable state. With each evolutionary development of this sort, the previous stable state is destroyed. In *divergence change*, the system also passes from one stable state to another through divergences, but each divergence increases the complexity of the system, as previous states do not disappear as in stratigraphic change but continue to exist. However, these old states are "enslaved" materially and cognitively to the new, dominant stable state, in the form of "memory." In *hermeneutic change*, the system undergoes divergences, but these are not between alternative states of social-spatial order but between different configurations of the same order. See discussion in Yuval Portugali, *Merhav, Zman ve-Hevrah be-Eretz Yisrael ha-Qdumah*, vol. A, Morfologiyah Merhavit (Tel Aviv: Ha-Universita Ha-Ptuha, 1999), pp. 118–121.

99. Compare Starrett - *Putting Islam*, p. 96. See also Suliman Al-Manadhri, *al-Suk al-Arabiyyah Al-Mushtarakah* (Al-Qahirah: Maktabah Madbulah, 1999), pp. 185–195.

100. For example, on the export of Saudi ideas to Gaza and the West Bank, see Geraldine Brooks, *Nine Parts of Desire: The Hidden World of Islamic Women* (New York: Anchor Books, 1995), pp. 154, 163 (hereinafter: Brooks - *Nine Parts*).

101. *Europa-1998*, p. 2939.

102. See *Al-Sharq al-Awsat*, 2 March 1992.

103. See the comprehensive article in *Al-Jazirah al-Arabiyyah*, December 1991.

104. See Douglas and Malti-Douglas, p. 5.

105. A. Al-Fardi, *The Development of Commercial Advertising in Saudi Television from 1986–1988*, unpublished Ph.D. thesis (Denton: University of North Texas, 1989).

106. A. Al-Yusuf, *Commercial Advertising in Saudi Arabia: A Content Analysis*, unpublished M.A. thesis (Tallahassee: Florida State University, 1989).

107. F. Al-Kheraiji, *The Culture of Television Advertising: An Historical and Empirical Analysis of the Content of Television Commercial and of Saudi Viewers' Responses to Advertising*, unpublished Ph.D. thesis (England: University of Leicester, 1992).

108. Safran Al-Makaty et al., "Attitudes Toward Advertising in Islam," *Journal of Advertising Research*, 36, no. 3 (1996), pp. 16–27.

109. See *Europa-1998*, p. 2939.

110. See, for example, *Sayyidati*, 781 (24.2–1.3.1996), pp. 8–11.

111. *Ben's Media Directory*, vol. 3 (1998), p. 398.

112. *Europa-1998*, p. 2939.

1. *Ilm al-Miqat*, The Science of Times: Timepieces and History

1. I am indebted to Avi Goldsobel for this story.

2. See Ibrahim Al-Ati, *Al-Zaman fi al-Fikr al-Islami* (Bayrut: Dar al-Muntahab al-Arabi, 1993), p. 5 (Hereinafter: Al-Ati - *Al-Zaman*).

3. Ibid., p. 7.

4. See fascinating discussions on the concept of time in its historical context in Gerhard Dohrn Van-Rossum, *L'Histoire de l'Heure: L'Horlogerie et l'Organization Moderne du Temps*, tr. Olivier Mannoni (Paris: Éditions de la Maison des Sciences de l'Homme [1992] 1997); Robert Levine, *A Geography of Time* (New York: Basic Books, 1997); Carlo M. Cipolla, *Clocks and Culture, 1300–1700* (New York: Walker, 1967); David S. Landes, *Revolution in Time: Clocks and the Making of the Modern World* (Cambridge: Belknap Press of Harvard University Press, 1983).

5. Shams al-Din Muhammad bin Abd al-Rahman al-Sakhawi, *Al-Ilan bi-al-tawbikh liman Dhamma al-Ta'rikh* (Damascus: Matba`ah al-Turki [902/1497] 1349/1930), p. 7.

6. Cf. Avshalom Elitsur, *Zman ve-Toda`ah: Tehiyot Hadashot al Hidot Atikot* (Tel Aviv: Misrad Habitahon, 1994), p. 45 (Hereinafter: Elitsur - *Zman*).

7. Al-Ati - *Al-Zaman*, p. 6.

8. Cf. Muhammad Awad Husayn, *Sina`at al-Ta'rikh*, Al-Majlad al-Khamis (Kuwait: Majalat Alam al-Fikr, 1974).

9. No. 793, 18–24.5.1996, p. 103.

10. Mawlana Wahiduddin Khan, *Women Between Islam and Western Societies* (New Delhi: Al-Risala Books, 1997), p. 20.

11. See chapter 7 on pens and writing.

12. On the relationship between Arab space and Aristotelian philosophy, see Frank Peters, *Aristotle and the Arabs: The Aristotelian Tradition in Islam* (New York: New York University Press, 1968).

13. Avraham Vachman, *Bniyah Agulah ve-Ortagonalit*, MA thesis (Haifa: The Technion, 1959).

14. Rolan Barthes, *Mythologies* (Paris: Éditions du Seuil, 1957) (Hereinafter : Barthes – *Mythologies*).

15. Johannes Fabian, *Time and the Other* (New York: Columbia University Press, 1983), p. 34.

16. See, for instance, no. 790, 27.4–3.5.1996, p. 21.

17. Brooks - *Nine Parts*, p. 97.

18. Roland Barthes, *La Chambre Claire: Note Sur la Photographie* (Paris: Cahiers du cinema, 1980).

19. Cf. Jean Baudrillard, *Fatal Strategies*, trans. Philip Beichman and W. G. J. Niesluchowski (New York: Semiotext[e]/Pluto, [1983] 1990), p. 8 (Hereinafter: Baudrillard - *Fatal*).

20. See, for instance, no. 880, 17–23.1.1998, p. 73.

21. Theodore Zeldin, *An Intimate History of Humanity* (New York: Harper Collins, 1995) (Hereinafter: Zeldin - *Intimate*).

22. Ibn Sina (Avicenna), Abu Ali al-Husayn b. Abd Allah. *al-Najah fi al-Hikmah al-Mantiqiyyah wa-al-Tab'iyyah wa-Alilahiyyah,* vol. 2. trans. Muhyi al-Din Sabri al-Kurdi. Cairo: Dar al-Sa'adah, 1938, p. 115.

23. Joachim Maria Machado De Assis, *The Posthumous Memoirs of Bras Cubas* (New York: Oxford University Press, 1997).

24. On bathhouses in Arab culture, see also the chapter on cosmetics.

25. See, for example, the interview with Abd al-Karim Ghani, an `ud player and singer famous in the Gulf states: no. 880, 17–23.1.1998, p. 120.

26. Lila Abu-Lughod, *Veiled Sentiments: Honor and Poetry in a Bedouin Society* (Berkeley: University of California Press, 1986).

27. See Stokes on arabesque music in Turkey as the music of an oppressed discourse: Martin Stokes, *The Arabesk Debate: Music and Musicians in Modern Turkey* (New York: Clarendon Press [Oxford], 1992), p. 12 (Hereinafter: Stokes - *Arabesk*).

28. Roger Penrose, *The Emperor's New Mind: Concerning Computers, Minds and the Law of Physics* (Oxford: Oxford University Press, 1989).

29. See Stokes - *Arabesk*. See also J. Blacking, "The Structure of Musical Discourse: The Problem of the Song Text," *Yearbook for Traditional Music*, 14, pp. 15–23.

30. T. W. Adorno, *Introduction to the Sociology of Music* (New York: Continuum, 1976); "On Popular Music," *Zeitschrift für Sozialforschung*, 9, pp. 17–49.

31. Translated in P. Cachia, "A Nineteenth Century Arab's Observation on European Music," *Ethnomusicology*, 17 (1973), 1, pp. 441–451.

32. Zeldin - *Intimate*.

33. Ibid.

34. Women in Saudi Arabia are not allowed to drive; see the chapter on cars.

35. Douglas and Malti-Douglas, p. 33.

36. Zeldin - *Intimate*.

37. Ibid.

38. See Brooks - *Nine Parts*, p. 50.

39. Mona Mikhail, "Love and Sex: A Study of the Short Fiction of Naguib Mahfouz and Yusuf Idris," in her *Images of Arab Women* (Washington, D.C.: Three Continents Press, 1979), p. 95.

40. No. 879, 10–16.1.1998.

41. Mohammad Ilyas, *Astronomy of Islamic Times for the Twenty-First Century* (New York: Mansel, 1989), p. 3 (Hereinafter: Ilyas – *Astronomy*).

42. Ansari estimates that "Islamic sciences" existed as early as 750. See S. M. R. Ansari, "A Brief Survey of Islamic Sciences," in *Introduction to Islamic Sciences* (Aligarah: Aligarah Muslim University, 1983), p. 35. For further discussion see Amr Fruj, *Ta'rikh al-'Ulum Inda al-Arab* (Beirut: Dar al-Ilm lil-Malayin, 1970.

43. Ilyas - *Astronomy*, p. 9, footnote 6.

44. See Yasin Aribi, *Ashkalat Athbat al-Zaman fi al-Falsafah al-Islamiyyah* (Tripoli, Libya: Majalat Al-Hikmah, 1976); Muhammad Atif Al-Iraqi, *Al-Falsafah al-Tabi'iyyah Inda Ibn Sina* (Cairo: Dar al-Ma'arif, 1971).

45. R. B. Serjeant, "Star-Calendars and an Almanac from South-West Arabia," *Anthropos*, 49 (Sankt Augustin: Anthropos Redaktion, 1954), pp. 433–459 (Hereinafter: Serjeant - Calendars). Reprinted in R. B. Serjeant, *Farmers and Fishermen in Arabia: Studies in Customary Law and Practice*, ed. Rex Smith (Great Britain: Variorum, 1995).

46. G. Ryckmans, *Rites et Croyances Pré-Islamiques en Arabie Méridionale* (Louvain, 1942), p. 175.

47. Ilyas - *Astronomy*, p. 4.

48. No. 849, 14–20.6.1997, p. 71.

49. No. 880, 17–23.1.1998, p. 5.

50. Sotheby's, *Important Clocks, Watches, Wristwatches and Barometers* (London: Thursday, 14th December 1995).

51. No. 880, 17–23.1.1998, inside cover.

52. See, for example, Serjeant - *Calendars*, p. 441.

53. Douglas and Malti-Douglas, p. 23.

54. No. 827, 11–17.1.1997, p. 29.

55. On the difference in nuance between the two words see Jamaluddin Muhamad Bin Mukkaram Ibn Manzur. *Lisan al-Arab*. Cairo: Matba'ah Bulak, 1882, vol. 17, p. 60, and vol. 16, p. 183.

56. See, for instance, Iffat Muhammad al-Sharqawi, *Adab al-Ta'rikh Inda al-Arab*, vol. 1 (Fikrat al-Ta'rikh: Nashatuha wa-Tatawuruha) (Cairo: Maktabah al-Shabab, [1978?]), pp. 142–143; Al-Ati - *Al-Zaman*, pp. 195–198.

57. No. 853, 12–18.7.1997.

58. No. 880, 17–23.1.1998.

59. Douglas and Malti-Douglas, p. 11.

60. See, for example, the ketchup advertisement in the chapter on food.

61. Advertisement for Rama watch, 25–31.1.1997, p. 27.

62. This relates to the history of the development of shapes, described in the beginning of this chapter.

63. No. 827, 11–17.1.1997, inside cover.

64. Al-Ati - *Al-Zaman*, p. 9.

65. Ibid., p. 65.

66. Abu al-Ala' Ahmad bin Abd Allah bin Suliman al-Ma'ari, *Risalah al-Ghafran*, ed. A'isha Abd al-Rahman, vol. 3 (Cairo: Dar al-Ma'arif, 1963), p. 426.

67. Edward T. Hall, *The Silent Language* (Garden City, N.Y.: Doubleday, 1959), p. 15.

2. The Camel and the Wheel: Automobiles in the Desert

1. On the connection of camels and cars, see Richard W. Bulliet, *The Camel and the Wheel* (Cambridge: Harvard University Press, 1977) (Hereinafter: Bulliet - *The Camel*); Dawn Chatty, *From Camel to Truck: A Study of the Pastoral Economy of the Al-Fadl and the Al-Hassana in the Beqaa of Lebanon*, thesis submitted to the University of California (Los Angeles: 1974); Muhammad C. H. Koya, *Camel to Cadillac* (New Delhi: Sterling, 1979). On markings and "advertisement" on camels, see Henry Field, *Camel Brands and Graffiti: From Iraq, Syria, Jordan, Iran and Arabia* (Baltimore: American Oriental Society, 1952).

2. Mohamad Riad El Ghonemy, *Affluence and Poverty in the Middle East* (London: Routledge, 1998), p. 126 (hereinafter: El-Ghonemy – *Affluence*). All over the Middle East, this rise caused significant increases in air pollution and in traffic accidents.

3. 10–16.5.1997, pp. 88–89.

4. Albert Hourani, *A History of the Arab People* (New York, NY: Warner Books, 1992) (Herefater: Hourani - *Arab*).

5. Point de Vue, 17–23.3.1999, no. 2643, pp. 30–33. To drink a cup of coffee in the desert with his male friends, the sheik arrives in a modern helicopter, which appears in the photograph behind the men.

6. Bulliet - *The Camel*.

7. See Ben-Zion El-Qala`y and Yehiel Qara, *Pninei Arav* (Jerusalem: Misrad ha-Bitachon, 1993).

8. Ihsan Muhammad Al-Hasan, *Al-A'ilah wa-al-Qarabah wa-al-Zawwaj: Dirasah Tahliliyyah fi Taghayyur Nizam al-A'ilah wa-l-Qarabah wa-al-Zawaj fi al-Mujtama` al-`Arabi* (Beirut: Dar Al-Tali`ah, vol. 2, 1985), p. 64.

9. See Hourani - *Arab*.

10. Yitzhak Ignác Goldziher, *Hartsa'ot al ha-Islam* [translation of *Vorlesungen über den Islam*] (Jerusalem: Mosad Bialik, [1925] 1969), p. 149; for a list of sources and versions of this Hadith, see Uri Rubin, "Pre-existence and Light: Aspects of the Concept of Nur Muhammad," *Israel Oriental Studies*, 5 (1975), pp. 62–119.

11. Ibid.

12. On Faisal's special status in modern Arab nationalism and collective memory, see Ernest Clarence Dawn, *From Ottomanism to Arabism* (Urbana: University of Illinois Press, 1973); and George Antonius, *The Arab Awakening: The Story of the Arab National Movement* (Beirut: Khayats, 1945).

13. Geertz - *Interpretation*, p. 404.

14. See Muhammad Murad, "Al-Aa'ilah wa-'Alaqat al-Qarabah fi al-Mujtama` al-`Arabi." *Al-Mujtama` al-`Arabi al-Hadith wa-al-Mu`asar* (Beirut: Dar Al-Farabi, 1998), p. 160.

15. This fact, along with the frequent advertisement of cars in *Sayyidati*, strengthens the view that the journal is not exclusively a women's weekly, but a "family" weekly.

16. Brooks - *Nine Parts*, p. 197.

17. Ibid., p. 198.
18. E. A. Doumato, "Gender Monarchy and National Identity in Saudi Arabia," *International Journal of Middle Eastern Studies*, 19 (1992), pp. 31–47.
19. Brooks - *Nine Parts*, p. 146.
20. No. 796, 8–14.6.1996, pp. 80–81.
21. No. 796, 8–14.6.1996, p. 63. The name is transcribed as "Afalun"; see the chapter on writing and calligraphy.
22. No. 886, 28.2–2.3.1998, p. 63.
23. Bernard Lewis, *The Middle East and the West* (New York: Harper & Row, 1964); Bernard Lewis, *The Muslim Discovery of Europe* (London: Weidenfeld & Nicolson, 1982). See also clothing as a symbol of the East-West encounter in Iran: Kate Millet, *Going to Iran* (New York: Coward, McCann, & Geoghegan, 1982), p. 57.
24. Geoffrey Lewis, *Turkey* (London: Ernest Benn, 1965), p. 94.
25. No. 879, 10–16.1.1998, p. 77.
26. No. 879, 10–16.1.1998.
27. No. 812, 28.9–4.10.1996, p. 75.
28. No. 829, 25–31.1.1997, p. 129.
29. No. 841, 19–25.4.1997.
30. 27.4–3.5.1996, p. 59.
31. Ibid.
32. No. 821, 30.11–6.12.1996, p. 132.
33. The connection of automobiles and poetry also occurred in another Arab state, Iraq, where Saddam Hussein's "poet laureate," Abd al-Raziq Abd al-Wahid, received a new car whenever he composed a poem that pleases the ruler. See *Yedi'ot Ahronot*, 28.12.1998, p. 20.
34. Marcel P. Kurpershoek, *Oral Poetry and Narratives from Central Arabia*, vol. 1 ("The Poetry of Ad-Dindan–A Bedouin Bard in Southern Najd") (Leiden: E. J. Brill, 1994), pp. 152–153 (Hereinafter: Kurpershoek - *Oral Poetry*).
35. See the table summarizing the contents of the poems, ibid., pp. 30–31.
36. Ibid., p. 13.
37. Marcel P. Kurpershoek, *Oral Poetry and Narratives from Central Arabia*, vol. 3 ("Bedouin Poets of the Dawasir Tribe: Between Nomadism and Settlement in Southern Najd") (Leiden: E. J. Brill, 1999), pp. 110–114.
38. Brooks - *Nine Parts*, p. 119.
39. Kurpershoek - *Oral Poetry*, p. 5.

3. *Sihah wa-Afiyyah:* Food Ads
from the *Futur* to *Hilwayat*

1. El-Ghonemy - *Affluence*, p. 125.
2. Ibid.
3. No. 850, 21–27.6.1997.

4. For the changes the name undergoes in Arabic transcription, see the chapter on pens and writing.
5. El-Ghonemy - *Affluence*, p. 128.
6. No. 823, 14–20.12.1996.
7. R. B. Serjeant, "Fisher-folk and Fish-traps in al-Bahrain," *Bulletin of the School of Oriental and African Studies*, 31, 1968, pp. 486–514. Reprinted in R. B. Serjeant, *Farmers and Fishermen in Arabia: Studies in Customary Law and Practice*, ed. Rex Smith (Great Britain: Variorum, 1995).
8. No. 853, 12–18.7.1997.
9. For example, no. 785, 23–29.3.1996.
10. El-Ghonemy - *Affluence*, p. 128.
11. No. 793, 18–24.5.1996, p. 149.
12. Barthes - *Mythologies*, p. 103.
13. No. 820, 23–29.11.1996, p. 167.
14. See, for example, Fisher and Fisher's discussion of slavery in Mecca, where white Caucasian slaves (male and female) enjoyed a higher status than black slaves. Saudi Arabia was the last country to outlaw slavery (in 1962), replacing it, like many Western countries, with widespread foreign labor. Allan G. B. Fisher and Humphrey J. Fisher, *Slavery and Muslim Society in Africa* (London: C. Hurst & Co., 1970), p. 107. See also Bernard Lewis, *Race and Color in Islam* (New York: Harper & Row, 1971); Bernard Lewis, *Race and Slavery in the Middle East* (New York: Oxford University Press, 1990).
15. In the shadow theaters (*karagöz*), it was customary to mar the "perfection" of the puppets by piercing holes in their bellies, in order to indicate that they were not flesh-and-blood human figures.
16. Brooks - *Nine Parts*, p. 204.
17. Pierre Bourdieu, "Sport and Social Class," trans. Richard Nice, in *Social Science Information*, 17, no. 6 (1978), p. 820 (Hereinafter: Bourdieu - *Sport*).
18. No. 815, 19–25.10.1996, p. 137.
19. Bourdieu - *Sport*, p. 831.
20. Starrett – *Putting Islam*, p. 31.
21. No. 789, 20–26.4.1996, p. 157.
22. No. 796, 8–14.6.1996, p. 111; no. 822, 7–13.12.1996, p. 197.
23. No. 785, 23–29.3.1996.
24. El-Ghonemy - *Affluence*, p. 132.
25. Ibid.
26. Ibid.
27. No. 821, 23–29.11.1996, p. 195.
28. No. 796, 8–14.6.1996, p. 119.
29. No. 793, 18–24.5.1996, p. 137.
30. See, for example, no. 800, 6–12.7.1996, p. 149; no. 824, 14–20.12.1996, p. 231; etc.
31. No. 823, 14–20.12.1996, p. 231.
32. No. 822, 7–13.12.1996, p. 209.

33. Much like the diminutives used to refer to athletes in the Tour de France, pointed out by Barthes (Barthes - *Mythologies*, p. 138).
34. No. 845, 17–23.5.1997, pp. 113, 115.
35. No. 418, 7–13.6.1997.
36. No. 846, 24–30.5.1997, p. 155.
37. No. 848, 7–13.6.1997, p. 93.
38. No. 789, 20–26.4.1996, p. 135.
39. No. 880, 17–23.1.1998.
40. No. 844, 10–16.5.1997, p. 139.
41. Egyptian Arabic retains the /g/; see further discussion in the chapter on writing and calligraphy.
42. No. 849, 14–20.6.1997.
43. No. 827, 11–17.1.1997, p. 121.
44. No. 822, 7–13.12.1996, p. 207.
45. No. 418, 7–13.6.1997.
46. No. 786, 30.3–5.4.1996, p. 133.
47. No. 827, 11–17.1.1997, p. 129.
48. No. 827, 11–17.1.1997, p. 115.
49. No. 791, 4–10.5.1996, p. 141.
50. No. 880, 17–23.1.1998.
51. No. 827, 11–17.1.1997, p. 109.
52. No. 827, 11–17.1.1997, p. 119.
53. No. 886, 28.2–2.3.1998, p. 79.
54. See the chapter on timepieces.
55. No. 793, 18–24.5.1996, p. 133.
56. Zeldin - *Intimate*, p. 109.
57. No. 829, 25–31.1.1997, p. 147; no. 879, 10–16.1.1998.
58. No. 827, 11–17.1.1997.
59. No. 829, 25–31.1.1997.
60. No. 827, p. 11–17.1.1997, p. 99.
61. No. 822, 7–13.12.1996, p. 187.
62. No. 879, 10–16.1.1998, p. 155.
63. No. 879, 10–16.1.1998, p. 151.
64. No. 841, 19–25.4.1997, p. 101.
65. The various uses of *qishtah* recur in another company advertisement: no. 886, 28.2–2.3.1998.
66. See, for example, the Yves Saint-Laurent facial cream advertisement in no. 846, 24–30.5.1997.
67. No. 814, 12–18.10.1996, p. 160.
68. No. 879, 10–16.1.1998, p. 157.
69. No. 788, 13–19.4.1996, p. 123.
70. No. 816, 19–25.10.1996, p. 183.
71. Brooks - *Nine Parts*, p. 144.

72. No. 880, 17–23.1.1998.

73. No. 886, 28.2–2.3.1998, p. 71.

74. No. 879, 10–16.1.1998, p. 175.

75. Ali Jawad, *Tarikh al-Arab Qablah al-Islam*. Baghdad: Al-Majma al-Ilmi al-Iraqi, 1959, p. 666.

76. Ibid., p. 669.

77. See Shukri Araf, *Al-Shajarah, Islamiyya[n] wa-Arabiyya[n]* (Ma'aliyah: Ila al-Amq, 1995), pp. 21–45.

78. Ibid., p. 29.

79. See Marcel Mauss, *The Gift* (New York: Norton, 1967).

80. No. 796, 8–14.6.1996, p. 89.

81. See Shahla Haeri, *Law of Desire: Temporary Marriage in Shi'i Iran* (Syracuse, N.Y.: Syracuse University Press, 1989).

82. See an imaginary "interview" by reporter Khayri Ramadan with Princess Diana, in which both the questions and the answers are fictitious, in *Al-Ahram al-Arabi* (special end-of-year edition for 1997).

83. No. 820, 23–29.11.1996, p. 183.

84. No. 822, 7–13.12.1996, p. 193.

85. No. 843, 3–9.5.1997, p. 107.

86. No. 800, 6–12.7.1996, p. 137. On the graphic "rhyme" in this slogan, see the chapter on writing.

87. Brooks - *Nine Parts*, p. 173.

88. C. M. Hann, *Tea and the Domestication of the Turkish State* (England: Eothen Press, 1990).

89. Ibid., pp. ix, 9–10, 78–79.

90. No. 829, 25–31.1.1997, pp. 134, 136.

91. No. 829, 25–31.1.1997, p. 145.

92. 5–11.4.1997, p. 75. See further discussion in the chapter on home appliances, in the context of a coffee grinder ad.

93. No. 781, 24.2–1.3.1996, p. 73.

94. No. 822, 7–13.12.1996, p. 213.

95. No. 792, 11–17.5.1996, p. 145.

96. On one such conflict between the Anza and Al-Shararat tribes, see Saad Abdullah Sowayan, *The Arabian Oral Historical Narrative: An Ethnographic and Linguistic Analysis* (Wiesbaden: Otto Harrasowitz, 1992), p. 99.

4. *Ughmuri Ahasisaki*: Cosmetics and Personal Care Products

1. No. 807, 24–30.8.1996, p. 97.

2. See "Rococo," in Harold Osborne, *The Oxford Companion to Art* (Great Britain: Oxford University Press, [1970] 1990), pp. 985–988.

3. On hybrids in "modern" culture, see: Bruno Latour, *We Have Never Been Modern* (Cambridge: Harvard University Press, 1993).

4. No. 827, 11–17.1.1997.

5. No. 807, 24–30.8.1996, p. 3.

6. No. 880, 11–23.1.1998, p. 67.

7. No. 880, 17–23.1.1998, p. 13.

8. No. 829, 25–31.1.1997, p. 117.

9. No. 907, 25–31.7.1998, p. 91.

10. No. 843, 3–9.5.1997, p. 95.

11. No. 880, 17–23.1.1998, p. 61.

12. No. 879, 10–16.1.1998, p. 173.

13. No. 880, 17–23.1.1998, p. 60.

14. No. 827, 11–17.1.1997, p. 85.

15. No. 853, 12–18.7.1997, p. 63.

16. See also another product, in no. 851, 28.6–4.7.1997, p. 89.

17. No. 829, 25–31.1.1997, p. 117.

18. Walter Armbrust, et al. *Mass Culture and Modernism in Egypt* (Cambridge and New York: Cambridge University Press, 1996), p. 131.

19. Roni Zirinski, "The Muslim Diana: The Transformation of a Western Cultural Heroine in Egypt" (Haifa: Haifa University, 1998, unpublished), pp. 12–27.

20. No. 841, 19–25.4.1997, p. 55.

21. No. 853, 12–18.7.1997, p. 39.

22. No. 852, 5–11.7.1997.

23. Brooks - *Nine Parts*, p. 27.

24. No. 827, 11–17.1.1997, p. 51.

25. No. 796, 8–14.6.1996, p. 137.

26. No. 786, 30.3–5.4.1996, p. 111.

27. No. 822, 7–13.12.1996, p. 109.

28. Webster, vol. 3, p. 2017.

29. No. 845, 17–23.5.1997, p. 25.

30. No. 886, 28.2–2.3.1998, p. 9.

31. No. 801, 13–19.7.1996, p. 60.

32. Brooks - *Nine Parts*, pp. 56, 60.

33. No. 886, 28.2–2.3.1998.

34. 22–29.3.1996, p. 119.

35. No. 843, 3–9.5.1997, pp. 71, 73, 75.

36. No. 841, 19–25.4.1997, p. 93.

37. No. 796, 8–14.6.1996, p. 26.

38. No. 886, 28.2–2.3.1998, p. 47.

39. No. 822, 7–13.12.1996, p. 163.

40. No. 804, 19–25.8.1996, pp. 18–19.

41. No. 812, 28.9–4.10.1996, p. 73.

42. No. 823, 14–20.12.1996, p. 189.

43. No. 879, 10–16.1.1998, p. 23.

44. No. 820, 23–29.11.1996, p. 159.

45. No. 886, 28.2–2.3.1998.

46. No. 879, 10–16.1.1998, p. 5.

47. No. 850, 21–27.6.1997, p. 91.

48. No. 850, 21–27.6.1997.

49. No. 880, 17–23.1.1998, p. 133.

50. Ibid.

51. No. 829, 25–31.1.1997, p. 7.

52. No. 879, 10–16.1.1998, p. 127.

53. No. 829, 25–31.1.1997.

54. No. 879, 10–16.1.1998, p. 55.

55. On the significance of green in Islam, see, for example, Malek Chebel, *Symbols of Islam*, photographs by Laziz Hamani (London: Editions Assouline, 1997), pp. 116–118.

56. No. 879, 10–16.1.1998, p. 57.

57. See, for example, no. 844, 10–16.5.1997, p. 25.

58. No. 843, 3–9.5.1997, p. 5.

59. Ibid.; see also an ad for Yves Saint-Laurent lipstick, in no. 880, 17–23.1.1998.

60. Michel Foucault, however, has shown how "repression" of sexuality in Victorian times was in fact a medley of continuous discourses about sex.

61. No. 841, 19–25.4.1997, p. 95.

62. No. 821, 30.11–6.12.1996, p. 195.

63. No. 886, 28.2–2.3.1998.

64. No. 808, 31.8–6.9.1996, inside cover.

65. No. 879, 10–16.1.1998.

66. This Canadian perfume, *L'Air d'Or*, contains drops of 23-carat gold (in the late 1980s, a 32-ounce bottle cost US $8,500). See *Canadian Business* 16 (January 1897), pp. 19–21.

67. See the discussion in chapter 5, "Home and Away."

68. No. 880, 17–23.1.1998, p. 83.

69. No. 827, 11–17.1.1997, p. 15.

70. No. 827, 11–17.1.1997, p. 15.

71. No. 852, 5–11.7.1997, p. 71.

72. No. 851, 28.6–4.7.1997, p. 67.

73. No. 879, 10–16.1.1998, p. 51.

74. No. 907, 25–31.7.1998.

75. No. 853, 12–18.7.1997.

76. No. 879, 10–16.1.1998.

77. No. 827, 11–17.1.1997, p. 35.

78. No. 880, 17–23.1.1998, p. 121.

79. No. 827, 11–17.1.1997.

80. No. 880, 17–23.1.1998, p. 139.

81. No. 886, 28.2–2.3.1998, p. 29.

82. See advertisements for *Animale Animale,* no. 829, 25–31.1.1997, p. 115; Davidof's *Cool Water,* no. 827, 11–17.1.1997, p. 13; Chanel's *Allure,* no. 796, 8–14.6.1996, pp. 16–17; *Lolita Lempica,* no. 879, 10–16.1.1998.
83. No. 880, 17–23.1.1998, p. 7.
84. No. 829, 25–31.1.1997, p. 26.
85. No. 418, 7–13.6.1997.
86. No. 886, 28.2–2.3.1998, p. 127.
87. No. 879, 10–16.1.1998.
88. No. 796, 8–14.6.1996, p. 87.
89. Muhammad Abdul Jabbar Beg, "Workers in the Hammamat in the Arab Orient in the Early Middle Ages," *Revisita Degli Studi Orientali,* 158, (1972), pp. 77–80,.
90. No. 823, 14–20.12.1996, pp. 104–105.
91. Brooks - *Nine Parts,* p. 177.
92. See, for example, Kurpershoek - *Oral Poetry,* p. 5.
93. No. 849, 14–20.6.1997.
94. No. 418, 7–13.6.1997.
95. No. 850, 21–27.6.1997, p. 11.
96. Brooks - *Nine Parts,* p. 56.
97. Ibid., p. 59.

5. Home and Away: Electronics, Leisure, and Recreation

1. No. 822, 7–13.12.1996, p. 181.
2. No. 879, 10–16.1.1998, p. 145.
3. No. 823, 14–20.12.1996, p. 215.
4. No. 827, 11–17.1.1997.
5. No. 780, 17–23.2.1996, p. 131.
6. No. 827, 11–17.1.1997, p. 111.
7. No. 829, 25–31.1.1997, p. 131.
8. No. 829, 25–31.1.1997, p. 143.
9. No. 812, 28.9–4.10.1996, p. 85.
10. No. 844, 10–16.5.1997, p. 141.
11. No. 880, 17–23.1.1998, p. 167.
12. No. 827, 11–17.1.1997.
13. No. 823, 14–20.12.1996, p. 227.
14. No. 822, 7–13.12.1996, p. 139.
15. No. 827, 11–17.1.1997, p. 43.
16. No. 844, 10–16.5.1997, p. 131.
17. No. 848, 7–13.6.1997, p. 123.
18. No. 801, 13–19.7.1996, p. 130.
19. No. 820, 23–29.11.1996, p. 137.
20. No. 880, 17–23.1.1998, p. 57.
21. No. 841, 19–25.4.1997.

22. No. 879, 10–16.1.1998, p. 113.
23. Brooks - *Nine Parts*, p. 196.
24. Ibid, pp. 144–145.
25. Ibid.
26. No. 793, 18–24.5.1996, p. 169.
27. No. 786, 23–29.3.1996, pp. 84–85.
28. No. 841, 19–25.4.1997, p. 83.
29. No. 879 10–16.1.1998.
30. See an ad in the weekly *Arab* (no. 74 [December 1996], p. 10), under the heading, "Generous hospitality in accordance with our noble Arab tradition."
31. Brooks - *Nine Parts*, p. 169.
32. No. 823, 14–20.12.1996, p. 207.
33. No. 829, 25–31.1.1997, p. 123.
34. Brooks - *Nine Parts*, p. 48.
35. No. 780, 17–23.2.1996, p. 95.
36. No. 815, 19–25.10.1996, p. 83.
37. Brooks - *Nine Parts*, p. 172.
38. No. 846, 24–30.5.1997, p. 71.
39. Brooks - *Nine Parts*, p. 174.
40. No. 850, 21–27.6.1997.
41. No. 843, 3–9.5.1997, p. 93.
42. No. 418, 7–13.6.1997.
43. In *Surat al-Fil*: "Have you seen what your Lord has done to the people of the elephant?" This is apparently a reference to a war against the Ethiopians before the rise of Islam.
44. See Abu Bakr Ahmad Al-Khatib Al-Baghdadi, *Ta'rikh Baghdad*. Vol. 1 (Cairo: Maktabah al-Khaji, 1931), pp. 100–104.
45. No. 827, 11–17.1.1997, p. 65; no, 843, 3–9.5.1997, p. 67.
46. No. 827, 11–17.1.1996.
47. No. 845, 17–23.5.1997, p. 21.
48. No. 852, 5–11.7.1997, p. 77.
49. No. 853, 12–18.7.1997, p. 131.
50. No. 780, 17–23.2.1996, pp. 88–89.
51. Brooks - *Nine Parts*, p. 175.
52. Ibid., pp. 172–173.
53. No. 841, 19–25.4.1997, p. 101.
54. No. 841, 19–25.4.1997.
55. No. 827, 11–17.1.1997, p. 29.
56. No. 879, 10–16.1.1998, p. 161.
57. No. 827, 11–17.1.1997, p. 5.
58. No. 879, 10–16.1.1998.
59. Ilyas - *Astronomy*, p. 5.
60. See, for example, the Rolex advertisement in no. 907, 25–31.7.1998.
61. No. 827, 11–17.1.1997, p. 99.

62. The Islamic prohibition on interest lending has necessitated the development of a unique banking system, based legally on joint enterprise with lenders and their participation in bank profits, as a substitute for interest.

6. The Calligraphic Ad: Pens, Writing, and Grammar

1. No. 844, 10–16.5.1997, p. 109.
2. No. 780, 17–23.2.1996, p. 37.
3. No. 880, 17–23.1.1998, p. 165.
4. No. 823, 14–20.12.1996, p. 195.
5. See Derrida - *Of Grammatology.*
6. The night on which the angel Gabriel forced Muhammad to read the *Surat al-'Alaq,* the chapter of Creation, although he could not read. For a discussion of the Prophet's illiteracy, see Norman Calder, "The Ummi in Early Islamic Juristic Literature," *Der Islam,* 67 (1), 1990, pp. 111–123.
7. Annemarie Schimmel, *Calligraphy and Islamic Culture* (New York: New York University Press, 1984).
8. See M. R. Sawignai and G. Horsfield, "Le Temple de Ramma," *Revue Biblique,* 44 (1937), pp. 245–278; Giulio Lepschy, *History of Linguistics,* vol. 1 (London and New York: Longman, 1994), p. 164.
9. Arabic calligraphy plays a significant role in Arab-Muslim collective memory. Jordanian television ran, during evening prime time (22.1.1999, 22:00–23:00), a program titled "Islam and the Journey of Arabic Writing" (*Al-Islam wa-rihlat al-kitabah al-'arabiyyah*), dealing with Arabic writing from the Jahiliyya period to the time of Muhammad and the beginning of Islam. The program showed letters "written" by Muhammad, and important buildings (including some in Europe) that bear Arabic calligraphic inscriptions.
10. No. 879, 10–16.1.1998, p. 175.
11. No. 880, 17–23.1.1998, p. 61.
12. No. 796, 8–14.6.1996, p. 63.
13. No. 786, 30.3–5.4.1996, p. 111.
14. No. 796, 8–14.6.1996, p. 26.
15. Brinkley Messick, *The Calligraphic State: Textual Domination and History in a Muslim Society* (Los Angeles: University of California Press, 1993), p. 21.
16. Ibid., pp. 84–87.
17. No. 880, 12–23.1.1998, p. 61.
18. No. 886, 28.2–2.3.1998.
19. No. 841, 19–25.4.1997, p. 83.
20. No. 820, 23–29.11.1996, p. 167.
21. No. 815, 19–25.10.1996, p. 137.
22. No. 804, 19–25.8.1996, pp. 18–19.
23. No. 820, 23–29.11.1996, p. 183.
24. No. 879, 10–16.1.1998, p. 156.

25. No. 786, 30.3–5.4.1996, p. 111.
26. No. 814, 12–18.10.1996, p. 7.
27. No. 879, 10–16.1.1998.
28. No. 850, 21–27.6.1997.
29. No. 418, 7–13.6.1997.
30. No. 822, 7–13.12.1996, p. 207.
31. No. 827, 11–17.1.1997, p. 119.
32. No. 843, 3–6.5.1997, p. 95.
33. No. 880, 17–23.1.1998.
34. No. 796, 8–14.6.1996, p. 63.
35. No. 812, 28.9–4.10.1996, p. 73.
36. No. 801, 13–19.7.1996, p. 23.
37. No. 880, 17–23.1.1998, p. 61.
38. No. 843, 3–9.5.1997, p. 35.
39. No. 827, 11–17.1.1997, p. 81; no. 788, 13–19.4.1996, p. 71.
40. No. 843, 3–9.5.1997, p. 55.
41. No. 829, 25–31.1.1997, p. 143.
42. No. 801, 13–19.7.1996.
43. No. 844, 10–16.5.1997, p. 139.
44. No. 816, 19–25.10.1996, p. 183.
45. See chapter 3 on foodstuffs.
46. No. 886, 28.2–2.3.1998, p. 71.
47. No. 879, 10–16.1.1998.
48. No. 827, 11–17.1.1997.
49. No. 879, 10–16.1.1998, p. 99.
50. No. 827, 11–17.1.1997.
51. No. 879, 10–16.1.1998, p. 175.
52. For example, no. 886, 28.2–2.3.1998, p. 47; no. 845, 17–23.5.1997, p. 25; no. 880, 17–23.1.1998, p. 133.
53. No. 827, 11–17.1.1997, p. 99.
54. No. 788, 13–19.4.1996, p. 123.
55. No. 816, 19–25.10.1996, p. 183.
56. No. 418, 7–13.6.1997.
57. No. 800, 6–12.7.1996, p. 137.
58. This was one of the reasons for the delayed appearance of print in the Middle East; see the preface.
59. Fuat M. Sezgin, *Geschichte des Arabischen Schrifttums*, vols. 1–9 (Leiden: E. J. Brill, 1967–1984).
60. The Arabic writing system is mostly cursive (but six of the letters do not connect forward, that is, to the left).
61. No. 879, 10–16.1.1998, p. 147.
62. No. 886, 28.2–2.3.1998, p. 79.
63. No. 823, 14–20.12.1996, p. 190.
64. No. 879, 10–16.1.1998, p. 51.

65. No. 796, 8–14.6.1996, p. 87.
66. No. 823, 14–20.12.1996, pp. 104–105.
67. No. 807, 24–30.8.1996, p. 13.
68. No. 815, 19–25.10.1996, p. 147.
69. No. 815, 19–25.10.1996, p. 83.
70. See, for instance, the blessing *"iftara[n] hani'a[n]"* in an ad for Craft cheese, no. 879, 1–16.1.1998.
71. See, for example, the ad for Al-Taj sour cream, no. 886, 28.2–2.3.1998.
72. No. 880, 17–23.1.1998, p. 141.
73. No. 788, 13–19.4.1996, p. 71.
74. No. 879, 10–16.1.1998.
75. No. 827, 11–17.1.1997.

Epilogue: Hybridic Arabism

1. On "front" and "social front," see Erving Goffman, *The Presentation of Self in Everyday Life* (New York: Doubleday, 1959), pp. 22–30. "Fronts tend to be selected, not created" (p. 28). See also his analysis regarding the "definition of a situation" and "emergent team impression" (p. 80).
2. Ludwik Fleck, *Entstehung und Entwicklung einer wissenschaftlichen Tatsache: Einführung in die Lehre vom Denkstil und Denkkollektiv* (Basel: Bueno Schwabe & Co., 1935). Translated to English by Fred Bradley and Thaddeus J. Trenn as *Genesis and Development of a Scientific Fact* (Chicago and London: University of Chicago Press, 1979).
3. Marshall McLuhan, *Understanding Media*. See also Paul Benedetti and Nancy Dehart (eds.), *Forward Through the Rearview Mirror: Reflections on and by Marshall McLuhan* (Cambridge, Mass.: MIT Press, 1997), p. 163.
4. Edward T. Hall, *Beyond Culture* (New York: Anchor Books, 1976), p. 16.
5. El-Ghonemy - *Affluence*, pp. 127–128.
6. Brooks - *Nine Parts*, p. 175.
7. Zeldin - *Intimate*, p. 167.
8. José Saramago, *Toldot Hamatsor al Lisbon*. Hebrew translation of *História do Cerco de Lisboa* by Miriam Tivo'n (Tel Aviv: Hotsaat Hakibuts Hameuhad, 1998), p. 45.
9. Kurpershoek - *Oral Poetry*, p. 10.
10. William Lancaster, *The Rawala Bedouin Today* (Cambridge: Cambridge University Press, 1981), pp. 102–103.
11. English translation: In every society, politics depend on the existence of cultural representaions, which define the relations between political actors, allowing individuals and groups to raise claims against each other and against the entire political body. See Keith Michael Baker, *Au Tribunal de l'Opinion*, trns. Louis Evrard (Paris: Édition Payot, [1990] 1993), p. 46.
12. Labid ibn Rabi`, in Al-Bustani (ed.), *Al-Majani Al-Hadithah* (Beirut, 1946), p. 103.
13. Baudrillard - *Fatal*, p. 74.

14. Margaret Mead and Rhoda Métraux, *The Study of Culture at a Distance* (Chicago: University of Chicago Press, 1953), p. 399f.

15. See Baudrillard - *Evil*, p. 16.

16. 1856–1919; the creator of the "Land of Oz," where everything is possible and fantasies become reality, and also the founder of the magazine *Shop-Window*, dedicated to the design of shop windows. See Zeldin - *Intimate*, p. 304.

Bibliography

A. Newspapers

Al-Ahram al-Arabi
Al-Jazirah Al-Arabiyyah
Al-Sharq Al-Awsat
Arab News
Point De Vue
Sayyidati

B. Almanacs and Official Publications

Ben's Media Directory, vol. 3, Tombridge, Kent, 1998.

"Saudi Arabia." in: *The Europa World Year Book 1998*. London: Europa Publications Limited, vol. 2, 1998, pp. 2927–2944.

Saudi Arabia, Ministry of Planning. *The Third Development Plan, 1980–1985*. Riyadh: 1981.

Saudi Arabia, Ministry of Planning. *Summary of Saudi Arabian Third Five Year Development Plan*, 2nd ed. Riyadh: 1985.

Saudi Arabia, Ministry of Planning. *Fourth Development Plan 1985–1990*. Riyadh: 1986.

Saudi Arabia, Ministry of Planning. *Fifth Development Plan 1990–1995*. Riyadh: 1990.

Sotheby's. *Important Clocks, Watches, Wristwatches and Barometers*. London: (Thursday, 14th December, 1995).

C. Arabic

Ibn Manzur, Jamaluddin Muhamad Bin Mukkaram. *Lisan al-Arab*. Cairo: Matba'ah Bulak, 1882.

Ibn Sina (Avicenna), Abu Ali al-Husayn b. Abd Allah. *al-Najah fi al-Hikmah al-Mantiqiyyah wa-al-Tab'iyyah wa-Alilahiyyah,* vol. 2. trans. Muhyi al-Din Sabri al-Kurdi. Cairo: Dar al-Sa'adah, 1938.

Al-Baghdadi, Abu Bakr Ahmad Al-Khatib. *Tarikh Baghdad, aw Madinah al-Salam*, vol. 1. Cairo : Maktabah al-Khanji, 1931.

Al-Hasan, Ihsan Muhammad. *Al-A'ilah wa-al-Qarabah wa-al-Zawwaj: Dirasah Tahliliyyah fi Taghayyur Nizam al-A'ilah wa-al-Qarabah wa-al-Zawaj fi al-Mujtama' al-Arabi*, vol. 2. Beirut: Dar Al-taliah, 1985.

Al-Manadhri, Suliman. *Al-Suk al-Arabiyyah al-Mushtarikah*. Cairo: Maktabah Madbulah, 1999.

Al-Ma'ari, Abu al-Ala Ahmad bin Abd Allah bin Suliman. *Risalah al-Ghafran*, vol. 3. trans. A'isha Abd al-Rahman. Cairo: Dar al-Ma'arif, 1963.

Al-Sakhawi, Shams al-Din Muhammad bin Abd al-Rahman. *Al-Ilan bi-al-Tawbikh li-man Dhamma al-Ta'rikh*. Damascus: Matba'ah Al-Turki, [902/1497] 1349/1930.

Al-Iraqi, Muhammad Atif. *Al-Falsafah al-Tabi'iyyah inda Ibn Sina*. Cairo: Dar Al-Ma'arif, 1971.

Al-Qasimi, Khalil al-Azam Jamal al-Din. *Qamus al-Sina'at al-Sha'miyyah*. Paris: Mouton & Co., 1960.

Al-Sharqawi, Iffat Muhammad. *Adab Al-Ta'rikh inda al-Arab*, vol. 1. Fikrat al-Ta'rikh: Nashatuha wa-Tatawuruha. Cairo: Maktabah Al-Shabab, [1978?].

Jawad, Ali. *Tarikh al-Arab Qablah al-Islam*. Baghdad: Al-Majma al-Ilmi al-Iraqi, 1959.

Husayn, Muhammad Awad. *Sina'at al-Ta'rikh*. Kuwait: Majalat Alam al-Fikr, 1974.

Murad, Muhammad. "Al-Aa'ilah wa-'Alaqat al-Qarabah fi al-Mujtama' al-'Arabi." *Al-Mujtama' al-'Arabi al-Hadith wa-al-Mu'asar*, (Beirut: Dar al-Farabi, 1998), pp. 159–197.

Nasr, Salim wa-Dubar, Qlud. *al-Tabaqat al-Ijtima'iyyah fi Lubnan*. Beirut: Mu'assasah al-Abhath al-Arabiyyah, 1982.

Araf, Shukri. *Al-Shajarah, Islamiyyan wa-Arabiyyan*. Ma'aliyah: Ila al-Amq, 1995.

Aribi, Yasin. *Ashkalat Athbat al-Zaman fi al-Falsafah al-Islamiyyah*. Tripoli, Libya: Majalat al-Hikmah, 1976.

Ghalib, Abd al-Rahim. *Mi'ah Am min Ta'rikh al-Sahafah Lisan al-Hal*. Beirut: Jarus Press, 1988.

Fruj, Amr. *Ta'rikh al-'Ulum Inda al-Arab*. Beirut: Dar al-Ilm lil-Malayin, 1970.

Sabat, Khalil. *Ta'rikh al-Taba'ah fi al-Sharq al-Arabi*, vol. 2. Cairo: Dar al-Ma'arif, 1966.

Sheikhu, Luis. "Ibn Rabiah, Labid." in: Al-Bustani, Fuad Afram (ed.), *al-Majani al-Haditha*. Beirut: al-Matba'ah al-Kathulikiyyah, 1946.

D. Hebrew

Elitsur, Avshalom. *Zman ve-Toda'ah: Tehiyot Hadashot al Hidot Atikot*. Tel Aviv: Misrad ha-Bitahon, 1994.

El-Qala'y, Ben-Zion and Qara, Yehiel. *Pninei Arav*. Jerusalem: Misrad ha-Bitachon, 1993.

Gurevitch, David. *Postmodernism: Tarbut ve-Sifrut be-Sof ha-Me'ah ha-Esrim*. Tel Aviv: Dvir, 1997.

Gilbar, Gad. *Kalkalat ha-Mizrah ha-Tichon ba-Et ha-Hadashah*. Tel Aviv: Misrad ha-Bitahon, 1990.

Glazman, Lea. "Ezrach Kama'stan ve-Hofesh ha-Nviha: Hearot ve-Hirhurim be-Shulei Dmuto vi-Ytitsirato shel ha-Mashorer Nizar Qabani (1923–1998)." *Itun 77*, 228 (Feb. 1999), pp. 23–27.

Goffman, Erving. *The Presentation of Self in Everyday Life*. New York: Doubleday, 1959.

Goldziher, Yitzhak Ignác. *Hartsa'ot al ha-Islam*. Ttranslation of *Vorlesungen über den Islam*. Jerusalem: Mosad Bialik, [1925] 1969.

Drori, Yosef. "Igeret ha-Bsorah al Kibush Yerushlayim." *Katedrah*, Hotza'at Yad Yitzhak ben Tsvi, 46 (Dec. 1987), pp. 7–12.

Vachman, Avraham. *Bniyah Agula ve-Ortagonalit*. MA thesis. Haifa: The Techniyon, 1959.

Halfi, Rahel. "Semyotika Hi." In: Stavi, Zisi (ed.). *66 Meshorerim–Mivhar Hamishim Shnot Shira Ivrit Hadasha*. Tel Aviv: Yedi'ot Ahronot,,1996.

Moreh, Shmuel. *ha-Ilan ve-ha-Anaf*. Jerusalem: Magnes, 1997.

Simon, Aqiva Ernst. "Ha-Historyographiya." in: *Historyonim ve-Askolot Historiyot: Kovetz Hartza'ot*. Jerusalem: ha-Universita ha-Ivrit, 1963.

Oz, Amos. *Kol ha-Tiqvot: Mahshavot al Zehut Yisra'elit*. Jerusalem: Keter, 1998.

Portugali, Yuval. *Merhav, Zman ve-Hevrah be-Eretz Yisrael ha-Qdumah*, vol. A. Morfologiyah Mevratit. Tel Aviv: ha-Universita Ha-Ptuha, 1999.

Shvedran, Binyamin. *Neft Ha-Mizrah Ha-Tichon: Brachah ve-Iyum*. Tel Aviv: Am Oved, 1975.

Shabtai, Aharon. *Ahavah*. Tel Aviv: Am Oved, 1987.

Snir, Reuven. "ha-Sifrut ha-Irvit Ba-Me'ah ha-Esrim: Model Histori-Funktsionali-Dinami." *ha-Mizrah ha-Hadash*, vol. 36, 1994.

E. European languages

Abdel Jaber, Tayseer. "Inter Arab Labor Movements: Problems and Prospects." In: El-Naggar, Said (ed.). *Economic Development of the Arab Countries*. Washington DC: IMF, 1993.

Abdul Jabbar Beg, Muhammad. "Workers in the Hammamat in the Arab Orient in the Early Middle Ages." *Revisita Degli Studi Orientali*, 158, (1972), pp. 77–80.

Abu-Lughod, Lila. *Veiled Sentiments: Honor and Poetry in a Bedouin Society*. Berkeley, CA: University of California Press, 1986.

Abu-Lughud, Lila. "Zones of Theory in the Anthropology of the Arab World." *Annual Review of Anthropology*, 18 (1989), pp. 267–306.

Adorno, T. W. *Introduction to the Sociology of Music*. Trans. E.B. Ashton. New York: Continuum, 1976.

Adorno, T. W. "On Popular Music." *Zeitschrift für Sozialforschung*, vol. 9, no. 1 (1941), pp. 17–49.

Ahmed, Leila. "Women and the Advent of Islam." *Signs* II, no. 4 (1986), pp. 665–691.

Al-Fardi, A. *The Development of Commercial Advertising in Saudi Television From 1986–1988*. Unpublished Ph.D. Thesis. Denton: University of North Texas, 1989.

Al-Kheraiji, F. *The Culture of Television Advertising: An Historical and Empirical Analysis of the Content of Television Commercials and of Saudi Viewers' Responses to Advertising*. Unpublished Ph.D. Thesis. England: University of Leichester, 1992.

Al-Makaty, Safran et al. "Attitudes Toward Advertising in Islam." *Journal of Advertising Research*, v. 36, no. 3 (1996), pp. 16–27.

Al-Najjar, Baquer Salman. "Population Policies in the Countries of the Gulf Cooperation Council: Politics and Society." *Immigration & Minorities* 27, 2 (1986), pp. 252–273.

Al-Rowaithy, Ateiyiah S. *The Effectiveness of the Saudi Arabian Government's Program to Modernize Saudi Society Through the Development of a Non-Oil Industrial Sector*. Unpublished Ph.D. thesis, Claremont, CA: Claremont Graduate School, 1986.

Al-Yusuf, A. *Commercial Advertising in Saudi Arabia: A Content Analysis*. Unpublished M.A. Thesis. Tallahassee: Florida State University, 1989.

Anderson, Benedict. *Imagined Communities*. Rev. ed. London and New York: Verso, 1991.

Ansari, S. M. R. "A Brief Survey of Islamic Sciences." In: *Introduction to Islamic Sciences*. Aligarah: Aligarah Muslim University, 1983.

Antonius, George. *The Arab Awakening: The Story of the Arab National Movement*. Beirut: Khayats, 1945.

Appleby, Joyce, Hunt, Lynn and Jacob, Margaret. *Telling the Truth About History*. New York: Norton, 1994.

Armbrust, Walter, et al. *Mass Culture and Modernism in Egypt*. Cambridge and New York: Cambridge University Press, 1996.

Asad, Talal. *The Idea of an Anthropology of Islam*. Center for Contemporary Arab Studies, Occasional Papers Series. Washington, DC: Georgetown University, 1986, p. 14.

Baker, Keith Michael. *Au Tribunal de l'Opinion*. trans. Louis Évrard. Paris: Édition Payot, [1990] 1993.

Barthes, Rolan. *Mythologies*. Paris : Éditions du Seuil, 1957.

Barthes, Rolan. *La Chambre Claire: Note Sur la Photographie*. Paris: Cahiers du cinema, 1980.

Baudrillard, Jean. *L'Echange Symbolique et la Mort*. Paris: Gallimard, 1976.

Baudrillard, Jean. *Fatal Strategies*. trans. Philip Beichman and W. G. J. Niesluchowski. New York: Semiotext[e]/Pluto, [1983] 1990.

Baudrillard, Jean. *The Transparency of Evil: Essays on Extreme Phenomena*. trans. James Benedict. London & New York: Verso, 1993.

Baudrillard, Jean. *The Consumer Society: Myth & Structure*. London: Sage, [1970] 1998.

Bédarida, François. "The Modem Historian's Dilemma: Conflicting Pressures from Science and Society." *Economic History Review*, 150, 3 (1987), pp. 335–348.

Benedict, Ruth. *Patterns of Culture*. New York: Houghton Mifflin, 1934.

Benedict, Ruth. *The Chrysanthemum and the Sword: Patterns of Japanese Culture*. Boston: Houghton Mifflin, [1946] 1989.

Benjamin, Walter. "Thesis on History." in: *Illuminations*. New York: Harcourt, Brace and World, 1968.

Berger, Peter L. and Luckmann, Thomas. *The Social Construction of Reality*. London: Penguin Books, 1967.

Birks, J. S., Secombe, I. J. and Sinclair, C.A. "Labor Migration in the Arab Gulf States: Patterns and Prospects." *International Migration*. 26 (1988), pp. 267–286.

Birks, J. S. and Sinclair, C. A. "The Domestic Political Economy of Development in Saudi Arabia." in: Niblock, Tim (ed.). *State, Society and Economy in Saudi Arabia*. London: Croom Helm, 1982, pp. 198–213.

Blacking, John. "The Structure of Musical Discourse: The Problem of the Song Text." *Yearbook for Traditional Music*, 14 (1982), pp. 15–23.

Bloch, Marc. *The Historian's Craft*. trans. Peter Putnam. New York: Vintage Books, 1953.

Bourdieu, Pierre. "Sport and Social Class." trans. Richard Nice. In: *Social Science Information*, 17, 6 (1978), pp. 819–840.

Brooks, Geraldine. *Nine Parts of Desire: The Hidden World of Islamic Women*. New York: Anchor Books, 1995.

Browne, Edward G. *The Press and Poetry of Modern Persia*. Los Angeles: Kalimat Press, 1983.

Buch, James. "Secular and Religious Opposition in Saudi Arabia." In: Niblock, Tim (ed.). *State, Society and Economy in Saudi Arabia*, London: Croom Helm, 1982, pp. 106–124.

Bulliet, Richard W. *The Camel and the Wheel*. Cambridge: Harvard University Press, 1977.

Buscombe, Edward. "Ideas of Authorship." *Screen*, vol. 14, no. 3 (1973).

Cachia, P. "A Nineteenth Century Arab's Observation on European Music." *Ethnomusicology*,17 (1973), 1, pp. 41–51.

Calder, Norman. "The Ummi in Early Islamic Juristic Literature." *Der Islam*, 67 (1) (1990), pp. 111–123.

Chartier, Roger. *Cultural History: Between Practices and Postmodernity*. trans. Lydia Cochrane. London: Polity, 1988.

Chatty, Dawn. *From Camel to Truck: A Study of the Pastoral Economy of the Al-Fadl and the Al-Hassana in the Beqaa of Lebanon*. Unpublished Ph.D. dissertation. Los Angeles: University of California, 1974.

Chebel, Malek. *Symbols of Islam*. photographs by Laziz Hamani. London: Editions Assouline, 1997.

Chenje, Anwar. "Arabic: Its Significance and Place in Arab-Muslim Society." *Middle East Journal*, 19 (1965).

Choucry, Nazli. "Asian in the Arab World: Labor Migration and Public Policy." *Middle Eastern Studies*, 27, 2 (1986), pp. 252–273.

Cipolla, Carlo M. *Clocks and Culture, 1300–1700*. New York: Walker, 1967.

Dabla, Bashir. "Migration and its Sociological Impact in Saudi Arabia and Kuwait." *Population Bulletin of ESCWA*, 29 (December 1986), pp. 77–92.

Danesi, Marcel. *Interpreting Advertisement: A Semiotic Guide*. Ottawa: Legas, 1995.

Dawn, Ernest Clarence. *From Ottomanism to Arabism*. Urbana: University of Illinois Press, 1973.

De Assis, Joachim Maria Machado. *The Posthumous Memoirs of Bras Cubas*. New York: Oxford University Press, 1997.

Derrida, Jacques. *Of Grammatology*. trans. Gayatri Chakravorty-Spivak. Baltimore & London: John Hopkins University Press, 1976.

Douglas, Allen and Malti-Douglas, Fedwa. *Arab Comic Strips: Politics of an Emerging Mass Culture*. Indianapolis: Indiana University Press, 1994.

Doumato, E. A. "Gender Monarchy and National Identity In Saudi Arabia." *International Journal of Middle Eastern Studies*, 19 (1992), pp. 31–47.

Dyer, Gillian. *Advertising as Communication*. London: Routledge, 1982.

Eco, Umberto. "Towards a Semiotic Inquiry into the Television Message." Reprinted in: *Working Papers in Cultural Studies*, no. 3, Birmingham University Center for Contemporary Cultural Studies, Autumn (1972).

Eco, Umberto. *A Theory of Semiotics*. London: Macmillan, 1976.

Edbury, Peter W. and Rowe, John Gordon. *William of Tyre: Historian of the Latin East*. Cambridge: Cambridge University Press, 1988.

El Ghonemy, Mohamad Riad. *Affluence and Poverty in the Middle East*. London: Routledge, 1998.

Engles, Fridrich. *The Origin of Family, Private Property and the State*. New York: International Publishers, 1973.

Fabian, Johannes. *Time and the Other*. New York: Columbia University Press, 1983.

Fergany, Nader. "Manpower Problems and Projections in the Gulf." In: El-Azhary, M.S. (ed.). *The Impact of Oil Revenues on Arab Gulf Development*. London: Croom Helm, 1984, pp. 155–169.

Ferguson, Ted. "The World Most Expensive Perfume." *Canadian Buisness*, v. 16 (Jan 1987), pp. 19–21.

Field, Henry. *Camel Brands and Graffiti: From Iraq, Syria, Jordan, Iran and Arabia*. Baltimore: American Oriental Society, 1952.

Fisher, Allan G. B. and Fisher, Humphrey J. *Slavery and Muslim Society in Africa*. London: C. Hurst & Co., 1970.

Fiske, John and Hartley, John. *Reading Television*. London: Methuen, 1978.

Fiske, John. *Reading the Popular*. London and New York: Routledge, 1989.

Fiske, John. *Introduction to Communication Studies*, 2nd ed. London and New York: Routledge, 1990.

Fleck, Ludwik. *Entstehung und Entwicklung einer wissenschaftlichen Tatsache: Einführung in die Lehre vom Denkstil und Denkkollektiv*. Basel: Bueno Schwabe & Co., 1935. Translated to English by Fred Bradley and Thaddeus J. Trenn as *Genesis and Development of a Scientific Fact*. Chicago and London: University of Chicago Press, 1979.

Foucault, Michel. *Discipline and Punish*. trans. Alan Sheridan. New York: Pantheon, 1977.

Foucault, Michel. *The Archaeology of Knowledge and the Discourse of Languages.* trans. Sheridan Smith. New York: Harper & Row, 1976.

Geertz, Cliford. *The Interpretation of Cultures: Selected Essays.* New York: Basic Books, 1973.

Goldberg, Jacob. "The Shi'i Minority in Saudi Arabia." In: Cole, Juan R. I. and Keddie, Nikki R. (eds.). *Shi'ism and Social Protest.* New Haven and London: Yale University Press, 1986, pp. 230–246.

Gombrich, Ernst. *Art and Illusion.* London: Phaidon Press, 1968.

Grace, George William. *The Linguistic Construction of Reality.* London: Croom Helm, 1987.

Habelton, H.G. "The Saudi Arabian Petrochemical Industry: Its Rationale and Effectiveness." In: Niblock, Tim (ed.). *State, Society and Economy in Saudi Arabia.* London: Croom Helm, 1982.

Haeri, Shahla. *Law of Desire: Temporary Marriage in Shi'i Iran.* Syracuse, N.Y.: Syracuse University Press, 1989.

Halbwachs, Maurice. *On Collective Memory.* Chicago: University of Chicago Press, [1968] 1992.

Hall, Edward T. *The Silent Language.* Garden City, N.Y.: Doubleday, 1959.

Hall, Edward T. *Beyond Culture.* New York: Anchor Books, 1976.

Hall, Stuart. "Culture, The Media and the 'Ideological Effect.'" In: Curan, James, et al. (eds.). *Mass Communication and Society.* London: Edward Arnold, 1977.

Hall, Stuart. "Encoding and Decoding in the Television Message." In: Hall, Stuart, et al. (eds.). *Culture, Media, Language.* London: Hutchinson, 1980.

Hann, C. M. *Tea and the Domestication of the Turkish State.* London: Eothen Press, 1990.

Herman, Edward S. and Chomsky, Noam. *Manufacturing Consent: The Political Economy of the Mass Media.* London: Vintage, 1994.

Hobsbaum, Eric. "Introduction: Inventing Traditions." In: Hobsbaum, Eric and Ranger, Terence (eds.). *The Invention of Tradition.* Cambridge: Cambridge University Press, 1983.

Hoppenstand, Gary. *In Search of the Paper Tiger.* Bowling Green, Ohio: Bowling Green State University Popular Press, 1987.

Hopwood, Derek. "The Ideological Basis: Ibn Abd Al-Wahhab's Muslim Revivalism." In: Niblock, Tim (ed.). *State, Society and Economy in Saudi Arabia.* London: Croom Helm, 1982, pp. 23–35.

Hourani, Albert. *A History of the Arab People.* New York, NY: Warner Books, 1992.

Ilyas, Mohammad. *Astronomy of Islamic Times for the Twenty-First Century.* New York: Mansel, 1989.

Jensen, Laron. "Widespread Affluence Makes Arabian Peninsula a Prime Market for U.S. Home and Leisure Products." *Business America,* 6 (April 1983), pp. 20–24.

Khan, Maulana Wahiduddin. *Women Between Islam and Western Societies.* New Delhi: Al-Risala Books, 1997.

Koya, Mohammed C. H. *Camel to Cadillac.* New Delhi: Sterling, 1979.

Kurpershoek, Marcel P. *Oral Poetry and Narratives from Central Arabia*, vol. 1, (The Poetry of Ad-Dindan – A Bedouin Bard in Southern Najd). Leiden: E. J. Brill, 1994.

Kurpershoek, Marcel P. *Oral Poetry and Narratives from Central Arabia*, vol. 3, (Bedouin Poets of the Dawasir Tribe: Between Nomadism and Settlement in Southern Najd). Leiden: E. J. Brill, 1999.

Lancaster, William. *The Rawala Bedouin Today*. Cambridge: Cambridge University Press, 1981.

Landes, David S. *Revolution in Time: Clocks and the Making of the Modern World*. Cambridge, MA: Belknap Press of Harvard University Press, 1983.

Landes, David S. "What Room for Accident in History? Explaining Big Changes by Small Events." *Economic History Review* 157, 4 (1994), pp. 637–656.

Lasswell, Harold. "The Structure and Function of Communication in Society." In: Bryson, L. (ed.). *The Communication of Ideas*. New York: Jewish Theological Seminary of America, Institute for Religious and Social Studies, 1948, pp. 37–51.

Latour, Bruno. *We Have Never Been Modern*. Cambridge: Harvard University Press, 1993.

Lepschy, Giulio. *History of Linguistics*. vol. 1. London and New York: Longman, 1994.

Lerner, Daniel. *The Passing of Traditional Society: Modernizing the Middle East*. Glencoe: The Free Press [1958], 1963.

Levine, Robert. *A Geography of Time*. New York: Basic Books, 1997.

Lewis, Bernard. *The Middle East and the West*. New York: Harper & Row, 1964.

Lewis, Bernard. *Race and Color in Islam*. New York: Harper & Row, 1971.

Lewis, Bernard. *The Muslim Discovery of Europe*. London: Weidenfeld & Nicolson, 1982.

Lewis, Bernard. *Race and Slavery in the Middle East*. New York: Oxford University Press, 1990.

Lewis, Geoffrey. *Turkey*. London: Ernest Benn, 1965.

Looney, Robert E. "Structural Change in the Arabian Gulf Impact of the Foreign Workers." *Population Bulletin of Escwa*, 37 (December 1990), pp. 129–172.

Looney, Robert E. "Patterns of Human Resource Development in Saudi Arabia." *Middle Eastern Studies*, 24, 4 (1991), pp. 668–678.

Lyotard, Jean-François. *The Postmodern Condition: A Report on Knowledge*. Minneapolis: University of Minnesota Press, 1984.

Malti-Douglas, Fedwa. *Woman's Body, Woman's Word: Gender and Discourse in Arabo-Islamic Writing*. Princeton: Princeton University Press, 1991.

Manheim, Karl. *Essays on the Sociology of Knowledge*. London: Routledge & Kegan Paul, 1964.

Mauss, Marcel. *The Gift*. New York: Norton, 1967.

McLuhan, Marshall. *Understanding Media*. London: Routledge & Kegan, [1964] 1967a.

McLuhan, Marshall. *The Medium Is the Message*. Harmodsworth, Middlesex: Penguin Books, 1967b.

McLuhan, Marshall. *The Global Village*. New York: Oxford University Press, 1989.

Mead, Margaret and Métraux, Rhoda (eds.). *The Study of Culture at a Distance.* Chicago: University of Chicago Press, 1953.

Mernissi, Fatima. *Beyond the Veil: Male-Female Dynamics in Modern Muslim Society.* Rev. ed. Bloomington: Indiana University Press, 1987.

Mernissi, Fatima. *The Veil and Male Elite: A feminist Interpretation of Women's Rights in Islam.* trans. Mary Jo Lakeland. Reading, MA: Addison-Wesley, 1994.

Messick, Brinkley. *The Calligraphic State: Textual Domination and History in a Muslim Society.* Los Angeles: University of California Press, 1993.

Mikhail, Mona. "Love and Sex: A Study of the Short Fiction of Naguib Mahfouz and Yusuf Idris." In: idem, *Images of Arab Women.* Washington, D.C.: Three Continents Press, 1979, pp. 91–112.

Millet, Kate. *Going to Iran.* New York: Coward, McCann & Geoghegan, 1982.

Moliver, Donald M. and Abbondante, Paul J. *The Economy of Saudi Arabia.* New York: Preager, 1980.

Osborne, Harold. *The Oxford Companion to Art.* Oxford: Oxford University Press, [1970] 1990.

Peirce, Charles Sanders. *Collected Papers.* Cambridge: Harvard University Press, 1958.

Penrose, Roger. *The Emperor's New Mind: Concerning Computers Minds and the Law of Physics.* Oxford: Oxford University Press, 1989.

Peters, Frank. *Aristotle and the Arabs: The Aristotelian Tradition in Islam.* New York: New York University Press, 1968.

Poster, Marc. *Cultural History and Postmodernity.* New York: Columbia University Press, 1997.

Robinson, F. "Technology and Religious Change: Islam and the Impact of Print." *Modern Asian Studies,* 27 (1993), pp. 229–251.

Roy, Delvin, A. "Saudi Arabian Education: Development Policy." *Middle Eastern Studies,* 28, 3 (1992), pp. 477–508.

Rubin, Uri. "Pre-existence and Light: Aspects of the Concept of Nur Muhammad." *Israel Oriental Studies,* 5 (1975), pp. 62–119.

Ryckmans, G. *Rites et Croyances Pré-Islamiques en Arabie Méridionale.* Louvain, 1942.

Said, Edward W. *Orientalism.* New York: Pantheon Books, 1978.

Said, Edward W. *Covering Islam: How the Media and the Experts Determine How We See the Rest of the World.* London and Melbourne: Routledge & Kegan Paul, 1981.

Saramago, José. *Toldot Hamatsor al Lisbon.* Hebrew translation of *História do Cerco de Lisboa* by Miriam Tivo'n. Tel Aviv: Hotsaat Hakibuts Hameuhad, 1998.

Sauer, Carl. *Agricultural Origins and Dispersals.* New York: American Geographical Society, 1952.

Saussure, Ferdinand de. *Course in General Linguistics.* Glasgow: Fotana & Collins, 1974.

Sawignai, M.R. and Horsfield, G. "Le Temple de Ramma." *Revue Biblique,* 44 (1937), pp. 245–278.

Schimmel, Annemarie. *Calligraphy and Islamic Culture.* New York: New York University Press, 1984.

Searle, John R. *The Construction of Social Reality*. New York: Free Press, 1995.

Serjeant, R. B. "Star-Calendars and an Almanac from South-West Arabia." *Anthropos*, 49, Sankt Augustin: Anthropos Redaktion, 1954.

Serjeant, R. B. "Fisher-folk and Fish-traps in al-Bahrain." *Bulletin of the School of Oriental and African Studies*, 31, 1968, pp. 486–514.

Serjeant, R. B. *Farmers and Fishermen in Arabia: Studies in Customary Law and Practice*. ed. Rex Smith. Great Britain: Variorum, 1995.

Sezgin, Fuat M. *Geschichte des Arabischen Schrifttums*. vols. 1–9. Leiden: E. J. Brill, 1967–1984.

Shannon, Claude Elwood and Weaver, Warren. *The Mathematical Theory of Communication*. Urbana: University of Illinois Press, 1949.

Shirazi, Faegheh. *The Veil Unveiled*. Gainsville, FL: University of Florida Press, 2001.

Sless, David. *In Search of Semiotics*. London: Croom Helm, 1986.

Sowayan, Saad Abdullah. *The Arabian Oral Historical Narrative: An Ethnographic and Linguistic Analysis*. Wiesbaden: Otto Harrasowitz, 1992.

Srebreny-Mohammadi, Annabelle and Mohammadi, Ali. *Small Media, Big Revolution: Communication, Culture and the Iranian Revolution*. London: University of Minnesota Press, 1994.

Starrett, Gregory. *Putting Islam to Work: Education, Politics and Religious Transformation in Egypt*. Los Angeles: University of Califonia Press, 1998.

Stehr, Nico. *Knowledge Societies*. London: Sage, 1994.

Stevenson, Nick. *Understanding Media Cultures: Social Theory and Mass Communication*. London: Sage, 1995.

Stokes, Martin. *The Arabesk Debate: Music and Musicians in Modern Turkey*. New York: Clarendon Press, 1992.

Uthaimeen, Yousef A. *The Welfare State in Saudi Arabia: Structure, Dynamics and Function*. Unpublished Ph.D. Thesis. Cairo: The American University, 1986.

Van-Rossum, Gerhard Dohrn. *L'Histoire de l'Heure: L'Horlogerie et l'Organization Moderne du Temps*. trans. Olivier Mannoni. Paris: Éditions de la Maison des Sciences de l'Homme, [1992] 1997.

Van Velsen, J. "The Extended-Case Method and Situational Analysis." In: Epstein, Arnold Leonard (ed.) *The Craft of Social Anthropology*. London: Tavistock Publications, 1967.

Vatikiotis, Panayiotis J. *The History of Modern Egypt: From Muhammad Ali to Mubarak*. Baltimore: Johns Hopkins University Press, 1991.

Woodward G.C. *Presentation and Influence in American Life*. Waveland: Prospect Heights, 1988.

Woodward, Peter W. *Oil and Labor in the Middle East: Saudi Arabia and the Oil Boom*. New York: Preager, 1988.

Young, Webb James. *How to Become an Advertising Man*. New York: API, 1963.

Zaman, J. Jay. "Peirce Theory of Signs." In: Sebeok, Thomas (ed.). *A Perfusion of Signs*. Bloomington: Indiana University Press, 1977.

Zeldin, Theodore. *An Intimate History of Humanity*. New York: Harper Collins, 1995.

Index